GORBACHEV

ZHORES A. MEDVEDEV

GORBACHEV

W · W · NORTON & COMPANY
NEW YORK · LONDON

First American Edition, 1986

ISBN 0-393-02308-7

W. W. Norton & Company, Inc., 500 Fifth Avenue, New York, N.Y. 10110
W. W. Norton & Company, Ltd., 37 Great Russell Street, London WC1B 3NU

1 2 3 4 5 6 7 8 9 0

Contents

Preface

For the first time in Soviet history, the leadership succession has meant more than the arrival of a new leader and the possibility of the implementation of new policies. The Gorbachev succession marks the appearance of a new political generation which differs from the old guard in style, knowledge and historical vision. Khrushchev, Brezhnev, Andropov and Chernenko began their ascent to power during the time of Stalin. By 1953 they were mature and experienced career Party men. Their Stalinist past was the most essential qualification for further promotion. Gorbachev, on the other hand, represents a younger post-war political generation, a generation which started its professional Party or state career during the more liberal Khrushchev era.

Political systems of the Soviet type are usually considered 'leader dominated regimes'. This is a valid description of the Soviet political system under Lenin, Stalin and Khrushchev. But Khrushchev's fall in 1964, and the emergence of Brezhnev, who delegated a significant part of his decision-making power to the bureaucratic apparatus, significantly eroded the personal power of the leader. In most other countries of the Soviet bloc, however, the Stalinist structure of leadership with its inevitable 'cult of personality' remains practically intact or has changed into an even more extreme form of personal, family or military dictatorship, as in North Korea, Cuba, Romania and Poland. The erosion of personal leadership in the Soviet Union has been closely linked with the character of the leader rather than with structural change. Insofar as there has been structural change within the system, it has become even more conservative in the process.

Brezhnev was interested in accumulating the superficial symbols of power in the form of awards, titles, honours and even material benefits of offices. He preferred to be 'head' of Party and state rather than the 'ruler'. Andropov tried to assume more personal power, but he did not have sufficient time to create a more efficient system. Far from trying to make the system more efficient, Chernenko made the declining prestige of the Soviet system of administration more obvious. The sharp contrast between the old and sick men who were in charge of the Soviet Union from 1974 to 1984 and the young, competent, dynamic and energetic Gorbachev immediately revived interest in the personality of the Soviet leader. It also aroused hopes for radical reform and change.

The end of every period of leadership in Soviet history has left society in a state of crisis. This has made each succession much more than a change of personality. Each new leader has employed very different methods to achieve his personal and political ambitions. In Stalin's time change was closely associated with methods of coercion and terror. The enormous machine of repression became the most important instrument of the personal power of the General Secretary. Khrushchev, on the other hand, ruled primarily through the Party apparatus. His main power base remained support from the Central Committee and from the regional Party barons whose position and lives he secured. The result was the emergence of an even more powerful bureaucracy. The interests of this group in a much higher level of security and stability found expression in Khrushchev's fall and Brezhnev's succession. In smaller countries of the Soviet bloc decision-making power remained in the hands of individual leaders. In the Soviet Union, however, with its more complex economic, political and military systems, the concentration of power in the hands of one man had already become difficult. Instead a new, inflexible, tenured Party and government elite began to take shape and form a privileged ruling class. It has taken almost 20 years to prove that this social and political class is sterile, inefficient and conservative. It inhibited social, economic and cultural renewal and it finally degenerated into a gerontocracy in which the only natural limit to its existence was infirmity and death. The final symbol of this degeneration has been the death of three General Secretaries in office within less than three years.

The instability and indecision associated with this decline seem to be over. Gorbachev's succession is clearly associated with the transfer of power from the old generation to a younger, better educated generation of political leaders, from the Party bureaucracy to a Party technocracy. In previous successions the consolidation of the power of the leader has usually been a long process, linked with the appointment and promotion to key positions in the government and Politburo of loyalists and friends, often poorly qualified for their positions. It is too early to say that Gorbachev's succession will not follow this pattern, but the deep economic and political crisis which developed slowly and surely from 1979 to 1984 has made it essential to promote not only loyal but also more competent, younger people with good managerial qualities. It is for this reason that the Gorbachev succession marks the beginning of an important political evolution within the Soviet Union.

Unlike Brezhnev and Chernenko, Gorbachev seems to want to increase the power and influence of the office of the General Secretary and to restore the image of a leader who is capable of inspiring people to work harder, perform better and achieve more substantial results. But his personal and charismatic appeal may not be able to work a miracle with the disillusioned Soviet people. Farmers and intellectuals alike want reforms, not resolutions, a more open and free society, not more restrictions and coercion. The technological and scientific revolution which has shaped the life of people in the West in the 1970s and 1980s has not had the same effect on the less flexible and more bureaucratic Soviet economic system. The methods and approaches which will be selected by Soviet leaders to deal with internal crises and international problems depend very much on Gorbachev's personal qualities, his political vision, knowledge, intelligence and the flexibility he shows in testing different models. It was probably politically inevitable that he should choose to use the tough and disciplinarian methods of Andropov to begin to get the Soviet Union moving again. It was probably equally inevitable that his honeymoon period with the Soviet and Western publics would prove to be very short. Will he be able to change the course of development of the Soviet Union? How wisely will he use the enormous power of his office? These are the questions which this biography tries to answer.

This book has been made possible by my long, personally motivated interest in political developments in the Soviet Union and the situation in Soviet agriculture, economy and science since the late 1940s, when the complete domination of Lysenko's pseudoscientific ideas in biology and agriculture made it difficult for any self-respecting scientist to continue genuine research without political and personal risk. To be a true scientist meant to be in political opposition to the system. To survive in a Stalinist society which, in its treatment of non-conformists and dissidents has remained essentially unchanged in the decades since Stalin, it was necessary to study not only science, but also the political system and its evolution.

I would like to thank my brother Roy, whose books on Stalin, 'Stalin's men' and Khrushchev and essays on the Brezhnev period and the Andropov and Chernenko succession have contributed greatly to my own understanding of political developments in the Soviet Union. He has also helped enormously by sending me articles from the Soviet professional and general press which have kept me well informed about major and minor events in the Soviet Union in the period of my involuntary exile from that country. I have also been able to read many unpublished *samizdat* works and to compare the internal official and unofficial sources of information with emigre and Western sources and to use my own judgement in selecting those which I have felt to be most reliable. 'Sovietology' and 'Kremlinology' exist because of the secretive nature of the Soviet system and the enormous efforts of the official Soviet press (both general and specialized) to distort the real history of the Soviet Union and to generate pseudo-information. However, Western perception of Soviet reality is often ideologically distorted or one-sided. This makes personal experience an invaluable attribute in selecting information. The other essential quality for writing about Soviet leaders is the patience to do the kind of detective work required to uncover details about their lives.

I would like to thank friends and colleagues, whose advice I have found it much easier to solicit while writing this book than it was when I worked on Andropov's biography three years ago. I would also like to thank Margot Light of the University of Surrey for her linguistic and editorial assistance during the writing stage of this book. I hope that the reader will find this more co-operative approach and the longer preparatory period reflected in the contents of this book.

Zhores A. Medvedev

ONE

The Making of a General Secretary

1
The General Secretary is dead, long live the General Secretary!

On March 11, 1985, for the first time in Soviet history, people were expected not only to mourn the death of their leader, but at the same time to congratulate the new leader. It was only in the Soviet Far East, in Kolyma and Kamchatka, separated by seven, eight and nine time zones from Moscow, that the name of the new leader did not arrive until the next day, during the early hours of March 12. On the surface it looked as if it had been the easiest succession on record. In fact, it was not that easy, and the speed of the announcement showed that the decision had been made in a hurry.

On March 12 all Soviet newspapers carried a picture of the deceased leader, Konstantin Chernenko, on page two, together with a list of his achievements. Gorbachev's photograph and biography appeared on page one. This was unusual. But there was something even more unusual about this death report and news of the succession compared to the recent reports in 1982 and 1984 after the deaths of Brezhnev and Andropov. There was no nomination speech. It was reported that Gromyko made the speech, but the text was not published. This could only mean that it had been spontaneous, not a carefully prepared speech. There was another difference, but this one took me longer to notice. The black mourning frame printed around the second page looked rather narrow. It was only half the width of the frames used for Brezhnev and Andropov (3 millimetres rather than 6). It was still, however, a millimetre broader than the frames used for the second page announcements of the death of senior Politburo members like

Marshal Ustinov, who had died a few months previously. But there was no doubt that it was less substantial than the normal deep mourning used for real leaders. The funeral commission, under Gorbachev's chairmanship, seemed to be in a hurry about the funeral arrangements. The lying-in-state was to be a day shorter than for Brezhnev and Andropov. The photograph of Politburo members paying their last respects to their deceased colleague showed nine people, rather than all ten remaining full members. Shcherbitsky, Ukraine Party secretary and Brezhnev's close friend, was missing. He had been in the United States since March 3, with a Supreme Soviet delegation. On March 8 he met President Reagan and he was due to meet other officials in Washington on March 9 and then to depart for Texas. The message to curtail his trip and return to Moscow reached him in California, too far from Moscow to make a non-stop flight. He had to change planes in Cuba and, as a result, he missed not only the Politburo meeting, but the crucial Central Committee Plenum as well.

Konstantin Ustinovich Chernenko died at 19.20 on March 10, 1985. The very fact that the Central Committee members were summoned to Moscow for a meeting the very next morning makes it clear that Gorbachev decided to discuss the succession at an emergency Politburo meeting immediately after Chernenko's death. Some foreign journalists living in Moscow reported that the Politburo meeting was convened three hours after the death.[1] From previous precedents it is understood that an extraordinary Plenum of the Central Committee to confirm the new leader is called only after consensus has been reached at Politburo level. The Plenum merely has to confirm the appointment. It takes at least ten hours to assemble a quorum of Central Committee members in Moscow from all parts of the Soviet Union. There are, however, no rules about what constitutes a quorum of the Politburo. In emergency situations the available Politburo members, even if they number only three or four, have the right to make decisions. When Lenin established the Politburo in 1919 the Central Committee consisted of 18 men and one woman, five of whom were appointed to the Politburo. Lenin's rules of procedure are still followed for Politburo meetings and they do not include the need to be quorate – there was a Civil War raging at the time and formalities were irrelevant. Trotsky and Stalin were often out of Moscow on Red Army business. Only three Politburo members normally tended to be in Moscow and one of them, Krestinsky, frequently opposed Lenin. Consequently, Lenin and Kamenev made many decisions in the name of the Politburo by themselves.

The absence of strict rules was an advantage for Gorbachev. On March 10 three Politburo members were away: Shcherbitsky was in the USA, Vorotnikov was in Yugoslavia and Kunayev was in Alma-Ata, a five-hour flight from Moscow and not less than six hours from the Kremlin. Andrei Gromyko was probably the only one of Gorbachev's supporters who had the interests of the country at heart, rather than his own personal fate. His position was secure anyway and, as the longest serving Foreign Minister in the world, defending Soviet interests was his profession. For all the others, the problem of who was to be the new General Secretary was also the problem of their future careers. Vitalii Vorotnikov, Prime Minister of the Russian Federation (RSFSR), was considered Gorbachev's ally, but his support was probably conditional. Geidar Aliyev, the very ambitious and successful First Deputy Prime Minister of the USSR, was his rival for the top job in the government when Tikhonov stepped down from the Prime Minister's post or died. Gromyko, working to build a majority for Gorbachev, probably found it easier to deal with Aliyev while Vorotnikov, Andropov's choice for the job, was still in Yugoslavia.

It was clear to everyone both in Moscow and abroad that Chernenko's own preference for his successor had been the Moscow Party secretary, Viktor Grishin. He was a safe choice for Brezhnev's former faction and both Shcherbitsky and Kunayev were ready to support him. Grigorii Romanov, Gorbachev's bitter rival, was also ready to back Grishin since his own chance to be elected had become slight. There was never any doubt about the position of the elderly, frail Tikhonov, a close friend of both Brezhnev and Chernenko. The remaining figure, the colourless Mikhail Solomentsev, chairman of the Party Control Commission, could probably be persuaded to back Gorbachev, but he was more likely to do so with his old rival, Vorotnikov, out of the way. It was the feud between Solomentsev, Prime Minister of the RSFSR until 1983, and his First Deputy, the younger and more active Vorotnikov, which had led to Vorotnikov's honorary exile to Cuba in 1979. Ambassadorial appointments were Brezhnev's favourite method of demoting high officials. Andropov, who recognized Vorotnikov's administrative talents, had brought him back to Moscow and given him Solomentsev's job. Solomentsev had been promoted 'upstairs', to the veteran's position of chairman of the Control Commission (where he replaced Arvid Pel'she who died in 1983 at the age of 84).

If Chernenko had lived for another month, Gorbachev would probably not have stood a chance of becoming General Secretary. For the first time in Soviet political history the illness of the General Secretary had provoked preparations for a well-rehearsed transfer of power with the General Secretary himself making the nomination. Brezhnev's faction, led after his death by Chernenko, had engineered a surprising comeback after Andropov's death. It was thought that Chernenko would survive until the XXVIIth Party Congress in February 1986. When his health deteriorated, the Congress was moved forward to November 1985.[2] Gorbachev could expect nothing positive from the approaching Congress. Agriculture, his responsibility for a number of years, might well become the main topic of discussion and he could hardly emerge in a favourable light. But by the beginning of 1985 Chernenko was weakening rapidly and it began to seem unlikely that he would survive until November. Preparations began for his formal resignation at the regular Central Committee Plenum in the second half of March. But even this proved too optimistic and the opportunity for an orderly transfer of power disappeared.

Getting a full Politburo consensus behind the nomination of a successor is never easy and Gorbachev's case was no different. There were five Politburo members who would, given sufficient time, block his nomination. He had the full and unconditional support only of Gromyko, and confirmation by a full Plenum of a Central Committee still dominated by Brezhnev's loyal followers (many of whom had no illusions that they would be retired or dismissed from their regional or ministerial positions before or after the next Congress, if Gorbachev were elected as General Secretary) was very uncertain. His best chance would be if a speedy Politburo decision could be made before Shcherbitsky, Kunayev and Vorotnikov returned, but even then Gromyko's great diplomatic experience was essential.

It was well known in the Soviet Union and abroad that Gorbachev had been second-in-command in the Soviet leadership since Andropov's death, but this did not guarantee his promotion in the case of Chernenko's resignation or death. There is a great difference between the first and second positions in any authoritarian system. The selection of a successor is always a complex process, fraught with difficulties. Although it had seemed that Gorbachev's influence had begun to grow after Andropov's death, he had been unable to increase his 'political capital' during 1984. Before Andropov's death it was clear that he was being groomed for succession at some future date. When Andropov died in February 1984, Gorbachev was a contender for power, but he simply did not have sufficient authority, a successful past history or the proper credentials for the job. He remained Central Committee secretary in charge of agriculture and head of the Central Committee's agricultural department. But agricultural performance had been extremely poor since his appointment at the end of 1978. 1983 was the fifth poor harvest in a row and it had become too difficult to blame the failure on the weather. Thus when Andropov died there were three days of heated debate in the Politburo, after which Chernenko emerged as General Secretary. But there were many conditions attached to his appointment and he had to make a firm promise to continue the 'Andropov line' and not to attempt to revive Brezhnev's already discredited policy. Chernenko's promotion was clearly a compromise and he was intended only to be an interim leader. It was a victory by default and his main advantage was his physical frailty. It was unlikely that he would live very long and therefore he would be unable to consolidate his power. The compromise was greeted with apparent relief by the members of the Central Committee. With Chernenko in charge, Andropov's anti-corruption line would no longer threaten them. Formal 'unity' was important to everyone. Despite the inevitable internal disagreements and feuds amongst these 300 members of the super-elite, it is unlikely that any of them would be interested in exploding the myth about the supreme wisdom of the Politburo, the infallibility of the Central Committee and the guiding force of the Communist Party.

Gorbachev became the formal second-in-command and was the official chairman of the Central Committee secretariat when Chernenko was ill or on vacation. (There is no formal position of chairman of the Politburo.) It was originally taken for granted that there had been a radical shift in Gorbachev's responsibilities. By established tradition, the second-in-command took charge of the 'ideology portfolio' and became responsible for propaganda and ideology, the control of the media and foreign relations within the socialist camp, where relations were based on Party links and ideology (as opposed to the traditional diplomatic relations with capitalist and Third World countries and China, which were managed by the Ministry of Foreign Affairs, in collaboration with the KGB and army intelligence). However, Chernenko considered ideological work his main area of competence and he was reluctant to give Gorbachev supervision over the Central Committee department of ideology. The General Secretary had the privilege of keeping one or other Party sector under his personal supervision. Moreover, Chernenko certainly understood that agriculture is the graveyard of potential leaders. The longer Gorbachev remained responsible for the unrealistic 'Food Programme' (which he had helped to create), the weaker his position would be, no matter what superficial signs of authority he acquired. Chernenko's scheme paid off handsomely in 1984, an extremely bad agricultural year. The figures for agricultural production were not reported at the end of the year, but reliable American estimates put the total 1984 Soviet grain harvest at 170 million metric tons, 70 million short of the planned target.[3] This was no higher than the average level in the 1960s and a record amount (50 million tons) of grain had to be imported to reduce the food and feed grain deficit. It was a personal disaster for Gorbachev. But a more serious blow was Ustinov's death.

Marshal Ustinov's death was not entirely unexpected. Since his absence from the Red Square parade on November 7, 1984 it had been reported that he had a 'cold'. The cold developed into pneumonia, but it was not fatal. By the time Gorbachev left Moscow for his successful trip to Britain, Ustinov was out of intensive care and had begun to recover. The official medical report made public later announced that during his convalescence he had shown symptoms of a possible 'rupture of an arteriosclerotic abdominal aneurism'.[4] His doctors decided that an emergency operation was required. The operation failed: Ustinov was 76 years old and still weak after his pneumonia. For Gorbachev Ustinov's death represented the loss of a friend and his strongest supporter. Ustinov was the most distinguished, prominent and powerful member of the Politburo. He was practically the only member whose position was not due to patronage and 'bureaucratic promotion', but legitimated by his unique and brilliant service to the country during the critical years of the war, when he was People's Commissar for armaments and the youngest member of the government. During those years Chernenko, already in his thirties, was a student at the Party Higher School in Moscow, training for his future propaganda work.

At the beginning of 1985 Chernenko had also disappeared from public view. The meeting of Warsaw Pact leaders scheduled for January was postponed and a programme of meetings with foreign leaders was cancelled. This was almost a repetition of what had happened at the end of Andropov's life. But Andropov had made Gorbachev his representative at Central Committee meetings and for other public functions, whereas Chernenko appointed Grishin as his spokesman. From now on it was a race between Gorbachev and Grishin. Mark Frankland later reported for the London *Observer* that 'for more than a month there had been rumours among the foreign community that the Moscow party chief, Victor Grishin, was the man to watch.'[5] Romanov, whose chances had still been considered fairly good in October, was certainly out of the game.

The main arena of the race was the approaching elections to the Supreme Soviet of the RSFSR on Sunday, February 24, 1985. The sequence in which Politburo members and candidate members make their election speeches is traditionally arranged according to seniority. The tradition dates back to the first elections to the Supreme Soviet on Sunday, December 12, 1937, when Stalin spoke on the Friday, two days before polling day. Watching the sequence is the best available indicator to diplomatic observers of the comparative standing of individual leaders. More junior and less influential members of the elite usually meet their constituents first. The later the speech, and the closer to the final speech of the General Secretary, the more senior the candidate. Prime Minister Nikolai Tikhonov made his speech on Thursday, February 21, as expected. Gorbachev's meeting with his constituents took place on Wednesday, February 20 and this, more than anything, showed that he still held the position of second-in-command. He had spoken on the Wednesday the year before, prior to the elections of the Supreme Soviet of the USSR, soon after Andropov's death. It was the timing of his speech then that had provided the clue to his prominence.

In 1984 Gorbachev had stood for election in his native rural district of Stavropol, where he had first been elected as a deputy in 1979. In the previous Supreme Soviet of the RSFSR he had represented the Altai *krai*, an important agricultural area, part of the famous virgin lands. But the Altai *krai* had performed very poorly in 1984 and his constituency had become a liability. Politburo members are usually nominated for election in a number of districts and they have the privilege of choosing which one to represent. Designed to demonstrate 'spontaneous popular support', the practice is, in fact, entirely staged and artificial. But it does give candidates the chance to change constituencies and Gorbachev availed himself of this much needed opportunity. He chose to stand for a central Moscow district (the Kiev district). The chairman of the Central Electoral Commission responsible for registering nominations was Yegor Ligachev, recently promoted by Andropov and a strong supporter of Gorbachev. However, the Kiev district was not vacant – since 1980 the Moscow city Party secretary, Leonid Borisov had represented the district. He had not fallen out of favour and there was no reason why he should not stand again. There *was* one vacant district in Moscow, the Cheremushkinsky. But it did not suit Gorbachev because it had been renamed after Brezhnev's death and was now known as the Brezhnev district. A deal was made: Borisov was nominated by the Brezhnev district, leaving the Kiev district vacant for Gorbachev. It was very important to Gorbachev that he should make his election speech in Moscow, rather than in Barnaul.

Gorbachev's speech on February 20 was very good. He concentrated on general aspects of social and cultural development since the previous election campaign in 1980. He paid particular attention to ideology, technical reconstruction of industry, especially local industry (he had visited some local modern industrial plants in his electoral district during the campaign), and the international situation. He mentioned agriculture only briefly, in two sentences. He could not, as is traditional on such occasions, compare agricultural performance between the two elections to show progress, since there had been no progress. Indeed, there had been a sharp decline. But some comparison had to be made, so he informed his audience that the combined results of the previous two years (1983 and 1984) had been better than the combined results of 1981 and 1982. This was an unimpressive argument, since all it really meant was that 1981 had been even worse than the disastrous harvest of 1984. But the agricultural situation was not the primary concern of the Kiev district in Moscow. Moscow receives priority supplies of both imported and domestically produced food and it does not suffer the real problems endured by rural areas.

Chernenko was to perform two days later, in the Kremlin Hall, before selected representatives of the Kuibyshev district of Moscow, which he had represented since 1980. Predictably, he was unable to make the speech himself and it was read on his behalf by Viktor Grishin, senior Politburo member and Moscow *obkom* secretary. Grishin's standing in the hierarchy was obviously higher than expected. His own election speech had been delivered two days before Gorbachev's (and a day before Gromyko's). Romanov and Shcherbitsky, both of whom had been more prominent than Grishin in the 1980 sequence of speeches, had now fallen behind him. This was a definite sign of Grishin's claim for succession.

Two days later, on Sunday, February 24, Moscow television showed Chernenko very briefly as he cast his vote. He could still, apparently, walk the few steps up to the ballot box to deposit his vote. But when the picture was published in the newspapers the next day it became apparent that the event had not taken place at an ordinary polling station (where people come in from the cold wearing their coats), but in a specially decorated room somewhere else. Of course, there was nothing illegal about this. Soviet electoral rules make it compulsory for everyone to vote and even the bed-ridden are given the opportunity to cast their ballot at home. A special team of officials visits all registered disabled voters with a ballot box. In hospitals the task is performed by nurses and doctors and all patients, except for the insane and the comatose, normally take part in elections. This explains how the poll reaches 99.99 per cent of registered voters (although in December 1937 the figure only reached 96.8 per cent).

On February 28 Moscow television filmed Chernenko again, this time receiving his mandate as an elected deputy to the Supreme Soviet. Grishin was present at the brief ceremony and Chernenko was well enough to say a few words. He thanked his electorate for the honour and promised to serve them well and to justify their trust. But he had little time left in which to do this. It was evident from the picture that he was a very ill man, although the nature of his illness was not clear. His heart seemed to be in reasonable condition, even if only because otherwise it would have been impossible to take the television shots.

Seweryn Bialer, an American scholar and expert on Soviet affairs, was in Moscow during this election. Later he published his recollections:

> . . . I left Moscow on March 3, seven days before Konstantin Chernenko's death. The mood was one of gloom, frustration, impatience and embarrassment – gloom about the country's huge problems, frustration with the inactivity of those who were supposed to lead, impatience with an 'old guard' of party leaders who refused to yield power and embarrassment that a great nation and great power was essentially leaderless.
>
> The embarrassment reached its apex in the macabre attempt to prop up, for election to the Supreme Soviet of the Russian Republic, what everybody knew was a living corpse: President Chernenko.[6]

The frustration and gloom noted by Bialer was not, however, reflected in the election results, published on March 2. In the 1980 RSFSR elections the uncontested block of Party and non-Party candidates had won a majority of 99.90 per cent.[7] Difficult though it is to imagine that this figure could be improved, it was even higher in 1985. 99.93 per cent of those who participated in the election expressed support for Chernenko's leadership. Newspaper editorials greeted the results as a new victory for Soviet democracy.

The television film and newspaper pictures were important. Chernenko was seen to be alive and in charge. He had not disappeared entirely as Andropov had done during his last six months in office. Preparations were underway for the regular Central Committee Plenum in March and rumours circulating in Moscow indicated the intention to arrange a formal retirement. There were some urgent state affairs which could only be dealt with by the Party leader. The most pressing was an extension of the Warsaw Pact, which had been signed for a period of 20 years with the option of an extra ten years on May 14, 1955 by Nikita Khrushchev and Nikolai Bulganin and which required the signatures of the General Secretary and the Prime Minister. This task could not be delegated to someone else. Chernenko was still alive and he could be dressed up in his three gold Hero's medals (Brezhnev had five, Andropov one and Gorbachev has none) and have the privilege of nominating his successor. It was perfectly clear that his choice was Grishin, a neutral figure and not 100 per cent a creature of Brezhnev's making (as Chernenko himself was). Grishin was 70 years old and known to be moderate in matters concerning his colleagues, although a hardliner with regard to Party policy. He was not a secretary of the Central Committee, which some Western experts believe is a requirement for top level promotion. There were, however, no binding rules about this matter. The Central Committee has, in theory at least, a free choice and it may even, if necessary, ignore the recommendation of the Politburo. This happened, for example, in June 1957, when the Plenum overruled the Politburo's majority decision of June 18, 1957 to dismiss Khrushchev. The Plenum re-instated him during its meeting from June 22 to 29.[8]

Politburo members and candidate members are also registered members of primary Party organizations where they pay their monthly Party dues and exchange, when necessary, their Party cards. They are invited to attend local Party meetings and conferences and they sometimes fulfil this duty, compulsory for all local Party members. When they do so, Grishin is their formal local Party boss. He chairs the meetings of the Moscow Party, even if more senior members of the Politburo are present.

Rumours about voluntary retirement and an orderly transfer of power had been rife in the last years of Brezhnev's rule and the last months of Andropov's life. But the nature of their health problems did not make accurate prediction possible. Brezhnev was able to stand for several hours on the mausoleum on November 7, 1982, only three days before his death. It is known that the doctors had told Andropov as late as December 1983 that with kidney dialysis he could live another five years (he told this to some private visitors). It seems that more accurate prediction was possible in Chernenko's case and there were more medical details in the rumours about his illness in January and February. But people still expected him to live for a few months, not a few days. He had problems with his lungs and his liver which were certainly irreversible and incurable, but the decline in his condition would be slow. There were many good reasons for him to step down voluntarily and have proper intensive medical care. He would continue to be chairman of the Presidium of the Supreme Soviet for a few months. There was nothing to indicate that the end was close. His letter to American veterans was published on March 2. There were some unofficial reports that Gorbachev had made his customary brief visit to his native village, Privolnoye, in the Stavropol *krai*, where his mother still lived to celebrate his birthday on March 2.[9] On March 3 Shcherbitsky departed for Washington and on March 4 Vorotnikov left for Yugoslavia. On March 7 the traditional meeting on the eve of International Woman's Day (which is genuinely celebrated in the Soviet Union by men and women alike) took place in the Bolshoi theatre. It was clear from the meeting, however, that Gorbachev was no longer merely acting as second-in-command, but that he had taken full control over all affairs. His name was listed *first* of the six Politburo members present at the meeting (Aliyev was the second). This is normally the privilege of the General Secretary, while all other members are listed alphabetically.

International Woman's Day was Chernenko's last conscious day. He lost consciousness on March 8, 1985 and was in a coma until his death two days later.[10] A coma is usual in the case of liver (hepatic) failure. Cirrhosis (as a result of progressive chronic hepatitis) was listed as the first of the causes of his death in the medical statement. Apparently he had lived with hepatitis for many years, perhaps even all his life, since hepatitis is endemic in Siberia where he was born. This may explain why he was not even fit enough for army service in a political capacity during the Great Patriotic War. The medical statement also confirmed the Western diagnosis of lung emphysema (first made by Dr David Owen, leader of the British Social Democratic Party, when he attended Andropov's funeral).

Details about the events on the day that Chernenko died are sketchy. A coded message was apparently sent to Shcherbitsky through the Soviet Embassy in Washington. But Shcherbitsky did not leave America immediately. It may be that his plane was not ready, or that the flight plan needed to be arranged with the American air controllers. Or perhaps there were other reasons. In any case the 12-hour time difference between California and Moscow would have made it impossible for him to arrive in time for the Central Committee meeting on March 11. There were rumours in Moscow that Gromyko deliberately delayed sending the message to the Soviet Embassy and that he also asked Fidel Castro to meet Shcherbitsky when he stopped in Havana en route for Moscow. It was unpredictable how long the Central Committee meeting would last and Shcherbitsky's presence could result in complications. Relations between Gorbachev and the Party bosses of the Ukraine and Kazakhstan (Shcherbitsky and Kunayev) had been very poor since the end of 1983, when Gorbachev and Ligachev had been entrusted by Andropov with the task of supervising regional re-elections in Party organizations to eliminate corruption and inefficiency. The largest number of regional barons dismissed and replaced during the 'house-cleaning' operation was in the Ukraine and Kazakhstan.[11]

Vorotnikov arrived in Moscow from Titograd after midnight. Kunayev only made it at dawn on March 11. But the Politburo decision had already been made and only the Central Committee could overrule it. There were rumours that the Politburo decision had not been taken without dispute. Some rumours, later reported in the Western press, claimed that Romanov had nominated Grishin[12] and that Grishin, in turn, nominated Gromyko. Candidate members of the Politburo do not have the vote, but they do have the right to participate in discussions. Similarly, Central Committee secretaries who are not already Politburo members normally attend special meetings, but they only have a consultative voice. These were the rules established by Lenin and it is likely that they still operate. One consistent rumour maintained that Viktor Chebrikov, head of the KGB, strongly objected to Grishin's nomination and made it clear that Grishin was possibly not entirely innocent of corruption. It was known that there had been several arrests in Moscow for corruption in the trade system and illegal sales of flats. Upon investigation the trail had led to the Moscow City Council, and this could easily be connected with the Moscow *gorkom* and *obkom*, both of which were chaired by Grishin. Moreover, his past in the Council of Trade Unions in the 1960s was far from spotless. Yegor Ligachev also had some strong objections. No-one, apparently, expected an easy Central Committee meeting and Gromyko, who was selected to make the nomination, did not prepare a formal nomination speech. This was a time for plain speaking.

The current rules of extraordinary or even regular Central

Committee meetings are not quite clear. In the post-Stalin period, when Khrushchev was trying to restore 'inner-Party democracy', he tried to establish some procedural rules. At that time many reports of Central Committee meetings were published in full in the same way that the proceedings of Party Congresses were published. In the early 1960s Khrushchev also established a secret ballot for electing the General Secretary and members of the Politburo. The rules were incorporated into the Party statutes, but Brezhnev later scrapped them. The practice of publishing Plenum proceedings was discontinued, to be replaced by official 'communiques' and the texts of the main speeches only. But it seems that Central Committee decisions are often made by consensus, without any formal vote. When voting is required, it is done openly and not in secret. The difference between a consensus decision and one which has required a vote can be detected in the wording of the results. If a formal vote has been taken and the result has been a unanimous decision, it is reported as *yedinoglasno* (literally 'in one voice'). In the case of a consensus decision or a formal vote where there has been some dissent, the word used is *yedinodushno* (literally 'as one soul'). Both words are translated into English as unanimous. In both 1982 when Andropov was elected and 1984 when Chernenko was elected, the election was reported to have been *yedinoglasno*. The official report of Gorbachev's election maintained that the decision had been *yedinodushno*. In the usual political vocabulary of Russian, however, the word *yedinoglasno* is only used when formal voting has taken place and everyone has cast the same vote (for example, when laws are passed in the Supreme Soviet). *Yedinodushno*, on the other hand, is usually used for general support, when formal voting has been unnecessary (a certain kind of long applause is sometimes taken as a substitute for voting, for example), or when a formal vote has resulted in an overwhelming majority but not unanimity. After the formal polling during a Supreme Soviet election, for example, the press talks of a *yedinodushnoye* decision, because the positive votes constitute some 99.9 per cent of those eligible to vote. But this is clearly not really a unanimous decision, because there are 0.1 per cent spoiled or negative votes. Nonetheless, the support is so overwhelming that officials consider it improper to talk about a majority, or even an overwhelming majority. Or perhaps those who vote against are simply not taken seriously.

Gromyko's nomination speech was eventually published in some Party journals about a fortnight after he made it. It was, apparently, heavily edited. Some statements which were reported in the Western press to have been made by Gromyko (for example, 'this man has a nice smile, but he has iron teeth')[13] did not appear in the official text. Nonetheless, it was an unusual speech and it was easy to understand why it had not been published in the general press immediately. A public which is used only to certain stereotype statements being made in the Central Committee on such occasions may have found it surprising. In previous nomination speeches (the one made by Chernenko nominating Andropov, for example, or the one made by Tikhonov nominating Chernenko) the speaker first acclaimed the achievements of the deceased leader (who was already lying in state) and mourned the country's grievous loss. The second part of the speech usually concerned the nominee, and described his work and the offices he had held during his Party career. The intention was to make it clear how well qualified he was for the post. Gromyko, however, did not talk about Chernenko at all. It was as if he had never existed. This alone would have made his speech unsuitable for publication on March 12 with the other documents relevant to the event. But this was not all. In talking about Gorbachev, Gromyko did not mention his experience, achievements or previous posts. It was simply impossible to mention agriculture. All that Gromyko could do was to talk about Gorbachev's personal qualities. But there are many nice people around, so Gromyko represented him as a near-genius:

> . . . If, let's say, a scientific forum was taking place in this hall now, everyone would probably say that this man has an analytic approach to problems. And this is the exact truth. His ability in this respect is brilliant. He can separate a problem into sections and parts before coming to a conclusion. But he is not only good at analysing problems. He also makes generalizations and draws conclusions. Policy sometimes requires that one not only separates out problems or parts of problems into sections . . . but that one draws conclusions, so that they can be used to arm our policy. He has often demonstrated this ability at Politburo meetings and at meetings of the Secretariat of the CC.

But this apparently was not enough. So Gromyko made a strong plea for Party unity, appealing to his colleagues not to show dissent since this would please the foreign enemies of the Soviet Union:

> . . . there are various telescopes, figuratively speaking, focused on the Soviet Union; there are many of them, big and small, a short distance away and far away. More, perhaps, far away than near. And they look to see whether they can at last find any fissures in the Soviet leadership . . . A unanimous [*yedinodushnoye*] opinion in the Politburo that this time we, the Central Committee of the Party and the Politburo, will not give our political opponents satisfaction on this count [*Applause*].[14]

But it was this very speech (and particularly the fact that it was not published immediately) which fuelled speculation that there was discord by friend and foe alike. The speculations were well based. The history of the Communist Party of the Soviet Union has been full of repressions and full of splits, from the original split of the Russian Social Democratic Workers' Party into Bolsheviks and Mensheviks, to the power struggle in the 1920s, and other splits in the 1930s, 1940s and 1950s. There had clearly been a split in the Politburo on the night before the Central Committee meeting. The disappearance of Romanov from all official functions only a few weeks after the Plenum and his later early 'retirement' shows only too well what the nature of the split was. There were unofficial reports that Kunayev also made a statement at the Plenum, but it was never published anywhere.[15] Apparently, he went overboard in presenting Gorbachev as some kind of superman. This was considered too excessive – if Gorbachev was such a giant, people might ask why his great achievements had gone unnoticed until he was 54. In any case, public expectations might be raised too high. People had already grown weary of 'personality cults' which proved false.

I watched the broadcast in London on BBC1 of Chernenko's funeral on March 13 (as I had watched Brezhnev's and Andropov's). In November 1982 the London *Observer* colour magazine had asked me to watch Brezhnev's funeral carefully and to comment on the arrangements. The magazine expected many photographs from a photographer specially assigned to this job in Moscow. It was the first official funeral of a Soviet leader since

Stalin's death and the *Observer* was preparing a cover story 'How They Buried Leonid Brezhnev'. The editor wanted someone who had watched Stalin's funeral on Russian television in 1953 and who could spot any striking differences. In my commentary I wrote that the absence of grief amongst public and officials in 1982 was the most obvious difference.[16] Stalin's funeral was deeply emotional. Molotov, whose wife had been sent to prison by Stalin, did not try to hide his tears and his voice trembled. Khrushchev, who was soon to denounce Stalin as a criminal, also shed some tears which seemed sincere. The only person who was absolutely composed and quiet was Beria. All the speeches spoke not of the 'loss', but of the great tragedy and the irreparable loss. Brezhnev's funeral was more efficient and formal. Surprisingly, Andropov's funeral was also emotional, but it was the public (carefully selected and organized groups of the public are present at Red Square on these occasions) which showed emotion rather than the leaders standing on Lenin's mausoleum. They seemed to be very positive about Andropov's policy and deeply disappointed that fate had not given him a fair chance to continue. There was little emotion at Chernenko's funeral. In the few pictures of the public, they seemed to be expressing relief rather than grief. Nobody seemed to mourn the death of the poor, ill man. People probably remembered how weak and frail he had been when he made Andropov's funeral oration the previous winter. The only people who were visibly grieving for Chernenko were his wife, Anna, and other members of his family. The leaders on the mausoleum chatted to one another and even smiled.

In all other respects Chernenko's funeral seemed identical to the previous two at first. But when the leaders had lined up on the mausoleum for the funeral meeting, something seemed to be missing. There was not a single man in uniform. At Brezhnev's and Andropov's funerals there was not only Ustinov in the main group, but also a group of marshals (four for Brezhnev and three for Andropov) and the controversial Marshal Nikolai Ogarkov was easily recognizable. This time there were only civilians, although the deceased leader had been head of the Supreme Military Council and head of state and the presence of marshals to honour his last voyage was certainly his due. It is very unlikely that there was a military boycott, but just what the this striking absence means is not clear.

The funeral speeches were rather formal and measured, indicating a 'business as usual' approach. It is customary that one speech stresses the intellectual contribution made by the deceased leader. The President of the Academy of Sciences of the USSR, Professor Anatolii Aleksandrov had fulfilled this task at Brezhnev's funeral. Andropov who, while head of the KGB, had enjoyed writing poetry, was lauded from the mausoleum by the Chairman of the Writers' Union, Grigorii Markov. At Chernenko's funeral this role was played by Fedor Fedoseev, head of the social science section of the Academy and former director of the Institute of Marxism-Leninism. This seemed fair enough – Fedoseev had also delivered a eulogy at the funeral of Suslov, former chief ideologist, in January 1982.

When the traditional bearing of the casket to the grave site behind the mausoleum began, the Politburo members departed from tradition. At previous funerals they had helped to carry the coffin. This time they formed a group and walked behind the coffin, which is the usual procedure when ordinary Politburo members or other important figures are buried in Red Square without cremation. Suslov had been buried in this way, but Stalin, Brezhnev and Andropov had been borne part of the way to their graves by the Politburo, who considered the task an honour and took turns according to seniority (at Andropov's funeral Chernenko and Gorbachev had been the first bearers). Now they walked in ranks of four behind the coffin and nobody seemed to want the honour of bearing their comrade's casket. Although all these signs could be accidental, it seemed as if Chernenko was receiving a 'second class' funeral.

If it was a pre-arranged second class funeral, a second class commemoration decree was to be expected. In Brezhnev's case the governmental decree to perpetuate his memory was published less than ten days after the funeral.[17] Naberezhnye Chelny, a rather large city with a population of 414,000 in the Tartar Autonomous Republic, was renamed Brezhnev. It was an industrial city where a new truck plant had been built during Brezhnev's tenure. There were many other provisions as well, including the renaming of a district in Moscow and several squares in other cities. Several plants, navy and passenger ships and one ice breaker were named after Brezhnev, as well as a tank division, a number of schools, etc. Andropov's commemoration decree was far more modest and it was published more than a month after the funeral.[18] Rybinsk, a fine old Russian city in the Yaroslavl region on the Volga river, was renamed Andropov. This was where the late leader had started his Komsomol work in 1933 and graduated from the local technical college. The population of Andropov is 249,000. There was no Moscow district renamed after Andropov, but one avenue changed its name. Streets in other towns were also renamed, as well as one guard division, some industrial plants and a few schools (but no naval ships). One of the plants, the Rostov plant of combines and agricultural machinery was very large indeed.

It was a month and a half before Chernenko's commemoration decree was published on April 26, and people could see how his work had been evaluated on this scale.[19] A Siberian town called Sharypovo was named Chernenko. Nobody I know has ever heard of this town and it was not mentioned in Chernenko's official biography. Nor is it listed with the towns and cities with a population of more than 50,000 in the 1983 Soviet statistics yearbook.[20] It does not appear in the list of Soviet towns and cities with a population of more than 15,000 in the 1970 census records or in the latest edition of the Great Soviet Encyclopedia (the volume containing *sh* was published in 1978). On some very detailed maps a village called Sharypovo can be found, about 400 km from Krasnoyarsk and rather far from any other centre and from the Trans-Siberian railway. It was by accident that I found in *Izvestiya* that it had become a town only recently because an atomic power station will be constructed there at some future date.[21] *Izvestiya* reported that the road being built to the site violates the plans and the law and the case is now in the Procurator's hands. There were no military units named after Chernenko, except the frontier post on the Chinese border where the 20-year-old Chernenko was on active duty in the early 1930s. Nor have any avenues in Moscow been renamed, although a street which has yet to be built in one of the new suburbs will be called after him. A few schools, pioneer clubs and industrial plants have been given his name. This was even less than a second class commemoration. It was almost as if Chernenko was being treated as an illegitimate leader who could not expect a prominent place in Soviet history. It would be easier now for Gorbachev to make an impression.

2
Childhood and youth

Mikhail Sergeevich Gorbachev (pronounced Gorbachyoff), the eighth leader of the Soviet Union,[1] was born on March 2, 1931 in the village of Privol'noye in the Krasnogvardeisk district of Stavropol *krai*. His parents were peasants. His grandfather was a member of the Party and the chairman of the first collective farm founded in Privol'noye in 1931. His father, Sergei Andreevich, was prior to the war a machine operator in a local Machine-Tractor Station. He served in the army during the war and later worked as an economist and party local official.[2] He died in 1976. Gorbachev's mother, Maria Panteleyvna, is now 74 years old and still lives in Privol'noye. If he has siblings, nothing is known about them. He may well have been an only child. Although Russian peasant families are traditionally rather large, this does not apply to the late 1920s and 1930s. In these years of rural discontent, collectivization, terror and starvation, the rural birthrate declined sharply and the infant mortality rate rose (rural mortality was higher then than in the 19th century).

Stavropol had not yet become a separate territorial and administrative unit in 1931. It was still part of the large North Caucasian *krai*, which covered the area between the Azov, Black and Caspian seas and which was the most important grain producing area for the urban population of the Russian Federation (RSFSR). Privol'noye is situated in the dry, fertile steppe area between the low parts of two great Russian rivers – the Don and the Volga. The village probably dates from the late 18th century, when the southern plains of Russia were colonized by peasants, many of them refugees from the serfdom of the Russian empire. Earlier settlers in the area, known as Cossacks, date from the 16th and 17th centuries, but most of them lived along the Dnieper,

Don, Kuban and Volga rivers (and later along the Ural and Terek rivers). The oldest trade and transport routes between the Nordic countries and the Byzantine Empire were these rivers and the peasants who fled from the yoke of serfdom or from famine also often travelled southwards by boat and spontaneously colonized the large and fertile lands of the south. They were usually organized into autonomous peasant–military communes each with its own elected leaders. The steppes of the low plains of the Manych Depression, however, were settled later, during the rule of Catherine the Great. Stavropol was built in 1777–8 as a fortress to secure the new frontiers of the Russian Empire against the mostly Moslem inhabitants of the mountain areas of the North Caucasus. Serfdom, which was only abolished in Russia in 1861, did not reach as far as Stavropol province. The peasants lived as free farmers and there was plenty of land for everyone. The name of the village where Gorbachev was born, Privol'noye, means 'free' or 'spacious'. The area is, indeed, sparsely populated. Sixty to seventy miles to the north are the rather dry, often salinated Salsk steppes (in the eastern part of Rostov region) and next to the north-east border of Krasnogvardeisk district is the Kalmyk Autonomous Republic. As late as the 1950s there were still vast tracts of virgin steppe land in Stavropol *krai*.

The October Revolution did not immediately change life much in villages like Privol'noye. Soviet power was established in the North Caucasus by the end of 1917. However, during the summer of 1918 'White' officers of the old Tsarist army and the Cossacks who were hostile to the food requisitioning policy of the new Soviet government rebelled. This marked the beginning of a Civil War which was to last three years. The memory of the Civil War is enshrined in the names of many villages and towns in the area – the Krasnogvardeisk district, for example, is named after the Red Guards, and Ipatovo (the district Gorbachev has represented in the Supreme Soviet since 1979) after the local Civil War hero, Ipatov, who was executed by the Cossacks in 1919. The war in the North Caucasus ended in 1920. In 1921 there was a severe drought and the combined effects of war and drought were calamitous – in the famine of 1921–2 more than 5 million people (most of them from the Volga basin) died of starvation or epidemics. Privol'noye was very close to the main disaster area and thousands of refugees from the famine-stricken Volga provinces passed through the village on their way to the more prosperous parts of the North Caucasus.

The New Economic Policy, introduced in 1921 to encourage individual private agriculture, was greeted enthusiastically by peasants all over the country. Agriculture recovered rapidly and the North Caucasus, together with the lower and middle Volga area, again became the most important food producing region in the country. It was officially designated as the main grain producing area. At that time Stavropol was a small district town and the main administrative capital of the territory was Rostov-on-Don. The Krasnodar area and several other areas which later became autonomous republics (for example, North Osetia, the Chechen-Ingush Republic and the Kabardin-Balkar Republic) also formed part of the administrative territory supervised by the North Caucasian *krai* Party Committee in Rostov.

Stalin's programme of forced collectivization shattered the previously little affected life of rural Russia. His industrialization plans had favoured heavy industry at the expense of the light and consumer-oriented industries. As a result, industry would not be able to produce sufficient consumer goods to satisfy rural demands. Without goods to offer in return, it would be difficult to persuade peasants to sell the food required for the developing towns. Stalin's remedy was simple: the peasants' land, horses, cattle and implements would be confiscated and they would be forced into collective farms (*kolkhozy*). The *kolkhozy* would then be forced to sell the necessary food. Because the main resistance to the programme came from the wealthier peasants (*kulaks*), it was decided that they should be eliminated as a class. Confiscation of property, mass deportation and execution followed, not only of *kulaks*, but often of less wealthy peasants. This mass terror had reached its peak in 1931, the year that Mikhail Gorbachev was born.

Stalin was determined that the collectivization of grain producing areas should be completed before the beginning of the spring sowing season in 1931. A daily watch was kept on the pace of collectivization from January 1931 and the press reported weekly figures of the new *kolkhozy* which had been formed. 730,000 peasant households were collectivized in January, 1,500,000 in February and 1,700,000 in March.[3] In April, when the agricultural season had begun in the North Caucasus, the pace slowed down.

However, at the end of March, it was reported that 86.4 per cent of all rural households in the North Caucasus had been collectivized.[4] Gorbachev's birth and the creation of a *kolkhoz* in Privol'noye probably occurred simultaneously: his parents were probably new *kolkhozniki.* Gorbachev's grandfather was an activist of collectivization and the chairman of the newly created *kolkhoz.* Collectivization resumed after the harvesting season, and was said to have reached 90 per cent by the end of August.[5] The fate of the remaining 10 per cent of peasant households remains unconfirmed. But since of the 23 million peasant households in Russia in 1929, only 17 million were registered after the completion of collectivization in 1934, it is not too difficult to surmise what happened. Of the missing 6 million households, some (*kulaks* and their families, and '*kulak* sympathizers', in other words, anyone who resisted collectivization) were arrested and deported. Others died in the famine which affected the Ukraine and other grain producing areas, including the North Caucasus. This famine was not a natural disaster. It was man-made, entirely the result of collectivization and the forced procurement of excessive amounts of grain and other produce from the newly created collective farms.

1931 was the peak year of collectivization and also a crucial year for the first Five Year Plan. The industrial output of 1931 exceeded that of 1930 by 21 per cent. This was the most rapid growth ever recorded in Soviet history. The highest rate of increase was in the heavy and machine tool industries. The growth of new industrial centres raised the demand for food and in response the government increased the procurement quotas of the weak, poorly organized *kolkhozy* and of individual peasants. In 1930 46 per cent of the total harvest in the North Caucasus had been taken by the state. In 1931 the proportion was 63.4 per cent, leaving far too little for the rural families which represented 80 per cent of the population.[6] These forcible procurements deprived peasants of the incentive to work and there were ominous signs of rural tension (later referred to as 'grain strikes') in 1932. Labour discipline on the *kolkhozy* was lax. The *kraikom* secretary in the North Caucasus, B. P. Sheboldayev, was a cruel man who was determined to use repression to ensure that the procurement quota was met in 1932. He also created his own personality cult in the area and the local press was full of extravagant tributes to him, often associating his name with Stalin's. Nonetheless, the grain collections in the Stavropol area and other parts of the North Caucasus were well below target. The *kolkhozniki* demanded advance payment in kind as a condition of their work on the collective farm. There was widespread slaughter of livestock and horses. The result was that 1932 was a disaster.

In October 1932 Stalin sent a special commission to the North Caucasus, headed by Kaganovich, and including Mikoyan, People's Commissar of Supply (before 1946 ministries were called People's Commissariats and ministers were referred to as People's Commissar), Yagoda, First Deputy Chairman of the OGPU (the political police), Gamarnik, head of the Political Directorate of the Red Army, and other officials. The Commission was given extraordinary powers and it introduced a kind of state of emergency in the area. Although Gorbachev was certainly too young to be affected by the economic and political situation in Stavropol area in the early 1930s, it must have had an enormous impact on his family, as it did on all the families in the area. Almost every family lost relatives, friends or neighbours during this period and Privol'noye was no exception. The repressions of the 1930s hit the rural areas of the North Caucasus particularly badly and Gorbachev must have been told a lot of stories about these events later. It may even explain why he decided to study law at the University of Moscow (a curious career for a peasant boy). In the early 1930s terror and lawlessness ruled the rural life of the North Caucasus. At the North Caucasus *krai* plenum on November 12, 1932, Sheboldayev demanded draconian measures against whole villages. The speech he made at the plenum reflects the prevailing situation and his cruel nature:

> We openly proclaimed that we would send off to northern regions malicious saboteurs and kulak agents who do not want to sow. Didn't we in previous years deport kulak counter-revolutionary elements from this same Kuban? We did, in sufficient numbers. And today when these remnants of the kulak class try to organize sabotage, oppose the demands of the Soviet regime, it is more correct to give away the fertile Kuban land to collective farmers who live in other *krais* on poor land, and not enough even of that poor land . . . And those who do not want to work, who defile our land, we'll send them to other places. That's fair. We may be told: 'What? Earlier you deported kulaks, and now you're talking about

> a whole village, where there are both collective farms and conscientious individual peasants? How can that be?' Yes, we must raise the question of a whole village, because the collective farms, because the really conscientious individual peasants, in the present situation, *must answer for the condition of their neighbours*. What kind of support for the Soviet regime is a collective farm, if right next to it another collective farm or a whole group of individual farms oppose the measures of the Soviet regime?'[7]

It is not surprising that during the winter of 1932–3, the Stavropol area, like the rest of the south of the country, was a famine disaster zone. The death toll from starvation was very high, and the highest mortality rate was amongst young children. In some villages all the children between the ages of one and two died. Mikhail Gorbachev survived, but it is possible that some of his relatives died. The Soviet writer, A. B. Kosterin, who visited the area in 1933 and 1934, described the situation:

> I had the occasion to go through dozens of villages in Stavropol, on the Don, Kuban, and Terek, and in Saratov, Orenburg, and Kalinin *oblasti* . . . Houses with boarded-up windows, empty barnyards, abandoned equipment in fields. And terrifying mortality, especially among children . . .
>
> On the deserted road to Stavropol I met a peasant with a knapsack. We stopped, greeted each other, had a smoke. I asked him, 'Where are you tramping, comrade?'
>
> 'To prison'.
>
> Astonishment kept me from saying or asking anything. I only looked my amazement at the old man. . . . He smoked calmly and quite unexcitedly told me his story. He was a middle peasant who had been sentenced to ten years. . . . for refusing to join a collective farm and for speaking against the plenipotentiary in the village meeting. The village policeman lacked the time or the inclination to escort him to Stavropol, so he was going alone.[8]

This brief excursion into the past of the Stavropol peasantry is relevant to Gorbachev's career as a political leader. Russian rural families have strong links. Their children know the tragedies and problems suffered by their native villages. Village boys who later become prominent do not lose these links. They continue visiting their villages, they often still have relatives there and they try to help their communities. Khrushchev, for example, was born in the village of Kalinovka in the Kursk region. He used to visit the village almost every year and he tried to make it prosperous – it received generous state help and was transformed into a modern agrotown. Although Andropov was not of peasant stock, his father was a railroad official at Nagutskaya station in the Stavropol area. The station was named after the nearby village of Nagutskaya, where the Andropov family had its roots. When Andropov became General Secretary in 1982, plans were immediately made to build a large modern hospital and a new high school in Nagutskaya village. They were built very quickly and were already operating when Andropov died in February 1984. Brezhnev was born in an industrial town, where his grandparents and parents laboured in a steel mill. When he became General Secretary, he selected many people for leadership positions (including ex-Prime Minister Tikhonov) who were from the same metallurgical complex where he had worked in the 1930s. He trusted them not because they were particularly competent and reliable, but because they were born in his province or town.

Following the adoption of the 'Stalin constitution' in 1936, there was an administrative re-arrangement of the Soviet Union in 1937. The North Caucasus *krai* was divided into Rostov region and several territories and Autonomous National Republics. The reorganization was accompanied by the wholesale arrest of the North Caucasus *kraikom*, including its secretary Sheboldayev, who was declared an 'enemy of the people' and executed.[9] In 1934 Stavropol was renamed Voroshilovsk (after Voroshilov, then Commissar for Defence and a member of the Politburo). It is, however, more convenient to continue using the old Greek name Stavropol, since it was restored during the war. The area was under occupation and the Germans restored the old names, particularly when new names had been derived from the names of Communist leaders or symbols. Many towns and areas reverted to their new names after the war, but Stavropol remained Stavropol, perhaps because Voroshilov had not acquitted himself very well during the war. Stavropol *krai* was a large, predominantly agricultural region, occupying 80,600 sq km (31,100 square miles). The population was mostly Russian, although there were some small Moslem national minorities, mainly Karachai and Circassians, in the mountain areas (which is why the area was called a *krai*).

Gorbachev was eight years old when Suslov, who was later to help him get the position of secretary of the Central Committee, was appointed first secretary of Stavropol *kraikom*. Suslov had been a member of the Communist Party since 1921 and had started working in the Party apparatus in Moscow in 1931. He was of peasant origin, born in a very poor family in Saratov province in 1902. He had worked in the Komsomol since 1918 and had been a member of the Committee of Poor Peasants (*Kombedy*) in his village. The *Kombedy* had been an important element of Soviet power in rural areas during the Civil War. In the 1930s Suslov participated in some of the purges in the Urals and in the Chernigov region. He was a member of Kaganovich's team, known for its ruthlessness. In 1937 he became one of the Rostov *obkom* secretaries, after the arrest of almost the entire *obkom*. He was promoted to Stavropol, again following the arrest of the *kraikom*. While there is no proven direct link between his activity and these repressions, they certainly enabled him to rise in the hierarchy.[10] In 1939 he was elected as a delegate from Stavropol *krai* to the XVIIIth Party Congress, where he was made a member of the Central Control Commission. In 1941, just before the war began, he was elected a full member of the Central Committee.

Since the late 1920s there had been primary schools (for children between the ages of 8 and 12) in almost every large village in the Soviet Union. Very large villages, like Privol'noye, usually also had 'pre-secondary' schools for the 12–15 year old age group. Peasant children began working in the *kolkhozy* at the age of 16 unless they were given the opportunity to continue their education at a town secondary school. Gorbachev was still at primary school when the German army invaded the Soviet Union in June 1941. Almost all the men in the villages who were in their twenties and thirties were mobilized immediately. At that time I lived in Rostov-on-Don, the former capital of the North Caucasus and the largest city in South Russia. I was 15 years old and had just completed my seventh school year. The war seemed far away and in July, together with my classmates, I was sent to one of the *kolkhozy* in the Don area to assist with the harvesting. The harvest was very good and we returned to Rostov at the end of August. The city had changed. People were in a panic. The Germans had occupied Taganrog, an important port on the Azov Sea, only 70 miles away. The Soviet army was retreating in apparent disarray and there was no sign of a strong defence. When Rostov was bombed several times, my mother decided to take us out of the city. Nobody seemed to know what was going on. We left Rostov on August 28, only a few days before the German army entered the city. In fact, the first occupation lasted only a few days. The Soviet army re-took the city after a week. But we did not return. We moved eastwards to Tbilisi, our native city, where I lived until February 1943, when I was called up for military service at what was then known as the North Caucasian Front.

However, my military career was shortlived. I was wounded by a German sniper near Krasnodar in May, I was emerging from a trench in an unsown field which was so fertile that the *chernozem* extended well below the bottom of the 2-metre deep trench. It was then that I recognized the natural beauty of the North Caucasus and the destruction caused by the war. It was this experience which made me decide to become an agronomist. There was certainly nothing in my family to prompt me to make this choice – my mother was a musician and my father an historian. Both they and their families had always been city dwellers. When I was invalided out of the army, I started a 5-year course at the Timiryazev Agricultural Academy in Moscow. Thus my knowledge of the war years in the North Caucasus and of post-war developments in agriculture comes directly from personal experience.

A new German offensive began in July 1942. Designed as a 'Blitzkrieg', it was launched in two directions – a shorter drive to Stalingrad to cut the communication lines between North and South Russia and a second drive towards Grozny in the North Caucasus and Baku on the Caspian sea, the only source of Soviet oil. Rostov was abandoned by the Soviet army for the second time on July 24, 1942. Less than two weeks later, on August 5, German troops entered Stavropol, about 200 miles away. By the end of August Soviet resistance had become better organized and the German offensive began to slow down. The German army did not succeed in breaking through to Grozny, its most important objective in the North Caucasus. The offensive was halted about 70 miles away. The occupation of Stavropol lasted for five months. A Soviet counter-offensive was launched at the beginning of January 1943 and it moved rapidly. Stavropol was by-passed by both offensives and the steppes to the north of the town, where

Privol'noye was located, never became a battle zone. Most of the towns and villages which were destroyed were along the railway and other roads and the other steppe villages were, for the most part, spared. There was probably no proper German occupation regime in Privol'noye – German units usually entered remote settlements only to find food and to hunt out and arrest Jews.

It seems certain that Gorbachev and his family remained in Privol'noye during the war. There was no organized evacuation of village people and the speed of the German offensive, absence of information and general chaos made most villagers reluctant to leave their homes. In any case, with the German army so deep inside Russia, there was a feeling amongst urban and rural people alike that there was no safe place to go. Suslov was at that time a member of the Military Council of the North Caucasian Front and in charge of the organization of the partisan movement in the area of Stavropol *krai*.

For the Moslem population of the North Caucasus and lower Volga areas the post-liberation period was more traumatic than the occupation had been. At the end of 1943 Stalin ordered the deportation of Moslem nations who were arbitrarily accused of 'collaboration with the occupying forces'. In November 1943 the entire Karachai population of Stavropol *krai* (about 80,000 people) were arrested and forcibly deported to special settlements in Central Asia. The Kalmyks, who lived even closer to Privol'noye (some of their settlements were only 30–40 miles from the village), were loaded into guarded freight trains and moved to Siberia by special troops of the NKVD within a period of four days at the end of December.[11] In 1944 the same fate befell the Chechen, Ingush, Karbardin, Balkar and Crimean Tartar peoples. The latter were the largest Moslem group in the European part of the Soviet Union. In all about one million people were deported and more than 15 Red Army divisions were involved in this repressive operation. It took place during a crucial phase of the war, when the soldiers were needed far more urgently at the front to fight against the German army than to repress defenceless old people, women and children. During Khrushchev's time, in the late 1950s, all the deported peoples, with the exception of the Crimean Tartars and the Volga Germans, were rehabilitated and allowed to return to their native areas. Stalin and Beria are held most responsible for this monstrous action, but Suslov must also have been directly involved, since it was usually announced that the deportation had been 'recommended' by the local *kraikom* and *raikom*. Of course, Gorbachev was probably too young in 1943 to understand what had happened to the Moslem people of the area, but in the late 1950s, when they began to return, he was already the first secretary of the Stavropol town Komsomol and a member of the *kraikom* Komsomol bureau. The restoration of the Karachai-Circassian Autonomous Region and the difficult job of finding them living space and jobs (many villages had been settled by people from Byelorussia and the Ukraine) must partly have been his responsibility.

In September 1943 Gorbachev resumed his schooling. From 1945 onwards he worked each summer as a temporary employee of the local Machine-Tractor Station (MTS), as an assistant combine operator. In the short biographies which were published before he came to power, his job in those years was defined as assistant combine operator. In March 1985, however, an official biography was published in which it was said that he worked as a 'machine operator at a machine and tractor station',[12] probably to emphasize that his work was more than just participating in the combine harvesting which usually lasted for a very brief period. His work was seasonal and he continued his secondary education, probably living in or commuting to the district centre. He never formally joined a *kolkhoz* – working in a MTS was considered state employment. During and after the war all the rural youth had to work in a *kolkhoz*, *sovkhoz* or a MTS. The Central Committee and government passed a decree on April 13, 1942 which reduced, as an emergency measure, the age at which rural children had to begin working from 16 to 12 years. This officially legalized the employment of children. Every boy or girl aged 12 to 16 was given a compulsory minimum number of *trudodni* (working day units) of 50 days, a third of the minimal adult quota. Manpower losses were extremely high and were felt particularly acutely in rural areas. Qualified industrial workers were often left to fulfil their military obligations by working in military industries. In 1943 the conscription age was raised to 50. Qualified mechanics, tractor drivers and combine operators were mobilized and replaced by women and by children like Gorbachev. It was not just a 'summer job', but hard work, often for as long as 11 or 12 hours a day. The school year could not start until the harvesting was over.

1946 was an extremely difficult agricultural year. The destruction wrought by the war was aggravated by a severe drought throughout most of the country. The total grain harvest was only 39 million metric tons – the level of 1921, also a famine year. Some parts of the Ukraine experienced serious famine and a major disaster was avoided only by drastic food rationing. In a few areas, however, the harvest was better and individual *kolkhozy* and *sovkhozy* managed to fulfil their plans. As a result Stalin passed a decree in December 1946 which promised decorations and generous rewards to *kolkhoz* peasants, *sovkhoz* and MTS workers, brigade and *kolkhoz* chairmen who fulfilled their plans and produced high yields of grain, technical crops or livestock products. Many successful rural workers and peasants accordingly received the title of Hero of Socialist Labour with the Order of Lenin and a Gold Star medal. Others were given the Order of the Red Banner of Labour, the Order of Honour and medals. Ever since then the rewarding of *kolkhozniki* and *sovkhoz* and MTS workers for fulfilling and overfulfilling their official plans and quotas has become institutionalized practice. It was (and is) expected that the prospect of this kind of award would stimulate the peasants to work harder and better.

Despite the new awards, the harvest of 1947 was poor and 65 million metric tons of grain were produced, well below the pre-war (97 million tons in 1937) and pre-revolutionary levels (86 million tons in 1913). The harvests of 1948 and 1949 were not much better – 67 million tons and 70.2 million tons.[13] In 1949 the village of Privol'noye had a very good harvest and overfulfilled its plan. Many of the local officials, peasants and brigade chairmen were nominated for government awards, among them the 18-year-old Gorbachev and his fellow combine operators. The list of awards decreed by the Presidium of the Supreme Soviet was published at the end of the year. Gorbachev had been awarded the Order of the Red Banner of Labour. It must have been a great boost to the morale and ambitions of the young peasant boy. Already in the Komsomol, he applied to become a candidate member of the CPSU in 1950. Joining the Party in the Soviet Union is a two stage process. The first stage, which cannot be undertaken until the age of 18, is to become a candidate member for at least a year. Candidate members are subject to Party discipline and may attend closed Party meetings, but they do not have any voting rights. Only after this probationary period has been judged successful can the candidate member apply for full membership. Officially Gorbachev only joined the Party in 1952, that is, the year that he became a full member. But for all practical purposes, he entered the ranks of the Party in 1950.

The year of German occupation had delayed Gorbachev's school career, but he finally graduated a year late in June 1950 and was given the opportunity to enter higher education. Had he failed the entrance examinations and missed this opportunity, he would have been conscripted into the army. Many boys reduce the risk of conscription by applying for places at provincial universities and institutions of higher education, where the competition is less fierce and the chances of success are higher. Gorbachev's award and his candidate membership of the Party probably influenced his bold decision to apply to the most prestigious higher education institution in the country – Moscow State University. There was strong competition for places in the Law Faculty – many demobilized young soldiers with military awards and medals were returning from the Soviet occupational forces in Eastern Europe, Manchuria and the areas where strong nationalist opposition movements still existed (Lithuania, Western Ukraine). However, the Order of the Red Banner of Labour was a rarity amongst applicants for Moscow State University and in a system in which there are special rules and instructions for admitting applicants, it certainly must have been a positive factor in Gorbachev's application. Although there were entrance examinations, it is doubtful that they were conducted in the spirit of genuinely fair academic competition. For one thing, the Ministry of Higher Education introduced regulations in 1949–50 to limit the admission of Jews and a few other social groups defined as 'unreliable' to universities and institutes of higher education. For another, active efforts were made to increase the proportion of provincial students studying at Moscow University. This is not to imply that Gorbachev did not have the requisite intelligence and ability – his subsequent career has proved that he was by no means deficient in either quality. But rural school education was certainly inferior to the standard of education in Moscow or Leningrad schools. Consequently, provincial applicants found the entrance examinations extremely difficult.

Gorbachev's choice of the Law Faculty remains a puzzle for his biographers. There was nothing in his life before 1950 to indicate an interest in the legal profession. His work in the MTS over several years would, it might be thought, have encouraged an interest in agriculture, agricultural machinery or general technical education and these fields offered many interesting choices. The needs of post-war industrial reconstruction had engendered active propaganda for technical education. Moreover, popular attitudes towards the legal profession in the Soviet Union are very different from Western attitudes. To become a lawyer in 1950 was to join a profession with very low prestige. Most young people did not even know that it was possible to become a defence lawyer. The only member of the legal profession who was widely known was the procurator – the legal defender of the interests of the state. Respect for procurators was particularly low amongst the rural population, which had, over the years, experienced coercion and legal excesses rather than justice. Procurators were associated with the arbitrary repressions, and the unjust, extortionate and restrictive legislation to which the villages had long been subject. Gorbachev's choice may have indicated a desire to cut his links with agriculture, or perhaps it was an early symptom of his political ambitions. As it turned out, knowledge and training in agriculture would be far more useful to his political ambitions than his legal expertise.

University years

In 1950 Moscow State University, founded in 1755 by the scientist, poet and linguist, Mikhail Lomonosov, was the most important centre of higher education in the Soviet Union. In 1946 Stalin had decided, as part of a programme stimulated by the American success in building an atom bomb, to invest heavily in Soviet science. A new campus was built for Moscow University on the Lenin Hills, in the south-west suburbs of the city. The central skyscraper on the new university campus has dominated the Moscow skyline since 1948. The faculties which moved out to the new campus were the natural sciences – mathematics, physics, chemistry and biology. The humanities – philosophy, history, law, literature, linguistics, etc. – remained in the old university buildings in the centre of Moscow, a block away from the Manezh and near the Kremlin and Gorky Street, and expanded into the space vacated by the sciences. The university library and the zoological and archeological museums also remained in what soon became known as the 'old university'. Science students were accommodated in the new luxury hostels on campus, where two students shared a room with modern facilities. Humanities students, however, still lived in old hostel accommodation far from the centre. The hostels tended to be overcrowded with four students sharing a room and a whole corridor sharing a toilet and wash room.

Soviet students usually receive a modest stipend from the state. The amount varies from institution to institution and depends on year of study and academic progress. In the 1950s the average stipend was between 200 and 300 old roubles (20–30 new roubles), barely enough to buy two meals a day in the university or institute canteen. To live above subsistence level parental support, a part-time manual job or private tutoring was essential. The villages were very poor, however, and it is unlikely that Gorbachev's relatives could afford to give him financial support. In Stalin's times food parcels were often sent from the towns to the villages, rather than vice versa. During the summer vacations Gorbachev returned to Privol'noye and worked as a combine operator. This probably provided him with the extra money he required.

Probably because of his Party candidate status and his good political record, Gorbachev did not live in ordinary, cramped student accommodation during his years at university. He shared a rather better room with a Czech student, Zdenek Mlynar, an able young man who was a member of the Czech Communist Party. Many Moscow institutions of higher education had fairly large communities of students from the Eastern European People's Democracies, as Poland, Czechoslovakia, Hungary, Romania, Bulgaria and East Germany were known. East Germany, however, did not usually send students to Moscow, partly because the hostility towards Germany had not yet disappeared and partly because there were excellent universities in Germany. The standard term for these East European students in Moscow student slang was 'demokraty'. At first the word was used ironically, but it soon lost any pejorative connotation – it was clear that the young men and women from Eastern Europe were better dressed, had more material comforts and enjoyed a great deal more freedom than their Soviet colleagues. There were many Chinese students in Moscow as well. The Chinese student community was probably the largest foreign community in Moscow. But they were under the strict control of their own mentors, they were not allowed to share rooms with Russians (the 'demokraty' often preferred to share with Russians so that they could learn the language more quickly) and they tended to keep to themselves. There was a sharp contrast between the behaviour and life style of the 'demokraty' and the Chinese students.

Zdenek Mlynar, who recently published two articles about his student friendship with Gorbachev,[14] believes that it was pure chance that he shared with Gorbachev. In fact, room-mates for foreign students are never selected randomly in the Soviet Union. Only 'trustworthy' Soviet students are distributed amongst the better rooms allocated to foreigners. Foreign students were kept under a certain amount of surveillance in Stalin's time (this probably still occurs), and it is not unlikely that Gorbachev would have been asked to give periodic reports on his room-mate. Then, as now, universities and other institutes which educated foreign students had a special member of staff who was called the dean of foreign students and whose job was to deal with their problems. They normally co-operate with the security system, and the information they acquire is sent back to responsible officials in Eastern Europe. If Gorbachev was, indeed, responsible for reporting on Mlynar, it is clear that they must have enjoyed very cordial, friendly relations, since Mlynar's rise in the Czechoslovak Communist Party was rather more rapid than Gorbachev's rise in the Komsomol and CPSU. In 1967, when Gorbachev was still in Stavropol, Mlynar became a secretary of the Central Committee of the Czechoslovak Party in Prague and one of the leading reformists of the Prague Spring of 1968. He emigrated to Austria in 1977.

In Mlynar's account of his student life in Moscow from 1950–5, he described how he and Gorbachev, who was his room-mate and classmate for the entire period, not only shared a room, but were in the same study group, took the same examinations and were awarded the same good degrees.[15] According to Mlynar, Gorbachev was intellectually able, without being arrogant. He was also loyal and honest and he possessed a natural air of authority.

He had never really known a foreigner before and he had surprisingly few of the inhibitions which were normally observed in Soviet students in their contact with foreigners. Mlynar sent him a postcard from Czechoslovakia in the summer of 1951 and Gorbachev reported that it had been delivered to him personally in the fields near Privol'noye by the local police chief – because it came from abroad it was suspicious. Mlynar believes that Gorbachev realized that the law had little relevance to the daily life of workers, since their obedience was guaranteed by coercion. His favourite quotation from his study of Marxist philosophy was 'Truth is always positive, real'. He was very active in university Komsomol work and became a full member of the Party in 1952. Mlynar, however, believed that the 'private' Gorbachev was very different from the official student of Stalin's law:

> In 1952 . . . we were studying the official history of Russia, we were led to believe that any ideas that deviated even slightly from the rigid party line were anti-party, and that any person who held such beliefs should be tried, executed, taken out of the history books . . . It was then that Gorbachev said to me 'Lenin did not have Martov arrested, he allowed him to leave the country'. Today such a remark would not be given much importance . . . But in 1952 those words signified that the student Gorbachev doubted that there were only two types of Russians, those who adhered strictly to the Party line and the criminals who did not. What is more, to confide an opinion of this sort to a foreigner, even to a friend, was unusual in those days.[16]

Far less generous recollections about Gorbachev were published by two Soviet emigres who also studied in the Law Faculty of Moscow State University in the early 1950s. Lev Yudovich, who now lives in the United States, recalls Gorbachev as the dogmatic Komsomol secretary of the Law Faculty who was responsible for ideology and propaganda and who always took a hard line when discussing problems of the behaviour of other Komsomol members.[17] Fridrikh Neznansky, formerly a Moscow investigator and procurator, who emigrated in the late 1970s and became known in the West as the author of thrillers based on the life of the Soviet elite (one of his co-authored novels, *Red Square*, was a bestseller in Britain soon after Brezhnev's death) was also one of Gorbachev's fellow students. He claims that he often heard:

> . . . the steely voice of the Komsomol secretary of the Law Faculty, Gorbachev, demanding expulsion from the Komsomol for the slightest offence, from inappropriately telling political anecdotes to shirking being sent to a *kolkhoz*.[18]

These differences of opinion are natural, of course. But it is certainly the case that Yudovich and Neznansky must themselves have been 'hardline' in the performance of their own duties. Their speeches as procurators must have reflected the political realities of the time, not the beliefs they now hold.

A few points need to be made about legal education in the Soviet Union. It is provided by the law faculties of some universities and by special Law Institutes. Out of the total 1.2 million students in the Soviet Union in the academic year 1950–51, there were 45,400 students of law.[19] It was not a popular profession and the number of law students declined in 1958–59 to 36,200, at a time when students of other professions almost doubled. The number of law students only began to grow after 1964. The decline reflected the problems of the profession after Stalin's death, when his crimes and the general lawlessness of the regime began to be exposed. Khrushchev's public denunciation of Stalin's crimes took place in 1956, when Gorbachev had already graduated. It seems likely that the events of 1953 to 1955 – Beria's arrest, the rehabilitation of the Kremlin doctors who had been arrested before Stalin's death, the return to the university Law Faculty of some Jewish professors who had been arrested and, sometimes, exiled – were discussed by students. However, the official content of the law courses remained unchanged until the end of 1956. Moreover, Stalin's draconian criminal code remained in force until 1958 and law textbooks continued to explain and comment on the law in the same way as before Stalin's death. It took until 1960 to prepare new legislation which reduced the previous extensive legislation on political, state and counter-revolutionary crimes to a few articles, only one of which (Article 70, on anti-Soviet propaganda) dealt with political crimes. Khrushchev's legislation in the political area was so mild that Brezhnev later found it very difficult to use the law against political dissent. As a result, several new laws were added to the Criminal Code during Brezhnev's time to give the KGB and the law-enforcement organs better opportunities to suppress dissent by using 'socialist legality'.

The main textbook on Soviet law which was approved for university use after Stalin's death and Beria's arrest was the two volume *Course of Soviet Criminal Law*, written by Professors A. A. Piontovsky and V. D. Men'shagin and published at the beginning of 1955. It reflected the legislation and practice valid in 1954.[20] Gorbachev, however, must have used the previous edition for most of his studies. The new edition was published just in time to give students graduating in 1955 a taste of the change in the way Soviet law was explained. Half of the first volume of this textbook is devoted to explaining how to deal with counter-revolutionary crimes against the state and crimes which are a particular danger to the Soviet system of administration. The active search for these crimes and the severe punishments are explained in terms of Stalin's theory about the class struggle of the overthrown classes. The show trials of 1929–31 and 1936–38 are presented as examples of true 'socialist legality'. An attempt is made to justify the mass arrests, deportations and executions of *kulaks* and other campaigns against 'enemies of the people'. Both this textbook and many other law books still reflected A. Y. Vyshinsky's dominance of the Soviet legal system. He was still a powerful and respected figure in 1950–54. He was Foreign Minister from 1949–1953 and Soviet representative at the United Nations in 1954. The Soviet press regularly published the long speeches he gave in New York. He died in New York in November 1954 from a heart attack and was buried in Moscow with full honours. He became well known in the West because of the part he played in the Metro-Vickers trial, when British engineers were accused of trying to wreck Soviet hydroelectric construction. But his notoriety stemmed from the fact that he was the General Procurator who conducted all the major show trials in Moscow in 1936–38, during Stalin's purges. He was an aggressive, vengeful, cynical person and he favoured confession rather than evidence of a crime. His determination to extract confessions from defendants led to the large scale use of torture during the investigation of crime. He was also opposed to professional courts and independent defence lawyers. He explained that in a socialist system, where judge, investigator and procurator all want to establish truth and justice, a defence lawyer is unnecessary. Defence lawyers try to mislead the court. Despite the fact that the Vyshinsky model of justice was discredited in 1956–58, the role of the defence lawyer has never become an important part of the Soviet juridical system.

In the early 1950s Vyshinsky was still considered the leading legal scholar and his books were required reading for students like Gorbachev. But law students also studied classical works, the history of law, Roman law, theory of law, state and administrative law, employment law, civil law, including the law that regulated the work of *kolkhozy* and labour law, etc. Probably the most relevant part of the curriculum in terms of Gorbachev's present position was international law. This covered the history of international law and modern international law. The Soviet version of international law combines the recognition of sovereignty and the validity of international agreements and treaties with a belief that national liberation and revolutionary movements and the anti-colonial struggle are legitimate. Some wars (civil wars of independence, national liberation wars and defensive wars) are considered just and should, therefore, be supported by communists. The course also includes some useful information about general international relations theory, rules of diplomacy, laws governing borders and territorial waters, international organization, etc.

In addition to lectures, seminars and examinations on various aspects of legal theory, law students have to undergo extensive practical training (usually after two years of study) in a selected field of specialization. This takes the form of working for two or three months in the legal services, either as an assistant procurator, or in courts, criminal investigation departments of the militia or in law offices in factories or elsewhere. No student can graduate before completing this practical apprenticeship. Students also have to pass a series of state examinations or, alternatively, write a long essay based on research into some aspect of the particular branch of the profession in which they have chosen to specialize.

Gorbachev almost certainly chose to do his apprenticeship in a procurator's office. Dina Kaminskaya, one of the few prominent defence lawyers in the Soviet Union, a graduate of the Moscow Law Institute and an active (but not successful) defence attorney for several prominent dissidents in the 1960s (including for Bukovsky in 1967), described the situation amongst students when they were preparing themselves for practical training:

> In our third year . . . when the time came for our first practical work, we were allowed to choose either the judicial system or the procuracy, which includes the investigatory apparatus. The overwhelming majority of my classmates asked to be sent to the procuracy, and a few wanted trial work, but I can remember no one in those days who planned to specialize in advocacy. A partial explanation for this, of course, was that we were so influenced by the lectures . . . If the defense attorney was ever mentioned in lectures, it was only in the role of a wretched, defeated opponent. . . . although we had not yet fully realized how abysmally low in status the profession of defense counsel was, we were very well aware of its unpopularity among the public at large.[21]

When the time comes to assign new graduates to jobs, the jobs for defence lawyers in law consultation centres are usually filled by non-Party members who are considered not quite trustworthy and therefore unsuitable to work in the procuracy or for the KGB. Defence lawyers are the pariahs of the legal profession. They also have very few procedural rights. They have access to the defendant only when the investigation has been completed and the case has been sent for trial. But even then, they can only see the defendant with the permission of the investigator, they cannot conduct their own, independent investigation and they can only invite witnesses for the defence with the consent of the judge.

Gorbachev graduated from Moscow University in June 1955. Since he was not offered a place as a graduate student, he had to go through the system of state distribution of jobs. For good students who have a range of positions to choose from, returning to their native regions to take up a local appointment is the most natural choice. We now know, of course, that Gorbachev made the decision not to seek employment in the procuracy, but to opt for professional Komsomol work. But five years at the best university in the Soviet Union had certainly transformed the young peasant boy who had left his village in 1950. His professional knowledge of the law, of philosophy, history, Marxism-Leninism, the history of the communist movement and of the Communist Party of the Soviet Union (CPSU) gave him considerable advantages for his future work in the Komsomol and Party. But he had also studied a skill which was to be particularly useful in his later career – law institutes are practically the only educational institutions which give students a formal training in the art of oratory, teaching them how to make an impressive speech, how to present a case, how to ask relevant questions and conduct interrogations. This training certainly paid off. Gorbachev is probably the best speaker there has been in the top Party echelons since Trotsky was expelled from the Politburo in 1926. Vyshinsky had also been a formidable orator, but he had never been a member of the Politburo (he was elected a candidate member of the enlarged Presidium of the Central Committee which replaced the Politburo in 1952, but he retained this position for only a few months, until Stalin's death).

It is extremely likely that after five years of sharing a room with a Czech intellectual, Gorbachev must have been profoundly influenced by Zdenek Mlynar. The personal knowledge of the culture and attitudes of a traditionally Western nation must have had almost the effect of a prolonged stay abroad in the early 1950s. If Gorbachev has become 'westernized' in his appearance, manners, dress and the image he projects of tolerance and cordial behaviour, all the small signs which mark him as different from the usual Komsomol and Party boss, it was probably Mlynar's doing. It was this mixture of cultured image and political orthodoxy which attracted his Party patrons like Suslov and Andropov and made them regard him as the epitome of the new style Party man which the country required. Paradoxically, Mlynar did not succeed in introducing lasting changes in Czechoslovakia during the Prague Spring, but indirectly he provided the Soviet Union with a new style leader by the influence he exerted on his provincial room-mate from the Stavropol village of Privol'noye. Whether this will make any substantive difference to the rigid Soviet system remains to be seen. But the image of the leader has certainly changed.

3
The young Gorbachev in Stavropol

In late June 1955, after graduating from the Law Faculty of Moscow State University, Gorbachev returned to Stavropol to take up his first professional position. Each year every regional administration informs the Ministry of Higher Education of the Soviet Union how many graduates and young experts it needs and what qualifications they should have, ranging from engineering, agronomy and teaching, to medicine and law. The Ministry receives similar requests from other ministries, the army, the diplomatic service and even from the Gulag prison camp system, which also needs a variety of professionals, including lawyers. The price of free education in the Soviet Union is that graduates have to fulfil a minimal term of three years' service in a place which is allotted to them by the state before they can choose where to work. Industrial managers, institutes and government agencies do not have the legal right to employ new graduates without permission from the distributing commissions which work in every college, institute or university at the end of the academic year and decide who will work where. However, universities and colleges each have a quota of places for the best graduates who will be encouraged to continue post-graduate education and study for higher degrees, do research or teach. Gorbachev does not seem to have been offered a post-graduate place and he selected Stavropol *krai* from the list of available provincial appointments. Graduates can select from a list of available positions and those who have achieved the best academic results are given first choice. Poor students are left till last in the distribution process and usually have to accept the least attractive posts in the least desirable places.

As a law graduate, Gorbachev should have been appointed to the procuracy, which is the largest section of the legal system in the Soviet Union. According to the constitution the procuracy has the power of supervising that the law is strictly and uniformly observed both by individuals and organizations. In theory it is independent, accountable in the first place to the Procurators General in the constituent union republics and then to the Procurator General of the USSR. In practice, however, procurators tend to be members of local Party organizations and to follow the Party line advised by the local Party committees. The Chief Procurator of a region or *krai* is normally also a member of the bureau of the regional Party committee.

When Gorbachev returned to Stavropol in 1955 all the procurators' offices throughout the country, from the Procurator General in Moscow down to the district level, were overloaded with the titanic job of reconsidering the charges and sentences against the victims of Stalin's terror. The arrest and execution of Beria and his 'gang' in 1953 had made a tremendous impact on the Gulag system. In 1954–5 his close accomplices were brought to trial in many parts of the country. During this period the process of rehabilitating those who had been imprisoned during Stalin's time was extremely slow and about 10 million people, almost 5 per cent of the population, were still in the Gulag. Most of them had appealed against the false accusations and had applied for rehabilitation. The atmosphere in the camps was extremely tense and rebellions occurred in some places. In addition to the appeals of the living, millions of relatives of those who had already died in the camps and prisons had applied for posthumous rehabilitation. I have a clear memory of this period because my mother and I applied for the posthumous rehabilitation of my father, who had died in a camp in Kolyma in 1941. In 1955 I visited the offices of the Procurator General in Moscow almost every month to enquire how far the re-investigation had proceeded. It was a lengthy business. By law the Supreme Court granted the rehabilitation, but only the procuracy had the right to reconsider cases and prepare them for presentation to the Supreme Court. The re-investigation had to be undertaken by the procuracy of the region or republic where the first investigation and trial had taken place. The North Caucasus had been particularly badly affected by the purges. Most of the *kraikom* and hundreds of district committee members had been arrested in 1937–8. In 1938 many *kolkhoz* and *sovkhoz* chairmen, agronomists and ordinary workers were arrested. The harvest had been poor and it was blamed on deliberate sabotage. There were several prisons and prison camps in Stavropol *krai* and between 1947 and 1952 the Stavropol-Moscow gas pipeline and several canals were built by Gulag labour.

The procuracy was unable to cope with the task of revising so many million sentences. The problem was only resolved by the wholesale rehabilitation of millions of prisoners after Khrushchev's secret speech at the XXth Party Congress in 1956. But in 1955 the task was not being performed very efficiently. Many senior procurators had themselves been responsible for accusations against those who were now demanding release. The backlog of cases was enormous and there was a great deal of pressure from the camps. All newly qualified lawyers were immediately assigned to the job of rehabilitation.

Gorbachev, however, did not want to use his professional skills in this particular field. The only way graduates can avoid compulsory appointments is to be taken into the local Party or Komsomol system. In 1954 and 1955 there were vacancies in the Komsomol, since many experienced Komsomol cadres had been transferred into the KGB, the Committee for State Security which Khrushchev had created to replace the discredited Ministry of State Security and Ministry of Internal Affairs previously run by Beria. General Ivan Serov, Khrushchev's old friend and former security chief of the Ukraine, became the first chairman of the KGB, but the whole security system was put under the supervision of Aleksandr Shelepin, First Secretary of the Central Committee of the Komsomol. (In 1958 Shelepin himself became head of the KGB.) Gorbachev applied for a vacancy in the Komsomol and was offered the position of head of a department of the Stavropol City Komsomol Committee. It was not a *nomenklatura* position which required approval of the area Party committee (*kraikom*) and therefore it was quite a humble position for a Moscow University graduate with good Komsomol experience. Nonetheless, it was a start.

The man who appointed Gorbachev and became his first boss was Vsevolod Murakhovsky, then first secretary of Stavropol City Komsomol Committee. Although Gorbachev's promotion was more rapid than Murakhovsky's (by 1970 Murakhovsky was

Gorbachev's deputy, at first in the city Party committee and later in the *kraikom*), they remained friends and when Gorbachev moved to Moscow in 1978, he recommended Murakhovsky for the job he was vacating of *kraikom* secretary, a position he held until October 1985, when Gorbachev moved him to Moscow and appointed him First Deputy Prime Minister. Murakhovsky played an important role in promoting Gorbachev through the Komsomol and Party ranks in 1955–60. He had been born in 1926. After serving in the army in 1944–50, he enrolled as a student at the Stavropol Teacher Training Institute. He graduated in 1954 and was elected secretary of the Stavropol city Komsomol committee.[1] He must have liked Gorbachev since he recommended him as his replacement when he was transferred to Party work in the Stavropol city Party committee (*gorkom*) in 1956 (a very early Party promotion for a young professional Komsomol worker). Thus it was only a year after he had returned to Stavropol that Gorbachev was made First Secretary of the city Komsomol committee.

Just before his promotion, Gorbachev married Raisa Titorenko, whom he had known when she was a student of philosophy at Moscow University. Zdenek Mlynar, Gorbachev's room-mate in Moscow, remembers that Raisa lived in the same hostel.[2] She came from Stavropol and graduated a year later than Gorbachev, returning to her home town afterwards to work first as a teacher. Later she became a sociologist at the local Teacher Training Institute. Mlynar, who knew Raisa and had a high opinion of her talents, maintains that Gorbachev and Raisa were already friendly when they were students. He believes that part of Gorbachev's success in Stavropol *krai* was due to his wife's influence and advice. Their only daughter was born in 1956.

In 1956 Stavropol was a small city with a population of 123,000.[3] Unlike in larger cities, the Komsomol organization was not divided into smaller districts, each with its own committee. The city committee thus dealt directly with primary organizations in schools, institutes, colleges, factories and offices. Professional Komsomol work does not have very high prestige in the Soviet Union because it does not involve any real decision-making and it does not have a tenured career structure. The Komsomol is a mass youth organization and membership does not carry any privileges. However, membership is essential for young people who want to join the Party. Membership is open to all young people from the age of 14 and it terminates automatically at the age of 27. Some people then join the Party, others merely stop paying their dues and leave the organization. Full-time professional Komsomol workers, however, do not have to terminate their membership when they reach the age of 27: regional or city secretaries may go on serving until they are 40, but they are expected to join the Party as well. When, finally, they do have to leave the Komsomol they usually try to obtain Party positions. If no suitable Party job is available, they are taken into the apparatus of the local Soviet or KGB, or else they revert to their original professions.

At the regional level, Komsomol positions are neither highly paid nor privileged. Moreover, the work is not very sophisticated. The main task of the Komsomol (as outlined in its rules) is propaganda: it aims 'to help the Party educate young people in the spirit of communism' and turn them into 'the Party's active helper and reserve'.[4] In general, the structure and activities of the Komsomol are modelled on the Party. The work includes holding annual and topical meetings and undertaking political education by means of lectures and publications. But since it is a youth organization, it is less formal than the Party and it also runs clubs and sports facilities, organizes competitions and provides the staff for summer camps for the Pioneers, the youth organization for even younger children. It also provides special patrols to assist the police in keeping public order, and it fulfils other public service functions. There are Komsomol organizations in every factory, plant, school, college, institute, *kolkhoz* and *sovkhoz*, as well as in army units. Gorbachev's work now involved visiting these local organizations, speaking at their meetings and conferences, supervising elections and appointments, arranging weekly meetings of the town Komsomol committee and being present at the weekly meetings of the Stavropol city Party committee. He must have done the work rather well because in 1958 he was first appointed head of the department of propaganda in the Komsomol *krai* committee, and then second secretary of the *krai* committee.

In 1959 his friend Murakhovsky became a secretary of the Stavropol *gorkom*, a position which also gave him membership of the bureau of the Stavropol *krai* Party committee, the main decision-making body in the area. In 1960 there were several major reorganizations of the Party apparatus in the Stavropol *krai*.

Nikolai Belyayev, a member of the Central Committee Presidium from 1957 and first secretary of the Kazakhstan Republic, was dismissed in January 1960 and demoted to Stavropol. Khrushchev had made him the scapegoat for the harvest failures in the virgin lands in 1959. He was replaced in Kazakhstan by Kunayev, a close friend of Brezhnev. Brezhnev had been the first secretary of Kazakhstan from 1954–56 and had purged the local cadres. In 1954 he made Kunayev, a metallurgist by training and president of the Kazakh Academy of Sciences, Prime Minister of the Kazakh Republic. As a doctor of technical sciences with good practical experience in the mining industry, Kunayev did not appear to be any better qualified to supervise agriculture in the virgin lands than Belyayev, an experienced administrator in the agricultural areas of Siberia and one of the first supporters of increasing the cultivated lands in the East. Belyayev had been a secretary of the Central Committee before his appointment to Kazakhstan in 1957. Although he was not responsible for the poor harvest in 1959, Khrushchev needed someone to blame and he chose Belyayev. He was recommended for Party work in Stavropol *krai*, and became first secretary of the *kraikom.*[5], He did not hold the position for very long, however, since Khrushchev did not hold with retaining people who had fallen out of favour in *nomenklatura* positions. At the end of June 1960 he was replaced as first secretary of Stavropol *kraikom* by Fedor Kulakov.[6]

In the general reorganizations which accompanied these changes, Gorbachev was promoted. He became first secretary of the Stavropol *krai* Komsomol committee and a member of the *kraikom* Party bureau. For a 29-year old Komsomol organizer this represented a very rapid rise. Since neither Belyayev nor Kulakov knew the local Komsomol people, it seems likely that Gorbachev's promotion must have been recommended by Murakhovsky.

For Kulakov, as for Belyayev, the position of *kraikom* secretary was a demotion. It represented exile from Moscow, where he had been Minister of Grain Products of the RSFSR. In 1960 Khrushchev had begun to reorganize the agricultural ministries, in the belief that they would operate better if they were closer to the land. The USSR Ministry of Agriculture was ordered to move to a rural area, Mikhailovsky state farm, 100 km from Moscow. The agricultural ministries of the RSFSR were moved even further away, to Yakhroma state farm, 120 km from Moscow. The ministries were now obliged to do more than supervise the administration of agriculture. They were to set up model farms to prove that the ministerial bureaucracy had links with real life and understood what the problems were. The general idea was probably quite good, but the reform was carried out in such haste that many prominent senior people preferred to resign, rather than to move to the villages. Almost all the ministers, including the very able USSR Minister of Agriculture, Vladimir Matskevich, were dismissed and sent to work in the key agricultural regions. Matskevich became chairman of the Executive Committee of the Soviet (*ispolkom*) in the Zelinograd region of Kazakhstan, while Kulakov was given a much better position in Stavropol *krai*.

By training Kulakov was an agronomist. He had graduated from an agricultural technical college and worked as a practical agronomist, including as head of the district agricultural department in the Kursk region. He had also studied as a correspondence student, graduating from the Moscow external agricultural institute which operates from the Timiryazev Agricultural Academy and offers five-year courses by correspondence. But he was a typical Party boss, tough, impressive and authoritarian. Matskevich, in contrast, resembled a professor and was more open to argument. I heard and saw both of them several times in the late 1950s, when they sometimes gave reports at the Timiryazev Agricultural Academy, explaining the new agricultural policy to the staff. I was working in the Academy at that time as a senior scientist. It was a time of heated agricultural debates.

Kulakov is still remembered in Stavropol. He was very ambitious and wanted to turn the area into a model of agricultural success. The first secretary of the Komsomol was important to his plans less as a propagandist than as an organizer of agricultural production. But the local leaders, young and old alike, apparently developed good relations with him and for the next 18 years Gorbachev's life and career were closely linked to Kulakov's ambitious ascent in the hierarchy.

As first secretary of the Komsomol *kraikom*, Gorbachev was selected as a delegate to the XXIInd Party Congress in October 1961. This Congress was a watershed in Soviet political history. In the West the 1956 XXth Party Congress is usually thought to have been a turning point, because it was then that Khrushchev made his secret speech denouncing Stalin. In fact, the speech was never published in the USSR and Party members read it as a 'closed document' which was circulated within the Party system only. Later the text was read to wider audiences at colleges, institutes and factories, but Stalin was never openly discredited. His embalmed body continued to lie in the mausoleum next to Lenin's, there were monuments to him all over the country and his birthday and the anniversary of his death continued to be recorded with articles in the press. Khrushchev himself had begun to take a milder line after June 1956, following the Chinese advice to treat Stalin's actions as 'errors' rather than 'crimes'. All this changed at the XXIInd Party Congress.

The Congress was attended by a wider representation from all levels of the Party than any previous Congress. Previous Congress sessions had been held in the Great Hall of the Kremlin, which can accommodate about 1,500 people. By 1961 the new Kremlin Palace of Congresses had been opened, with seats for 6,000 people. The number of delegates to the Congress had been increased to 5,000. Khrushchev's main report on October 17, the first day of the Congress, followed the traditional lines of analysing the past performance and future prospects of the economy, and discussing the international situation and the problems of the world communist movement. But Khrushchev also needed to explain the great changes in the Presidium of the Central Committee and in the Central Committee itself between the XXth and XXIInd Party Congresses (an extraordinary XXIst Congress had been held in 1959, but it considered only economic problems). The XXIInd Congress also had to consider the new Party Programme and Party Rules. There had been a plot to unseat Khrushchev in 1957, which had become known as the work of the 'anti-party group', consisting of Molotov, Malenkov and Kaganovich, all closely associated with Stalin's crimes. But the plot had also been supported by other leaders (Bulganin, Voroshilov, Pervukhin and Saburov) who were removed from the Presidium later. Khrushchev had to give a full explanation of their expulsion. This would make it easier for him to undertake a purge of the Central Committee.

To explain the dismissals, Khrushchev included the problem of Stalin's repressions in his official, open report. This meant that other speakers also had to deal with the problem. The most detailed and horrific description of Stalin's crimes (and the participation of Molotov, Malenkov, Kaganovich and Voroshilov in them) was given by N. V. Podgorny, K. T. Mazurov, D. S. Polyansky and others. Polyansky testified to Kaganovich's destruction of Party and Komsomol cadres in the North Caucasus. A detailed description of some of Stalin's crimes was given by A. N. Shelepin, formerly head of the Komsomol and now chairman of the KGB. After the Congress, Stalin's body was removed from the mausoleum and most of his monuments were demolished. Cities, towns, villages, factories, *kolkhozy* and *sovkhozy* which had been named after him were renamed. The restrictions on printed criticism of Stalin were partially lifted, opening a floodgate of publications concerning his misdeeds, errors and crimes. The most famous example was Solzhenitsyn's novel, *One Day in the Life of Ivan Denisovich*, which was published in 1962 and marked the high point in the cultural and political upheaval brought about by the XXIInd Party Congress.

It is traditional that when delegates return from Party Congresses to their regions, they report on the decisions of the Congress and their implications for local Party and Komsomol organizations. Accordingly, in November and December 1961 Gorbachev travelled around the Stavropol *krai*, organizing discussion of the XXIInd Party Congress decisions at conferences of Komsomol activists. Life was difficult for a professional Komsomol propagandist in 1962. Young people in the early 1960s had neither the inhibitions nor the inertia born of fear that kept the more experienced, older generation silent. They asked difficult and uncomfortable questions. The exposure of Stalin's crimes was more outspoken in 1962 than at any other time before or since. Many official dogmas of Party history were challenged. Even the Party's agrarian policy in the 1930s was under reconsideration. Traditional ideological work became difficult. There was no clear political line or instructions and, at the same time, there were many conservatives locally who tried to resist any real liberalization. Kulakov, for example, was not a liberal and had many reasons not to follow Khrushchev's new line. It must, therefore, have been difficult for Gorbachev to follow the controversial instructions from the Komsomol Central Committee (which underwent reorganization in 1961–2) without offending the more traditional and conservative views of the local Party bosses in Stavropol.

The time had come, Gorbachev felt, to choose between the Komsomol and a Party career. Aged 31, at the top of the *krai* Komsomol Committee and a member of the Komsomol Central Committee, he was still some distance from the natural end of his Komsomol career. He was also a member of the *kraikom* Party bureau and sixth in the Party hierarchy in Stavropol *krai*. Within a few years he could expect to become head of a department of the Party *kraikom* or, if he elected to remain in the Komsomol, he would probably be transferred to the Komsomol headquarters in Moscow. However, in March 1962 he was unexpectedly appointed Party organizer of one of the 16 territorial-production agricultural units in Stavropol *krai*. This seemed to be demotion: the job did not carry membership of the *kraikom* Party bureau and he would have to move out of Stavropol to one of the rural districts to supervise agricultural production. Moreover, he was poorly qualified for the job.

It is unlikely that this decision was made solely by Kulakov. Relations between Kulakov and Gorbachev were quite good. Gorbachev probably requested a transfer to professional Party work. In 1962 a number of positions of 'territorial Party organizer' became available as a result of yet another of Khrushchev's reorganizations of Party structure. Agriculture had been doing badly since 1959, partly as a result of Khrushchev's policies (particularly the abolition of the Machine-Tractor Stations in 1958 and the transfer of their machinery to the *kolkhozy* which did not have enough qualified personnel to run or service it). Reorganization of the agricultural administration in Moscow and the capitals of the constituent union republics also contributed to the problems. Unable and unwilling to acknowledge his own mistakes, Khrushchev now launched a new reorganization. At a Central Committee Plenum from March 5 to 9, 1962, he proposed replacing the traditional Party structure, based on geographical districts, by 'production' administrative units throughout the country. Each unit would consist of 25–30 *kolkhozy* and *sovkhozy* and it would be responsible for agriculture alone, rather than for all local affairs which had traditionally been the combined responsibility of the *raikom* and the district Soviet executive committee (*raiispolkom*). Khrushchev believed that if a large number of collective and state farms were united into a large 'production trust' or corporation under qualified professional leadership, each would work more efficiently. A group of inspectors – specialists in various aspects of agriculture – would be attached to each unit to advise the *kolkhozy* and *sovkhozy*. Each unit would also have a Party organizer who would not be elected but would be appointed as a representative of the *obkom* or *kraikom*. Stavropol *krai*, with a rural population of 1.4 million people, was divided into 16 territorial-production *kolkhoz-sovkhoz* units. Gorbachev was appointed Party organizer of one of them. His Komsomol career was now over.

The appointment to a more practical Party job which, to anyone else, would have seemed like demotion, speaks in favour of Gorbachev's integrity. His new work carried considerable risk, particularly for someone without any agricultural education. His peasant background and his experience of MTS work in the 1940s were insufficient for dealing with the more complex agricultural problems at the level of a large agricultural corporation. He probably did not realize that Khrushchev's reform was contradictory and controversial. But he must have realized that there was no real future in Komsomol work. In 1958, when he became second secretary of the Stavropol Komsomol *kraikom*, there was another extensive transfer of professional Komsomol workers to high-ranking KGB positions. The secretary of the Komsomol Central Committee, Aleksandr Shelepin, was made chairman of the KGB and he immediately began to retire military professionals from the KGB and to appoint local Komsomol leaders in their place. He had high political ambitions and was preparing the KGB as his power base. After the XXIInd Party Congress, Shelepin became a Central Committee secretary and his close friend, Vladimir Semichastny, was appointed chairman of the KGB. Semichastny had also previously been first secretary of the Komsomol Central Committee and he continued replacing older KGB cadres with Komsomol officials. The KGB and Komsomol systems began to work in close co-operation at all levels and it became normal to recruit Komsomol members as KGB informers. Shelepin and Semichastny continued to supervise and control the Komsomol apparatus and Shelepin was beginning to form his own faction in the Central Committee and in the regional networks of the Party, KGB and Komsomol. His supporters were comparatively young careerists who were ready to use the KGB for their own purposes. The KGB apparatus, quite small after the reorganization of the security and political police in 1953–4, had begun to grow again. As a *kraikom* Komsomol secretary, Gorbachev would have to follow the Shelepin-Semichastny line and it would be unlikely that he could establish good, friendly relations with this cynical group. Thus, leaving his comparatively important Komsomol position for a rather obscure agricultural Party job was probably related to developments within the Komsomol system as a whole, rather than to anything that happened locally in Stavropol. The creation of the new position of territorial Party organizer gave him the opportunity to transfer to Party work rather earlier than he might otherwise have expected.

His new job, however, proved to be very difficult and without clearly demarcated responsibilities. The previous district administration did not disappear and the *raikom* and *raiispolkom* in the area retained broad local responsibility for agriculture, local industry, schools, hospitals, the trade system, roads, banks, the legal system, social security, etc. The *kolkhoz-sovkhoz* territorial units, on the other hand, overlapped several districts and were to concentrate on purely agricultural matters. They were also instructed to establish new 'territorial' newspapers, and to select as headquarters a centrally located village. It soon became clear that it was impossible to concentrate on agricultural matters without interfering in other local problems. The territorial units began to duplicate the activities of the *raikom* and *raiispolkom*, becoming an unnecessary superstructure which merely increased local bureaucracy without resolving any of its problems. Once again, Khrushchev was unwilling to acknowledge his error and dismantle the territorial units. Instead he maintained that the traditional districts were old-fashioned and abolished them, replacing them with larger administrative units which coincided geographically with the new *kolkhoz-sovkhoz* territorial units. These new districts were often two or three times larger than the *raiony* they replaced. However, as multi-purpose administrative areas they were inefficient simply because there was no road and communication infrastructure which corresponded to them. For decades communications had developed around the *raion* centre and it was impossible to change the whole structure overnight, or at all without the investment of a great deal of money. As a result neither the local population nor the country's agricultural production derived any benefit from the reorganization. The new administrative areas were far too large and they were criticized by the public and by the *kolkhozy* for the poor service they provided and for their inefficiency.

Gorbachev was ill-equipped to deal with the complexities of agriculture and when the new districts were set up, he suddenly found himself responsible for all other aspects of district life as well. He had become a *de facto raikom* secretary, but with more *kolkhozy* and *sovkhozy* under his supervision and without a proper communication system to deal with all their problems. Fortunately, the weather was very good in 1962 and agricultural performance was correspondingly impressive. The total grain harvest in the country was 140 million metric tons, higher than it had ever been in a single year. Stavropol *krai* did very well. Nonetheless, during the summer Gorbachev must have realized that his prospects in the *kraikom* Party system would be poor unless he acquired a professional training and proper qualifications in agriculture. His knowledge of law was irrelevant to his job as a local Party boss in a grain-producing district. His work would be judged according to how successful agriculture was in the area he controlled. In September 1962 he enrolled in the department of agricultural economy at the Stavropol Agricultural Institute on a five-year external course. Once again he was a student, but this time by correspondence.

However, his practical experience in agriculture turned out to be short-lived. As soon as the harvesting season was over and all the state procurements and other obligations of his territorial unit had been fulfilled, he received an important promotion. In December 1962 he was appointed head of the department of Party organs of the *kraikom*. He was now in charge of Party cadres and in a position to influence the promotion and demotion of Party workers who were on the *kraikom nomenklatura* list. This appointment indicated Kulakov's confidence in him. He became a member of Kulakov's team and the two men remained closely linked until Kulakov's sudden death in 1978. His friend, Murakhovsky, who had been secretary of the Stavropol *gorkom* since 1959, did not enjoy such good relations with Kulakov. He had lost his *gorkom* job in 1961 and had been doing a minor job at the district level ever since. Now it was Gorbachev's turn to help him, but he could only do so by transferring him out of the Party network. In 1963 Gorbachev recommended him as a deputy of the

Stavropol *krai ispolkom*. In 1965 (by which time Kulakov had been transferred back to Moscow, but Gorbachev was still in charge of the *krai* Party cadres), Murakhovsky returned to the Party system as first secretary of the Kislovodsk *gorkom*. Kislovodsk was the largest of the resort towns in Stavropol *krai*, with a population of 80,000.

Gorbachev's new position as head of the *kraikom* Party organs department was more important in Stavropol than it would have been in many other, larger regions. In addition to being an agricultural area, Stavropol *krai* is famous for its mineral water and other resorts. There are hundreds of holiday centres, spas and sanatoria in the area. Many of them belong to special networks of 'state sanatoria' for high officials of the Central Committee or the government and some are designed for members of the Politburo and Secretariat. The Ministry of Defence, KGB, MVD, Committee for Atomic Energy and other important state institutions all have special sanatoria in Stavropol *krai*. There are also sanatoria for Party and state officials from other socialist countries and for foreign tourists. In the early 1960s resort towns in the area like Kislovodsk, Pyatigorsk, Essentuki, Zheleznovodsk and Mineral'nye Vody were growing rapidly. Because the area plays host to so many high Party and state officials who arrive at all times of the year for rest or specialized medical treatment, local Party and state appointments need to be co-ordinated closely with the cadre departments in Moscow. This must have presented Gorbachev with a uniquely good opportunity to establish contacts with people in the central Party apparatus. Many of the Party and state positions in the area are considered 'sensitive' from a political and security point of view. There is, of course, a significant presence of the KGB and ordinary militia. It was probably not an accident, for example, that the man who was appointed *gorkom* secretary of Zheleznovodsk in 1965 was a military hero, Shipakhin, who had been awarded a Gold Star medal during the war. (He was also Gorbachev's brother-in-law, having married Raisa's sister. Later he became a liability to Gorbachev, since he was partially implicated in a local corruption case in 1977. He was dismissed and demoted to a minor post in the local consumer system.)

Gorbachev occupied his cadre post in the *kraikom* Party system for more than four years. Essentially it was a desk job, with occasional trips to district centres. At the same time he continued studying at the Stavropol Agricultural Institute and his wife resumed her academic career. She began a sociological research project, 'On the formation of a new pattern of life for the *kolkhoz* peasantry', taking the life style of the local Stavropol peasantry as a model. The project was approved for graduate work and for four years Raisa collected data about incomes, consumption, attitudes, family budgets, educational background, life style, etc. This work must have helped her husband as well, particularly later when he became second secretary and then first secretary of the *kraikom*.

It is quite possible that Gorbachev knew in advance about the plan to remove Khrushchev from office. In a detailed account of Khrushchev's dismissal, Roy Medvedev writes:

> There is evidence to suggest that detailed discussion of the Khrushchev question took place among a group of members of the Presidium and the Central Committee in September, while they were on a hunting and fishing holiday in the south, near Manych lakes, as guests of the First Secretary of the Stavropol kraykom, F. Kulakov.[7]

It is clear that the main figures behind the anti-Khrushchev plot needed to get the support of the most influential members of the Central Committee. The 'hunting and fishing' holiday in the Manych lakes in Stavropol *krai* lasted for several days, but the participants spent more time in political discussion than in pursuing their sporting activities. The main instigator of the plot was Suslov. Shelepin and Semichastny provided him with backing from the KGB. But their main task was to convince Brezhnev, who was second-in-command, and Marshal Malinovsky, Minister of Defence. Both were considered trusted Khrushchev men. It was clear that the plot could only succeed on condition that Khrushchev was retired without anyone else sharing his disgrace. In other words, no other heads should roll. Other members of the Presidium could not be made responsible for his errors, even if they had a history of actively supporting all his reforms. Brezhnev was the person who could most obviously be trusted to succeed him and to keep to this line.

There was, however, one particularly influential person amongst Khrushchev's closest friends who would have to go with him – Vasilii Polyakov, Central Committee secretary for agriculture. He was not only Khrushchev's speech writer on agricultural affairs, but also closely linked with Trofim Lysenko's circle. It was Polyakov who had inserted a glorification of Lysenko into almost all Khrushchev's speeches on agriculture in the early 1960s. As editor of the central newspaper *Sotsialisticheskoye zemledeliye* (*Socialist agriculture*) in 1938–41, Polyakov had actively participated in formulating the damaging ideological accusations which were levelled against prominent geneticists and which resulted in them being purged. His deputy in the agricultural department and head of the section of agricultural sciences was A. A. Utekhin, a former student of Lysenko in Odessa and later his close assistant on the so called 'vernalization method'.[8] Polyakov was formally dismissed at the regular Plenum of the Central Committee in November 1964, a month after Khrushchev's fall. It was then that Kulakov was officially appointed to replace him as head of the agricultural department of the Central Committee. However, in practice Polyakov lost his post in October with Khrushchev and Kulakov immediately set about purging the agricultural department of Lysenko's supporters. Many other officials returned to Moscow from their provincial exile. One such person was Matskevich, Kulakov's colleague, who was once again appointed Minister of Agriculture. Many of Khrushchev's reforms, including the territorial *kolkhoz-sovkhoz* units, were dismantled.

Stavropol, however, once again became a place for the honorary exile of prominent Party workers. Kulakov was replaced as first secretary of Stavropol *krai* by Leonid Efremov, candidate member of the Presidium of the Central Committee (in 1966 the Presidium reverted to the name Politburo). He was a well-educated, liberal man, and an expert on agriculture since he had graduated from the Voronezh Institute of Agricultural Mechanization. He also had considerable experience of regional work, having served as *obkom* secretary in the Kuibishev, Kursk and Gorky regions. In 1962 he had been appointed second secretary of the Central Committee bureau for the RSFSR (Khrushchev himself held the position of first secretary, which was combined with the position of first secretary of the whole CC CPSU). After Khrushchev's fall the RSFSR bureau was abolished. Efremov was far more experienced and intelligent than Kulakov and it would have been more logical to give him responsibility for agriculture. There was no purge of Khrushchev's men in the Central Committee and, in any case, he was less associated with Khrushchev's policies than Brezhnev,

Podgorny, Kirilenko or Polyansky. But he was not a 'Brezhnev man', and nor did he belong to either of the other ambitious factions under Suslov or Shelepin. Brezhnev expected to deal with agriculture himself and he preferred Kulakov to the more independent Efremov. In the well established patronage system of the top echelons of the Party and state, Kulakov enjoyed the support of Kosygin and Suslov.

Efremov started work as first secretary of the Stavropol *kraikom* at the beginning of 1965. At the comparatively young age of 53, he had reasonable hopes that he would be promoted back to Moscow in the future, when things had changed. As secretary of an agricultural region, it was in his best interests to maintain good relations with Kulakov and to keep Stavropol as Kulakov's power base. The Soviet system of patronage is not only political, consisting of appointments and promotion of clients by patrons. It is a two-way system. Higher officials rely on the support of their followers in the regional Party and government systems, in return for which they help them to obtain priority economic supplies, investment funds and other resources for development. As head of the Central Committee agricultural department, Kulakov was in the key position to give Stavropol *krai* all the necessary assistance and to increase its quota of machinery, mineral fertilizer, and funds for irrigation works. This turned the Stavropol *krai* officials into something which could be described as Kulakov's 'team'. The economic success of the *krai* would, in turn, help Kulakov achieve further promotion. Thus his link with the *krai* would take a new form. But he also had a rather more traditional political link with the area. As Supreme Soviet deputy for one of the electoral districts of the area, it was his duty to take a close interest in local affairs and to give the *krai* all the necessary support.

The patronage system of promotion and interdependence began to take shape in Stalin's time. Khrushchev made extensive use of the system of appointing people who were personally loyal to him and they helped him in his power struggle in the 1950s. However, the existence of various 'clans' was most prominent during the Brezhnev era and it became possible to trace the personal connections between Brezhnev and many of the people who were promoted to high positions in the 1960s and 1970s. The brightest and ablest members of the Communist Party who had been promoted by the Revolution and the Civil War rather than through the ranks of the bureaucracy, had disappeared during Stalin's purges. In the 1950s and 1960s the Soviet state and Party bureaucracy consisted essentially of people of rather modest intellectual and political capabilities. Some of them, like Kosygin and Ustinov, for example, possessed excellent managerial talents which had been developed and tested during the war. But almost all of the others were easily replaceable. There were few outstanding people, despite the frequent use of the term to describe top officials. The Russian Revolution had produced two giant figures, Lenin and Trotsky. Others, like Bukharin or Voznesensky, had considerable potential and this was why Stalin eliminated them. By the 1960s there were no leaders of this calibre left in Soviet political life. Personal links and patronage became the commonest way in which people were selected and promoted.

In 1965 Brezhnev still maintained a low profile, acting as 'first amongst equals'. Kosygin, the Prime Minister, wanted to implement serious economic reforms, and he received more attention both inside and outside the country. Podgorny, chairman of the Presidium of the Supreme Soviet and, therefore, President of the Soviet Union, was a rather independent figure who had previously been Brezhnev's rival. Within the Central Committee Presidium, both Suslov and Shelepin had their own political ambitions. The long and painful disputes about Soviet Middle East policy in 1967 (which was a fiasco), about the liberal changes in Czechoslovakia in 1968 and about the rehabilitation of Stalin (in 1966–9) revealed deep differences within the Politburo. One cannot, of course, talk about 'hardliners' and 'liberals', since there are no liberals at that level. But some were clearly more 'soft' than others, not particularly because they were liberal, but because they wanted a quiet life.

Efremov and Gorbachev seem to have developed a good relationship. This was natural since Gorbachev did not fit the stereotype of a provincial Party *apparatchik* and Efremov did not act the role of a local Party baron. In the general reshuffle of Party positions after the XXIIIrd Party Congress (this was the Congress at which the Central Committee Presidium returned to its previous name of Politburo), to which Gorbachev was not a delegate, Gorbachev was given the opportunity to leave his desk job and move upwards. He was elected first secretary of the Stavropol *gorkom*. Although it was a promotion, this position was controlled by the *kraikom nomenklatura* and not by the Central Committee's list of appointments. Stavropol *krai* is an important area, but the town itself is not a key centre. In 1966 it had a population of 171,000,[9] and was 110th in the list of Soviet towns and cities by size of population. It is an attractive town with many parks and trees. The *gorkom* occupies an old two-storey mansion on Marx Prospect. A red flag waves permanently from the top of the roof and there are busts of Marx and Lenin facing the avenue on the edge of the park which surrounds the building. The local industry is predominantly concerned with food-processing and agriculture-related light industry (clothing, leather and wool textiles). There are several educational institutions in the town (teacher training, medical, agricultural), and agricultural research institutes, one of which studies sheep and goat husbandry and belongs to the Lenin Academy of Agricultural Sciences. There are the usual monuments to the Civil War and the Great Patriotic War, including a Monument of Glory with an eternal flame. The cultural life reflects the status of the city as the capital of the *krai*: there is a theatre, a circus and the *krai* museum. The city has a small air terminal and it is linked to the main Baku-Rostov railroad.

Gorbachev finally completed his correspondence course in 1967 and graduated from the Stavropol Agricultural Institute as an agronomist-economist. His new agricultural diploma opened the way to further promotion. Correspondence or external education in the Soviet Union (available for all subjects except for medical and technical sciences) normally includes the same subjects that full and part-time students take and the qualification has equal weight. Both full and external courses take five years, but the arrangements are more flexible for the latter. Every student is entitled to a month's extra leave with pay for seminars, practical work which cannot be done by correspondence (using computers or practical work with agricultural machinery, for example) and for examinations. Agricultural education is broadly based. Those who, like Gorbachev, specialize in agricultural economy, have to pass other subjects like plant and livestock breeding, agro-chemistry, agricultural machinery, field crops, etc. Agricultural economy itself, a single course for non-specialists, is divided into several courses for specialists, including general agricultural economy, organization, *kolkhoz* and *sovkhoz* finance, agrarian policy and statistics. Political economy and Marxist-Leninist materialist philosophy are compulsory subjects in all professional education.

By 1967 Raisa Gorbacheva's academic career was proceeding successfully. She was awarded the degree of candidate of philosophical sciences (the equivalent of a PhD) at the Moscow State Pedagogical Institute named after Lenin for a dissertation on sociology. The examination of a dissertation is formidable in the Soviet Union. The dissertation must be defended at an open meeting. A successful defence requires agreement by a secret ballot of the members of the academic council (consisting of 12–15 members). The council nominates two 'official opponents' who add their critical comments to the public report by the candidate. The research work is presented as a typewritten manuscript and 200 copies of a detailed synopsis of the work have to be printed and distributed to related institutes and departments for comment at least one month before the presentation. Even if the decision of the academic council is unanimous, it is not final. After the successful defence, the dissertation has to be submitted for official confirmation by the All-Union Qualification Commission, which holds an independent review and approves the work at a closed session of one of its specialized councils. The final diploma is issued by the Ministry of Higher Education. The reprint of the synopsis (a booklet of about 15–20 pages), has to be displayed for some time in the main State libraries before entering the stocks of the library. The full text of the thesis is deposited in the library of the institute which supported the research and in the central Lenin Library in Moscow, where it is available for other specialists to read. Anyone looking through the main catalogue of the Lenin Library could, at least until 1985, find an entry under R. M. Gorbacheva, listing a thesis on the new attitudes and interests of the Soviet *kolkhoz* peasantry, the formation of the new socialist men and women in the villages of Stavropol *krai.*[10]

In 1968 Gorbachev was elected second secretary of the *kraikom*. It was an important promotion, since he had skipped the position of third secretary. In regional and district Party organizations the secretarial positions are usually numbered. The first secretary has overall responsibility, the second secretary is responsible for agriculture and the third for ideology, including education and science. In a primarily agricultural region like

Stavropol *krai*, the first secretary is also closely involved in agricultural affairs. The position of second secretary is on the Central Committee *nomenklatura* and has to be approved by the Politburo and Secretariat. Gorbachev's new degree made his promotion possible. Proper educational qualifications became important during Brezhnev's tenure. Neither Stalin nor Khrushchev had paid much attention to the educational level of *obkom* or *kraikom* secretaries, actually preferring to deal with people who had no formal education. Brezhnev, on the other hand, tended to promote only those with proper higher education and those who did not already have qualifications had to register on correspondence courses. There were a number of *obkom* secretaries with PhD degrees and several Doctors of Science – Brezhnev prided himself that 'his' Central Committee was also an impressive 'Academic Council'.

In fact, Gorbachev did not have much luck as secretary responsible for agriculture. 1969 was an extremely poor year, through no fault of his. The North Caucasus suffered severe dust storms which hit the northern and eastern plains of Stavropol *krai* which were prone to wind erosion particularly badly. In January and February strong eastern winds blew millions of tons of the *chernozem* topsoil from the steppe areas to the hills and forests of the North Caucasus. The whole *krai* was badly damaged by this natural disaster. The extensive system of irrigation canals became choked with dust. The few forest belts which had survived from Stalin's 1948 programme of forestation (abandoned in 1953) reduced the damage, but drifts of soil, often more than 2 metres high, formed between the trees of the protective forest belts. Villages and towns were covered in dust. Gorbachev learned a lesson from this disaster. Two months later he was elected as a deputy to the Supreme Soviet for the first time, and he became a member of the Standing Commission for the Protection of the Environment. The task of the commission was to supervise, amend and prepare legislation on environmental protection for the entire country.

Gorbachev's old friend, Zdenek Mlynar, reports that Gorbachev visited Prague in 1969 soon after the Dubček government was finally toppled (a year after the Soviet invasion).[11] This is his first known trip abroad. Mlynar, who still lived in Prague, could not see him, since he had come as an official member of a Soviet delegation. The selection of high Party officials for delegations like this was normally made by Suslov, in his capacity of secretary for ideology and head of the special foreign travel commission of the Central Committee which gives final approval for all official trips abroad. Gorbachev's inclusion in the delegation indicates that he was considered sufficiently orthodox to be in Czechoslovakia at that troubled time. Mlynar had last seen Gorbachev in Moscow in 1967 when, according to Mlynar, he had expressed himself in favour of more independence for the East European Soviet allies.[12] At that time Novotny, the conservative Czech leader, was still in power although under criticism. When Alexander Dubček was elected first secretary of Czechoslovakia in January 1968, Zdenek Mlynar, a consistent reformer, became a secretary of the Czech Central Committee and a close ally and assistant to Dubček. After 1967 there was no further contact between him and Gorbachev. In 1968 Mlynar became the main spokesman for a democratic socialism in which opposition is tolerated and minorities are guaranteed the opportunity to voice critical opinions.[13]

Gorbachev did not remain second secretary for long. In 1970 Efremov returned to Moscow, to the position of first deputy chairman of the USSR State Committee on Science and Technology. It was a demotion in the Party hierarchy, but it was a highly prestigious governmental position. The Committee had been created in 1957 to co-ordinate all research and technological projects in the Soviet Union and it was more important than a specialized ministry. The chairman, Professor Vladimir Kirillin, an expert on thermophysics and a member of the Academy of Sciences, was also a deputy Prime Minister. His own deputy chairmen had the rank and privilege equivalent to those of full ministers in other ministries. Efremov's new job was far more sophisticated than the one he had left in Stavropol. It was also much quieter and safer. In 1985, at the age of 73, he retains the same position and, doubtless, his friendly relations with Gorbachev.

In a brief statement on page three of *Pravda* on April 11, 1970, it was reported that the Stavropol *krai* committee of the CPSU had elected Gorbachev as first secretary. He had now joined the Party's super-elite and could expect to be a full member of the Central Committee after the next Party Congress.

4
Kraikom secretary

The term *krai* refers to an administrative and territorial unit found in the RSFSR which is distinguished from the far more common *oblast'* not by size, but by the fact that there are non-Russian ethnic groups living in the area which are too small to be separated into an 'autonomous republic'. Instead the locality in which they live, which is often no larger than a *raion* (district), is called an autonomous region. Stavropol *krai* contains the Karachai-Circassian Autonomous Region. There are five more *krai* in the RSFSR (the others are Krasnodar, Altai, Krasnoyarsk and Primorsky). Stavropol *krai* also contains 26 *raiony*. The word *krai* is normally translated into English as territory (or, occasionally, area). In political literature, however, the Russian term *obkom* is usually transliterated to refer to a regional committee of the CPSU. It seems natural, therefore, to use the term *kraikom* to refer to a territorial Party committee, rather than spelling out the whole term each time.

The structure of the *kraikom* or *obkom* is modelled on the Central Committee apparatus. It consists of 30 to 40 members of the Plenum (most of them *raikom* secretaries), a bureau and a secretariat. The 9 to 11 members of the bureau usually consist of representatives of the local administration – the chairman of the *ispolkom*, the procurator, the local head of the KGB, the *gorkom* secretary, the secretary of the *krai* Komsomol, the chairman of the main city's Soviet (council), and the other *kraikom* secretaries. A small secretariat of 3 or 4 people presides over several departments (agriculture, industry, trade and other services, construction, ideology and propaganda, youth organizations) which form the *kraikom* apparatus. Every region has a four-page daily newspaper which publishes local and national news and a few TASS reports in its small international section. *Stavropol'skaya pravda*, for example, consists mainly of agricultural news. A second newspaper printed in Stavropol, *Kurortnaya gazeta* (the Resort Newspaper), is aimed at the vacationers, workers and residents of the resort districts and is slightly more entertaining. It is also controlled by the *kraikom* and *kraiispolkom*.

The *kraikom* apparatus supervises the local government network in the *krai* in the same way that the Central Committee apparatus supervises government work at the All-Union and republican level. This dual administration has persisted since Lenin's time. It is both the main distinguishing feature of the Soviet system and the phenomenon which creates a top-heavy bureaucracy and ensures that the system is innately conservative. Dual power (with the Party issuing directives and acting as a 'political commissar' while the experts did the actual job of administration) was a necessity in the 1920s when most professional experts were connected with the old regime and did not belong to the Bolshevik Party. The role of the Party apparatus declined in the 1930s when Stalin put the security system above both Party and government, but it was revived during Khrushchev's time, particularly when the government apparatus was decentralized and economic life was administered through regional economic councils. When Khrushchev fell from power the central government system was restored and enlarged. The parallel Party economic administration became redundant. All managers in the government system were by now Party members, not bourgeois experts who required supervision by Bolshevik commissars. Nonetheless, at the republican and All-Union levels the power of the Party and its ability to interfere in government work is greater than it was and it is increasing. The effect is often to make things worse, not better. The government has the expertise to introduce projects, test methods, distribute funds and employ suitable workers. The Central Committee tends to duplicate the same functions, but without the means (computers, design bureaux, laboratories, etc.) to make them efficient. Most decisions at the top level are now issued as joint resolutions of the Central Committee and the Council of Ministers.

At the lowest level, however, in most production units, the lead is taken by qualified economists, engineers and other professionals, rather than by the secretaries of the Party bureaux or committees. In primary Party organizations, Party bureaux are responsible for ideology and political supervision, not for the plan or for the organization of the actual work. Finances and material funds are received via the government system. If primary Party bureaux were to disappear, nothing would happen – plants, factories, collective farms, etc. would continue to function normally, to produce their goods or sow their seeds and harvest their crops. When a Party official from a higher level has to deal with problems in a factory, research institute or collective farm, he contacts the director or chairman, not the secretary of the Party bureau. Nonetheless, Party bureaux continue to exist in every work place in the USSR.

At the district level, the *raikom* secretary tends to have influence only over the agricultural sector. He is unlikely to have any authority over the directors of the industrial plants, colleges, research institutes, army units, experimental stations, theatres, or universities located in his district. It is only at the *kraikom* and *obkom* level that the real power of the Party becomes apparent. Central Committee directives and decisions are transmitted to the *obkom* or *kraikom* and implemented from there in whatever way the *obkom* or *kraikom* finds necessary. All major establishments within the region or territory are supervised by the *obkom* or *kraikom*. Thus at the very lowest level the role of the Party is irrelevant, while at the top and at the *obkom* and *kraikom* level the power of the Party is as strong as it has ever been, particularly because at *oblast'* level the co-ordination of governmental departments (i.e. the regional offices of various ministries) within the *ispolkom* system is not very good.

According to the Soviet constitution, each constituent republic and autonomous republic has a Supreme Soviet with corresponding government functions. Each forms a Council of Ministers. Thus autonomous republics like Bashkir, Karelia, Komi, Chuvash, etc., each smaller and economically less developed than Stavropol or Krasnodar *krai* and many other regions, have their own Councils of Ministers. At lower levels, however, the constitution specifies that 'the bodies of state authority in Territories, Regions, districts, city districts, settlements and rural communities shall be corresponding Soviets of Peoples Deputies',[1] each of which forms an executive committee (*ispolkom*). Thus the structure of a local executive committee is smaller, less adequate for co-ordinating the ministerial networks in the area and has less authority than the chairman of local government in a sparsely populated and economically less important autonomous republic. The funding of the apparatus of a local *ispolkom* depends on the state budget and is less flexible than the finances of the Party apparatus at the *kraikom* or *obkom* level. The result, inevitably, is that deficiencies in the local government adminstration are spontaneously compensated for by growth and bureaucratization of the Party apparatus at that level.

There is thus a strange situation in the Soviet administration. In Moscow and other republican capitals, a dual system exists with the government in a strong position (at least in the early 1970s when Kosygin was still in charge and comparatively independent) to affect policy. At the regional level, however, the government system is weak and the Party bosses rule like dictators. Further down the hierarchy, at the work place, the managerial functions of the secretaries of primary Party organizations are almost non-existent. As a result, decisions and information pass up and down the hierarchy very slowly, co-ordination between different regions is very poor and the dual administrative apparatus is expensive, inefficient and prone to corruption. The connections between power and responsibility, between management and credit for success or debit for failure have disappeared.

According to the Party rules, *obkom* and *kraikom* secretaries have equal status in the Party hierarchy, the same privileges and the same amount of power in the areas they control. In practice, however, their rank and prestige depend on the political and economic importance of the area. Moscow and Leningrad *obkom* secretaries, for example, have higher status than other *obkom* secretaries and are traditionally members of the Politburo. In matters of economic policy the *obkom* secretaries of industrial regions like Gorky, Sverdlovsk or Novosibirsk are more important than the *obkom* secretaries of agricultural areas. Stavropol *krai* is important as an agricultural area. In good years it can produce as much as 4 million metric tons of grain and sell 2 million tons to the state. Other areas, like Krasnodar *krai* or Rostov region can produce even more (up to 8 or 10 million metric tons) in a good year. The North Caucasus as a whole is the best agricultural area in the Soviet Union and the Party secretaries of the area are correspondingly important. However, the secretaries of three provinces are particularly prominent. Krasnodar *krai*, Stavropol *krai* and the Crimean region are designated All-Union resort areas and it is this that makes their Party secretaries particularly important.

Large as it is, the Soviet Union has only one attractive, warm natural resort area. It is situated around the eastern part of the Black Sea, the North Caucasus, Georgia and Crimea. Between 20 and 30 million people, including foreigners, visit these areas each year as tourists and holiday-makers. Thus the holiday industry is an important and separate branch of the local economy. Almost all important state and Party officials from the General Secretary and the Prime Minister, to other ministers, Central Committee members and marshals and generals of the armed forces have a summer residence or state *dacha* (the term *dacha* means summer residence) in the Black Sea area. The leaders of many other socialist countries and foreign communist parties are similarly provided with *dachas* in the Crimea or other regions of the Black Sea. There are also thousands of sanatoria of various types, rest homes, hotels and camping facilities. In 1948 I began doing research work in the biochemical laboratory of the Nikitsky Botanical Garden near Yalta and I also worked in the area in 1950–51, travelling along the Black Sea coast to the Batumi Botanical Garden in Georgia. After that, from 1951 until 1972, I often spent my summer vacation in the area. I therefore witnessed at first hand that the construction of state *dachas* for high officials and of special 'closed' sanatoria developed more rapidly and successfully than any other branch of the Soviet economy.

In Soviet socialist realist literature, the *obkom* and *kraikom* secretary is depicted as a legendary figure. Wise, energetic, straightforward, just, hardworking, he (never, in fact or in fiction, she) travels from one trouble spot to another in his *oblast'* or *krai*, putting things right and getting things moving. The only *obkom* secretary I really knew was the obverse of this literary figure. A. A. Kondrashenkov was, for many years, the *obkom* secretary of Kaluga (where I worked in two research institutes from 1963 to 1972). A candidate of agricultural sciences, he liked to travel around Kaluga region to get the local agriculture moving. His region was the first, in the 1960s, to use a new method for preparing fodder. The new product, called *senazh* (haylage), is still very popular and important. It is a cross between hay and silage, produced by packing wilted grass into trenches lined with polyethylene. But Kondrashenkov (who died recently in retirement) was neither wise nor straightforward. He was, in fact, a typical petty tyrant. His dream, like the dream of many *obkom* secretaries in agricultural areas, was to be transferred to Moscow, either to be secretary of the Central Committee agricultural department or to be minister of one of the several agricultural ministries. His PhD work (on the agricultural economy of the area, which was ghost-written for him at the Kaluga experimental agricultural station) was an essential qualification for this ambition.

Obkom or *kraikom* secretaries are elected on the basis of a recommendation from the Central Committee. The candidate is normally invited to Politburo and Secretariat meetings in Moscow and should have the approval of the Central Committee departments of Party organs (this department was chaired by I. V. Kapitonov in 1970) and agriculture. It has been suggested that Gorbachev was recommended for his *kraikom* first secretaryship by Suslov or Andropov. It seems unlikely, however, that either of them knew Gorbachev well in 1970. It is true that Andropov was born in the Stavropol *krai* and used to spend his holidays in the Kislovodsk KGB sanatorium and that Suslov, who had been Stavropol secretary in 1939–44, had a professional interest in matters relating to the North Caucasus. But they would have met the first secretary, not the second secretary, during their visits to the area. Although they would have seen his file and would have had to voice an opinion about him at the Politburo meeting, this does not necessarily mean that they recommended him. It is far more likely that Kulakov (a candidate member of the Politburo in 1970), in his capacity as Central Committee secretary for agriculture, and Efremov, whose opinion of the quality of local cadres would have been solicited, proposed him. In any case, Gorbachev was young (39) by the standards of Brezhnev's Central Committee, but he was the natural choice for the position and he probably did not require special patronage. It would be normal to assess the suitability of the second secretary for the position, particularly since he had all the necessary qualifications. If Brezhnev met him before making the final decision, he must have been satisfied.

As soon as Gorbachev became first secretary, he transferred

Murakhovsky from Kislovodsk to Stavropol and made him first secretary of the *gorkom*, to consolidate his power in the region. A few years later Murakhovsky was moved over to become second secretary of the *kraikom* and Gorbachev's immediate deputy. At the XXIVth Party Congress in 1971 Gorbachev was elected a full member of the Central Committee. Within a year he had taken the two most important steps in his political career. None of his previous positions had involved decision-making at the national level, or even at the level of the RSFSR. Now he had become not only boss of his area, but personally responsible for part of the national plans and programmes and he had a voice in the highest Party body, the Central Committee. His personal links with Kulakov, who became a full member of the Politburo in 1971, and later with Suslov, Andropov and Kosygin, were important factors in his future promotion. But friendly relations with senior colleagues were insufficient. The crucial ingredients for the promotion of *obkom* and *kraikom* secretaries are economic success in their own areas and the ability to attract national attention by undertaking new initiatives which can be adopted by other areas. These tasks are particularly difficult for secretaries of agricultural regions. State plans and programmes are almost always more ambitious than what can, realistically, be attained. As a result, most *obkom* and *kraikom* secretaries of agricultural areas content themselves with trying to survive in their jobs. But this would clearly not be enough for Gorbachev.

Success for Stavropol *krai* meant success for Gorbachev. Nothing mattered more than this. The area enjoyed an excellent climate and good soil, two important conditions for agricultural success. However, Gorbachev's neighbour and rival, Medunov, first secretary of Krasnodar *krai*, was more fortunate than Gorbachev in this respect. Krasnodar *krai* was the same size as Stavropol, but had a larger population and produced twice as much grain and many other products (for example, tea, wine and rice). While Gorbachev was friendly with Kulakov, Medunov enjoyed the friendship of Brezhnev, who quite often stayed in Krasnodar *krai*. Gorbachev had recently graduated from a correspondence course in agriculture, whereas Medunov was not only a professional agronomist, but also a candidate of economic sciences (he had got his PhD in 1968) and a graduate of the Central Committee Higher Party School. He had also served in the

Soviet army during the war. Gorbachev's other North Caucasus neighbour, Ivan Bondarenko, secretary of Rostov *obkom*, was an even more formidable rival for promotion. He was young (44), a professional agronomist with broad practical experience (he had been director of an experimental station and a teacher of agronomy) and had a good military record. He had been elected second secretary of Rostov *obkom* in 1962 and had also served as *ispolkom* chairman for several years. After becoming first secretary of Rostov *obkom* in 1966, he had made Rostov a great industrial and agricultural success. The overall economic potential of Rostov *region* was about three times greater than that of Stavropol *krai*. In 1972 Bondarenko was given the highest award in the country – the title of Hero of Socialist Labour, the Gold Star Medal and the order of Lenin.

It can thus be seen that there were other *obkom* and *kraikom* secretaries who were far more prominent and better known than Gorbachev and who, on the face of it, stood a far better chance of being promoted in any competition for the few, highly prized vacancies which might occur in Moscow.

Although Gorbachev's rise had been noteworthy in provincial terms, on an All-Union scale he was well behind many others. When he became a member of the Central Committee in 1971, no-one outside Stavropol *krai* had ever heard of him. Even Kondrashenkov, Kaluga *obkom* secretary, was better known, since there had been a press campaign to publicize the 'progressive' and economic methods of producing haylage which he had initiated in Kaluga. But it was the Rostov region, with its famous fertile Don area and the largest agricultural machinery plant in the world, that was in the forefront of agricultural progress. Krasnodar *krai* was also famous. It produced the highest yields of all crops and had become an experimental centre for producing the best varieties of wheat and other cereals for a Soviet-style 'green revolution'. Thus Gorbachev's neighbours seemed, in the Soviet scale of evaluating political potential, to be Party cadres of a higher calibre than Gorbachev. It is very important to keep this in mind, because it is not general public perception or foreign perception of Gorbachev as a leader that will determine his political success. It is the attitude of his close colleagues in the Party apparatus and in the government. And if they do not accept him now as a natural leader, with superior talent, skill and knowledge, he will be unable to have much impact on Soviet policy.

As the secretary of an agricultural region, Gorbachev's only possible line of promotion was through agriculture. Fedor Kulakov, his friend and supporter, was, at 52 years of age, the youngest Politburo member. If he failed and was demoted, Gorbachev would stand no chance of replacing him. If Kulakov succeeded and rose in the Party hierarchy, Gorbachev would probably move up with him, either in the Party apparatus or in the government. There was one problem, however: in the early 1970s Brezhnev was very actively consolidating his power by promoting personal friends and loyal allies. But Kulakov did not belong to the Brezhnev faction. He was more closely associated with Suslov and Kosygin. Andropov was not yet in the picture – he became a full Politburo member in 1973, two years later than Kulakov achieved full membership.

Both Kulakov and Efremov had been efficient and successful *kraikom* secretaries, although they had very different styles. They had left Stavropol *krai* in good shape for Gorbachev. Moreover, they were in the position to continue giving Stavropol economic and organizational support. Gorbachev tended to favour Efremov's quiet style rather than Kulakov's toughness and rudeness. He was too young to imitate Kulakov's authoritarianism and he had to learn the art of successful leadership. He remained a modest and intelligent leader of the area until the end of his tenure in Stavropol. Admirable though this was, it made him comparatively unknown, even in his own *krai*. Local newspapers and magazines rarely mentioned his name. They often wrote about the *kraikom* in general terms, but without creating the kind of myth about the *kraikom* secretary which was frequently invented in other regions, where the secretary created a mini-cult with himself as the central folk hero. Ironically, it was because the *krai* was successful that it was unnecessary to create a cult. Plans were usually fulfilled, the harvest was increasing, the procurement quotas were met in time and local light industry was doing reasonably well. Gorbachev's 'iron teeth' grew later, when he left the comparative prosperity and quiet of Stavropol *krai* and became responsible for the much less tractable rural and agricultural problems of the country as a whole and had to deal with many equals.

According to the census, there were 979,804 urban inhabitants in Stavropol *krai* in 1970 (living in 16 towns and 15 settlements) and 1,325,976 rural inhabitants.[2] At the time of the 1959 census the percentage of the rural population had been higher (69 per cent), although the total population was about the same (1,302,306). But the exodus from the villages was far lower than in the northern parts of the country, where towns and cities grew very rapidly. There are 4.2 million hectares of arable land in Stavropol *krai*. About half of it is used to cultivate grain and the rest is given over to fodder and technical crops (mainly sunflower and sugar beet). Comparatively large tracts of land are used to cultivate vegetables and fruit. The increasing demand from the booming health centres makes this necessary. *Kolkhozy* and *sovkhozy* do not find it easy to grow fruit and vegetables and this has stimulated the extensive development of private plots and allotments. Their owners sell the produce on private markets to the vacationers who more than triple the population in the resort areas during the summer and early autumn. As a result, the income that peasants earn from their private plots is often rather higher than their income from the socialist sector.

The growth of tourism and the health industry was particularly rapid during the 1970s, when the Soviet population became more affluent and more mobile. Between 1970 and 1978 the number of people who spent holidays in sanatoria, holiday homes, hostels and hotels and tourists centres grew from 16 to 35 million. Millions more rented private accommodation. The tourist boom created a sizeable black market in the south which was impossible to control. The demand for fresh food was so high that many collective and state farms in the North Caucasus began employing temporary outside brigades to produce, on the basis of shared profits, the vegetables and fruit which were in most demand. The private brigades (known as '*shabashnye*' which means easy profit) sprang up spontaneously in the North Caucasus in the late 1960s on the initiative of the Koreans who had migrated to the area from Central Asia (more than 100,000 Koreans were deported from the Far East to Central Asia in 1942, in anticipation of a possible Japanese attack). The Korean families leased land from the *kolkhozy* and *sovkhozy* and cultivated labour-intensive crops. They worked very hard and made high profits. In the 1970s the number of these 'free enterprise' brigades increased sharply, particularly in the Stavropol and Krasnodar areas.[3] Although the brigades violated strict Soviet laws, they were tolerated because there was no other way to satisfy the demand of millions of holiday-makers for fresh vegetables. The local *kolkhozy* and *sovkhozy* shared the profits of the tourist and health-treatment boom in the area.

In the main steppe areas of the eastern and northern parts of Stavropol *krai* agriculture was more traditional, specializing in the cultivation of grain. The grain harvest in the Soviet Union varies widely from year to year, but in 1973 for the first time in the history of Russia the level rose above 200 million metric tons, to 222.5 million. This was a remarkable reversal of the poor performance of 1972. The success contributed to Kulakov's prominence in the Politburo. The 1974 elections to the Supreme Soviet provided a clear indication of his rise in the Party hierarchy. As we have seen, the sequence of speeches made by members of the Politburo prior to elections is not random, but is arranged according to seniority with the less senior speaking first. There had been important changes in the Politburo in 1973. Voronov and Shelest had lost their positions and Grechko, Andropov and Gromyko, in charge of defence, the KGB and foreign affairs respectively, had been promoted to full membership. It had also become known that when Brezhnev was away (on holiday or abroad), it was Kirilenko and not Suslov who chaired Politburo meetings. From the sequence of election speeches in June 1974, however, it was clear that Suslov retained his official rank as second-in-command, the position he had held since Khrushchev's fall from power. He met his electorate on Wednesday, June 11, a day before Kosygin and two days before Brezhnev's speech which closed the campaign. Kirilenko's speech preceded Suslov's. But Kulakov's speech in Stavropol *krai* was also in the last week, on June 7. Western observers were quick to spot this. Since he was the youngest member of the Politburo, it seemed to augur a bright future. Longer serving members of the Politburo like Polyansky, Shelepin and Pel'she spoke before him and he also seemed to be senior to Grishin, Kunayev and Shcherbitsky, who had been members of the Politburo since 1971 and to Andropov and Ustinov.

Kulakov's electoral meeting in his Petrovsky constituency took place in the House of Culture in the small town of Svetlograd. The constituency included the centrally located Petrovsky district and six neighbouring districts. By law electoral constituencies consist of a population of about 300,000 and therefore they do not usually coincide with administrative units. One of the districts which formed part of Kulakov's constituency was Ipatovsky, later famous for its agricultural success. Gorbachev was present at the meeting and he made a speech praising Kulakov for the remarkable success of Soviet agriculture and advising the electorate to give him unanimous support. Kulakov, in turn, in a speech which was published in all the central newspapers, praised the *krai* for its successful economic development since the previous elections in 1969.[4] Industrial production had risen from 2.5 billion roubles in 1970 to 3 billion in 1973. The average grain yields had increased from 15 centners per hectare in 1970 to 18.1 centners. The *krai* had sold 2.1 million metric tons of grain to the state in 1973, a record for the area. There had also been successes in the production of meat and wool.

Gorbachev was also nominated as a deputy to the Supreme Soviet to represent Stavropol city and three surrounding rural districts, including Krasnogvardeisky district where Privol'noye, the village in which he had been born, was located. His own electoral meetings took place earlier and as a local candidate, he participated in several meetings. In the newly elected Supreme Soviet he was given a new appointment: chairman of the Standing Commission on Youth Affairs. This reflected his experience in Komsomol work.[5] The Supreme Soviet Standing Commissions (15 of them were formed in 1974, on agriculture, consumer goods, construction, health, etc.) have very broad constitutional powers, but they rarely exercise them. Theoretically, they are meant to 'make a preliminary review of matters coming within the jurisdiction of the Supreme Soviet of the USSR . . . to check on the work of state bodies and organizations.'[6] About 80 per cent of Supreme Soviet deputies serve on the commissions, but since they almost never meet between sessions of the Supreme Soviet, and most legislative acts are normally passed by the Presidium of the Supreme Soviet between sessions, they play a minor legislative role. The Supreme Soviet normally meets twice a year for two days each session, and the commissions meet immediately before each session if there is legislation to consider. The position of Commission chairman, therefore, is not very onerous.

Gorbachev did not acquire particular prominence during his

first five years as *kraikom* secretary. Some recent Western articles have suggested that he was important because he was able to travel abroad (to Belgium in 1972 and to West Germany in 1975) as head of official delegations. In fact, these visits were of minor importance and not at all unusual. In the 1970s many other *obkom* secretaries and members of the Central Committee travelled to the west with various delegations usually, and this was true of the delegations headed by Gorbachev, at the invitation of the local communist parties. When the invitation comes from an important Western party (the French, Italian or Greek Communist Parties, for example), the head of the delegation is usually a secretary of the Central Committee or a member of the Politburo. For smaller, less important communist or socialist parties, the delegation is usually small and headed by an *obkom* secretary. The visits are not only a privilege, but also a test of Party officials. We can conclude that Gorbachev must have proved himself trustworthy and reliable.

The main event at which the comparative prominence of *obkom* and *kraikom* secretaries became evident was the XXVth Party Congress in February 1976. It is a long time since discussions at Party Congresses have been spontaneous. Since the 1930s the speeches have been programmed well in advance and the texts have been censored to fit certain rules. It is a rare privilege to be nominated as a speaker. The normal procedure is that all the Party leaders of the constituent republics are given the opportunity to make a speech giving a national flavour to their praise of the General Secretary. By 1976 the Brezhnev cult had reached significant proportions and speakers competed with one another in the lavishness of their praise for Brezhnev. Eduard Shevarnadze, then Georgian Party secretary, it seems, came first in this particular competition, with Aliyev, the Azerbaijani secretary, a close second. Gorbachev did not make a speech, whereas both Medunov and Bondarenko, his North Caucasus neighbours, were invited to speak. The previous agricultural year had been extremely poor (only 140 million tons of grain were produced and about 30 million tons had been imported from the USA, Canada and other countries – it was the worst agricultural year of Brezhnev's tenure). Both speakers promised better results in 1976. Medunov announced that Krasnodar *krai* had undertaken to produce 10 million tons of grain and to sell more than 4 million tons to the state. Bondarenko promised 8 million tons, of which 4 million would be for state procurements. Brezhnev was very pleased and showed his intimacy with Medunov by interrupting his speech in a friendly way to ask that the production of rice be developed. The Congress resulted in the consolidation of Kulakov's position. His agricultural rival in the Politburo, Dmitri Polyansky, was made a scapegoat for the poor harvest in 1975 and was not re-elected to the Politburo.

Although Kulakov was Central Committee secretary for agriculture, he was not held directly responsible for the disastrous harvest in 1975. Polyansky had been a member of the Politburo since 1960 and was more directly involved in agricultural administration, serving as well as Minister of Agriculture and first Deputy Chairman of the Council of Ministers. He lost these positions and, in line with Brezhnev's favourite technique for dealing with disgraced officials, he was sent as Soviet ambassador to Japan (he was later transferred to Norway, where he is still Soviet ambassador). Polyansky's departure left Kulakov in overall control of agriculture. He and Brezhnev now had the problem of selecting a new Minister of Agriculture. It had become a key ministry, since by 1976 it consumed one quarter of the state budget. Brezhnev favoured his close friend Ivan Bodyl, first secretary of Moldavia, one of Brezhnev's power bases. Bodyl was an agronomist and veterinary surgeon by training. Kulakov, however, had strong objections. Brezhnev was determined to appoint one of his own men and Valentin Mesyats, second secretary of the Kazakhstan Central Committee and Kunayev's deputy, became Minister. He had previous experience of ministerial work in the RSFSR, but had been transferred to take responsibility for the virgin land areas in Kazakhstan in 1971 (this was the job in which Brezhnev had first achieved prominence in 1954–56). He was comparatively young (48 years) and a graduate of the Timiryazev Agricultural Academy in Moscow (where he was not remembered as a very bright student). He had been a staunch supporter of Lysenko. Although he and Kulakov were not friends, Kulakov did not feel threatened by him – he was unlikely to acquire a Politburo post in the near future and he would have to submit to Kulakov's authority. The overall co-ordination of the agricultural sector of government (previously done by Polyansky) which included the ministries of agriculture, procurements, tractors and agricultural machinery, meat and milk production, agricultural construction, etc., was charged to Zia Nuriyev, a Bashkir, previously secretary of the Bashkir Autonomous Republic and since 1973 one of Kosygin's deputy prime ministers.

Kulakov's influence increased after Polyansky's departure, but the administration of agriculture became no easier. Polyansky's experience and seniority had made it possible to co-ordinate the work of the various agricultural ministries and state committees around the Ministry of Agriculture. With the appointment of a more junior minister, the Ministry of Agriculture was effectively downgraded. The role of the Central Committee department of agriculture became more important, but it could not really replace the government system. Brezhnev was committing the same mistake that he had made in 1973, when he had turned Matskevich, an able and competent Minister of Agriculture, into the scapegoat for the bad harvest of 1972 (Matskevich was sent as ambassador to Czechoslovakia). In 1973 it had been considered essential to upgrade the position of the Minister of Agriculture and to ensure that it was held by a member of the Politburo. Now, less than three years later, there was another major reorganization because of a bad harvest and the result was a downgrading of the new minister. However, the harvest of 1976 was unexpectedly good and a new record amount of grain (223.8 million metric tons) was produced. It was no more due to the agricultural administration than the failure of 1975 had been, but this was not the view taken by the Central Committee. Moreover, despite the good harvest, many of the other important indicators of agricultural production (production costs of grain, meat, milk and other produce, the debts of the *kolkhozy* and *sovkhozy*, the continuing exodus of the rural population, etc.) were deteriorating.

By 1975 Brezhnev's health had become an issue. From December 1974 to February 1975 he disappeared from public view. It became known later that he had suffered a serious heart attack and was in hospital. By the time of the XXVth Congress he had recovered sufficiently to deliver a formidable six hour report. However, neither the Congress nor the steadily increasing Brezhnev cult could stifle speculation about succession. There were signs that Brezhnev and his faction were making preparations to guarantee the legacy of the Brezhnev leadership in the history of the Party and the country. Brezhnev wanted to ensure that he would not suffer Stalin's or Khrushchev's fate in Soviet political history. It was therefore important that he should nominate a successor who would continue the 'Brezhnev era' and not demolish the Brezhnev cult. Suslov, his former rival and the present second-in-command, was older than him and in poor health. Kirilenko, an old friend, was the same age as Brezhnev (70). Podgorny, another rival, was also older. The most senior member of the Politburo after these elder statesmen, and the most senior member of the secretariat, was the youngest member of both, Kulakov. The agricultural success of 1976 increased Kulakov's influence and he was supported by Suslov, Kosygin and Andropov. Moreover, if there was a power struggle, Podgorny would probably support him. Marshal Grechko, Brezhnev's close wartime friend, died in 1976 and was replaced as Minister of Defence by Ustinov, a rather independent figure. By the end of 1976 Brezhnev only had three loyal friends left in the Politburo: Kirilenko, Shcherbitsky and Kunayev. When Andropov, Gromyko, Romanov and Ustinov were promoted, many Western observers believed that this implied the ascendancy of Brezhnev's proteges.[7] In retrospect, however, it is clear that they did not belong to Brezhnev's faction and that they would not co-operate with him on many issues of internal policy. However, in terms of Gorbachev's future, what is interesting is that Kulakov became a contender for succession in 1977 and that his name was often mentioned in discussions about the prospects for change in the Soviet Union.

Kulakov was a man with a good intellect. Agricultural problems had been serious issues during the power struggle in 1953–54 and in 1964 and they continued to dominate the political agenda in the 1970s. Kulakov needed to consolidate his success, to prove that the crisis in agriculture was over and that the Soviet Union could retain high standards of living without importing embarrassing amounts of grain. The Soviet leadership as a whole linked its own credibility too closely to the promise of better food production and a better diet. The record harvest of 1976 created the illusion that this goal was attainable and that the superiority of socialist agriculture would finally be proved.

Kulakov adopted two principles as the centre of his 'agricultural miracle': one was a 'programmable, guaranteed production level' and the second was rapid harvesting. In his speech in Svetlograd in

1974 he had made it clear that he expected Stavropol *krai*, with its good irrigation system and high level of mechanization, to be a model of agricultural success irrespective of weather conditions. His priorities were correct. The main problem of Soviet grain production was the inability to reap the harvest quickly enough with resulting large losses of grain. When grain cereals mature, they must be harvested and threshed as soon as possible. The golden yellow fields which are the conventional visual symbol of a rich harvest are, in fact, already dead fields. Cereal plants are not designed by nature to stay ripe for very long. The actual grain is a seed which, if left too long, drops to the soil to grow again. Mature plants lose their resistance to wind and rain and can easily be flattened. If harvesting is delayed or extended, as much as 20 to 30 per cent of the grain can be lost. Kulakov's scheme was simple – to prove to everyone that the harvesting could be done quickly and efficiently and that this would save a lot of grain. The scheme needed to be tested as a large scale experiment and then recommended to the country as a whole. If it was successful, Kulakov would receive a great deal of kudos.

The experiment was prepared in 1976 in the All-Union Research and Technological Institute of Mechanization and Electrification of Agriculture in Zernograd in the Rostov region. Scientists there, under the supervision of the director of the institute, Professor M. S. Runchev, tested a number of computer models of harvesting, finally designing a scheme to co-ordinate all the work of a grain-producing region. It seemed realistic although it involved a formidable task of preparing machinery, people, the administrative structure and mobilizing all available resources. Although the scheme was developed in the Rostov region, Kulakov decided to test it in Stavropol *krai*, in the Ipatovsky district. It was a flat, purely grain-producing district and it cultivated winter wheat which matures synchronously. All these factors were important. But equally important would be local involvement and the enthusiasm of the district administration. Ipatovsky district, in the north of Stavropol *krai*, was part of Kulakov's Supreme Soviet electoral constituency. A special group of *krai*, district and rural deputies was formed to supervise the experiment and act in tandem with Party supervision. The 'Ipatovsky method', as it became known, was the main event of the 1977 agricultural season.

Harvesting in Stavropol *krai* and elsewhere in 1977 was usually done by a *beznaryadnoye zveno*. This was a small unit of people and machinery, consisting of a simple harvester, two combines and trucks to transport the grain. The units worked on the basis of individual quotes and were paid according to the amount they harvested. The direct relationship between efficiency and pay was assumed to act as an incentive to increase productivity. The new scheme was based on a larger unit, called a harvesting-transport complex, and composed of at least 15 combine harvesters in three groups, 15 trucks and groups of people specializing in delivering fuel, collecting straw, preparing fields beforehand and cultivating them immediately after the harvesting. There were also groups to take care of repair and servicing, catering, medical problems and ideological support (which included a radio service, newspapers, lectures, a special postal service in the fields and a daily newsletter to show how the complex worked). Two mobile houses were to be provided for each complex so that the work could continue round the clock and workers could sleep in the fields. There were also to be mobile showers and a small shop. In theory the complex would be able to co-ordinate all the work involved in harvesting – mowing, threshing, loading, delivering the grain to the elevators, making straw stocks – more efficiently than smaller units. However, the essence of the system was a well prepared preliminary programme which co-ordinated the work of all the complexes in the district. Each group and each individual member had to know his or her timetable for the whole harvesting period. It was expected that management and co-ordination would, in the future, be computerized.

Intensive preparations to implement the scheme were launched at the beginning of 1977.[8] The Ipatovsky district was perfectly suited for large mechanization units, particularly because its main crop was winter wheat. Winter cereals mature more evenly than spring crops, since the winter weather synchronizes plant development. The Stavropol *kraikom* supported the initiative and its agricultural department kept in close contact with the institute in Rostov. The district was divided into 54 harvesting zones, each with its own complex. The original scheme was slightly amended, and each complex was provided with reserve combines, in case of breakdowns during the intensive period of work. No delays could be tolerated if the district was to achieve a record. The ideological support groups were also made slightly larger, to show that it was the Party which was leading the whole project. Two professional agitators from the Party committee, eight part-time agitators, four 'political informants' and one lecturer were attached to each complex. A 'temporary mobile Party organization' and a 'temporary mobile Komsomol group' were formed to give Party and Komsomol members in the complexes the opportunity of organizing and attending meetings in the fields. Since 1977 was the 60th anniversary of the October revolution, the whole enterprise was dedicated to this jubilee. The summer turned out to be very dry, but this was perfect weather for the experiment. Rain or unreliable weather could easily spoil the co-ordination and delay work. The fields looked very promising. According to the official plan (based, as usual, on the performance of the previous year), Ipatovsky district was to deliver 120,000 metric tons of grain to the state. However, local Party officials had undertaken to overfulfil the plan and deliver 200,000 tons.

The experiment was a complete success. Previously, harvesting had often taken three or four weeks. In 1977 the Ipatovsky district completed the harvest in the second week of July (the earliest possible date for the North Caucasus) in a record 9 days. The 200,000 tons of grain which had been promised were delivered to the state. The results were reported to Brezhnev and *Pravda* published a Central Committee decision on July 16, 1977, 'On the Experiment of Ipatovsky District Party Organization in Harvesting'. The method was praised as an example of progressive technology and credit was given to the district and to the Rostov institute. The technique was described briefly and positive comments were made about the 'temporary Party and Komsomol groups' which had provided Party influence. The Central Committee recommended that the method be studied by all republican Central Committees and Councils of Ministers, as well as by other *ob-* and *kraikomy* so that they could support its introduction. An interview with Gorbachev was published prominently on the front page of the same issue of *Pravda*,[9] in which he gave credit to the whole *krai*. This was the first time he had received publicity in *Pravda*.

The fact that a special resolution of the Central Committee was published on July 16, only two days after the harvesting in Ipatovsky district ended, shows very clearly that the publicity had been prepared well in advance. The 'record' had been in the making for some time and the agricultural department of the Central Committee had been keeping it under close observation. The Central Committee decision was not only very rapid, but, unusually, it was not published as a joint Council of Ministers–Central Committee resolution. Moreover, no Central Committee Plenum had taken place. Thus the decision must have been taken by the Secretariat and approved by the Politburo. Normally when an economic record is achieved, congratulations arrive first and only later is there a Central Committee or other Party and government decision. The order was reversed this time. Brezhnev was at his summer residence in the Crimea and it took some time to arrange for him to send a congratulatory telegram to the Ipatovsky *raikom*. It was only published in the press two days after the Central Committee resolution urging all other regions to adopt the Ipatovsky method immediately for the rest of the harvesting season. [10]

A front page *Pravda* editorial on July 20, 'Follow the harvesting innovators', announced the beginning of a campaign to emulate the excellent, timely example of Ipatovsky district. This was an unrealistic gamble which miraculously paid off. It had taken almost a year for the Ipatovsky district to prepare its co-ordinated programme and make the task clear to each participant. The Rostov Institute had co-operated fully and had assisted in the implementation of the method. It was simply impossible to reorganize the harvesting plans in other regions at such short notice. Moreover, in the northern and eastern parts of the country most of the grain is sown in the spring and does not mature simultaneously. In any case, if it rained in September, the method would be unworkable, since poor weather demands selective harvesting. However, the authorities clearly felt that it was important to keep the momentum of the campaign going. In fact, the gamble paid off. It was reported later that 56,000 harvesting-transport complexes had been created across the country and that the productivity of each combine harvester had increased by 20 per cent. It is difficult to check how real these complexes were. 1977 was a very dry year and the total harvest (195 million tons) was lower than the planned target. However, the results may have been worse but for the Ipatovsky method – or at least, that was Kulakov's message.

More serious preparations for introducing the method more widely were launched at the beginning of 1978. Articles by V. V. Kalyagin and Gorbachev were published in *Agitator*, the Central Committee propaganda magazine. Gorbachev claimed that the new method allowed better use of mechanization because all available machinery was concentrated in a district at just the right time. Thus 'each farm in the district can carry out the harvesting in the most optimal time'.[11] Kalyagin, the secretary of Ipatovsky *raikom*, was awarded the title of Hero of Socialist Labour, together with a Gold Star Medal and the Order of Lenin. On February 4, 1978, *Pravda*, *Izvestiya* and other newspapers published official congratulations from the Central Committee, the Council of Ministers and the Presidium of the Supreme Soviet to Kulakov on his 60th birthday. This kind of greeting is standard for Politburo members and candidate members and they are usually linked with an award: the title Hero of Socialist Labour, for example, for a Politburo member who enjoys very high standing, or the Order of Lenin for less important members. In February 1978 Kulakov was rewarded with the highest award – Hero of Socialist Labour.[12] A few days later it was presented to him by Brezhnev at a special ceremony. Brezhnev was acting in his capacity as Chairman of the Presidium of the Supreme Soviet (Podgorny had been retired without any honours in 1977 and Brezhnev had assumed the post). All the Moscow-based Politburo members were present and Brezhnev made a speech praising Kulakov warmly for his contribution to the collective efforts of the Party leadership.[13]

In its decree of March 1, the Presidium of the Supreme Soviet made awards to many agricultural workers, *kolkhozniks* and Party officials in Staropol *krai* in recognition of its success in agriculture. Gorbachev received the order of the October Revolution. In May, the city of Stavropol itself was awarded the order of the October Revolution, to mark the bicentenary of its foundation. On the 12th of that month Mikhail Suslov arrived in Stavropol for the presentation ceremony, in the course of which he and Gorbachev exchanged warm congratulations (Gorbachev linked Suslov's name with many of Stavropol's successes). The award over, Suslov and Gorbachev visited other parts of the *krai*.

The agricultural season seemed promising in 1978. The weather was good and the organization of agricultural work seemed adequate. The Ipatovsky district planned to improve on its 1977 record. The promise was fulfilled. From a total sown area of 101,000 hectares, 240,000 metric tons of grain were delivered to the state procurement system within 7 days. It was an outstanding result, so remarkable that no district, including Ipatovsky district itself, would ever be able to repeat it. Since some of the grain must have been retained for animal feed and seed grain, the total harvest in 1978 was probably not less than 35–40 centners per hectare. The rest of Stavropol *krai* also did well and the prospects were good for other regions of the Soviet Union. The country seemed to be heading for a new record in agricultural production. The July estimates of the harvest made in the USA indicated the almost unthinkable level of 240 million tons. For the first time in Soviet history it looked as if the annual plan might be overfulfilled. Kulakov, who had engineered this unprecedented success, should have been proud and happy.

However, in July 1978, Kulakov was in no condition to enjoy his success. Something strange seemed to be happening in the Kremlin. The Ipatovsky harvest had been completed, but the announcement of the results was delayed. Then, suddenly, on July 17, 1978, Kulakov died. It was reported that the cause of death was that his 'heart stopped beating'. He had not suffered a heart attack or a stroke or any of the other medical problems related to illness or old age. His heart had simply failed, a curious fate to befall the youngest and ablest member of the Politburo. It is not, of course, impossible for people to die prematurely from heart disease. Ordinary Soviet citizens did not regard Kulakov's death as a particular tragedy. Under Brezhnev the Kremlin leaders lived rather private lives and very little was known about them. The only people who ever try to evaluate the consequences of changes in the Politburo caused by a death, promotion or demotion are Party *apparatchiki*, Moscow intellectuals and Western 'Kremlin watchers'. Kulakov's death produced speculation, but, curiously, not because of the unusual medical statement signed by Academician Professor Chazov and other prominent Kremlin doctors. Chazov had built the largest and most up-to-date 'state-of-the-art' cardiological unit in the world in the Kremlin hospital. Despite this, the hearts of Politburo members could clearly simply cease beating without any warning. Speculation only began after Kulakov's Red Square funeral. Everything seemed normal to the public. The body of the deceased lay in state in the Hall of Columns of the House of Unions. The funeral commission was chaired by Kirilenko, who made the first eulogy speech at the funeral. Gorbachev was also given the opportunity to speak from the Lenin mausoleum on behalf of the people of Stavropol *krai*, where Kulakov had first become prominent. He said that Kulakov's death was not only the loss of an important Party and state figure but also of a close personal friend.[14] This was the first opportunity that Soviet television viewers had ever had to see and hear Gorbachev, their future leader.

The reason why the funeral caused speculation was that Brezhnev, Kosygin and Suslov were absent. They had all been in Moscow on July 3 and 4, when a Central Committee Plenum had taken place. Even if they had already left for their respective summer vacations, it would have been appropriate for them to return for a day or two to pay their last respects to their dear comrade. They all signed the Central Committee's official obituary. There were some suggestions in the Western press that Kulakov's death may not have been entirely due to natural causes.[15] In Moscow there was a rumour that he had committed suicide and later publications claimed to know that he had cut his wrists.[16] Some of Brezhnev's biographers believe that there may have been a quarrel between Brezhnev and Kulakov in 1978.[17] Suicide is not entirely unknown amongst the Soviet super-elite, but it is difficult to explain what Kulakov's motives could have been. If he was so much out of favour that he might lose his job, this would have become clear at the Plenum on July 3–4, when agriculture was the main subject of discussion. He had not been criticized openly at the Plenum. Gorbachev had been one of the speakers (his speech was never published) and there is no doubt that he must have related the successes of Stavropol *krai*. It was already apparent that 1978 was going to be an extremely good agricultural year. Moreover, if there had been something seriously against Kulakov, he would neither have been buried with full honours, nor would he have been given a commemoration decree some time after his death. If one compares the medical reports of other deaths with the announcement of Kulakov's, the latter seems remarkably vague and ambiguous. The same team of doctors headed by Chazov had always given detailed descriptions (as they would in the future) of the cause of death of other leaders, perhaps just to exonerate themselves in case there was any suggestion of negligence or foul play. To announce that Kulakov died when his heart stopped is rather absurd. After all, the heart *always* stops when someone dies. But the suggestion of suicide also does not ring true. Kulakov's career is evidence of a very strong will. He clearly was a typical Party boss and a formidable character, but he was equally clearly a fighter, not a defeatist. What the real story is might not be known for a long time, but it seems unlikely that the whole truth was reported at the time.

Kulakov's death left Western Kremlin experts at a loss. They now had no idea who might be Brezhnev's successor. Speculating about the succession in 1980, Seweryn Bialer, for example, expressed confusion about the promotion in 1978 and 1979 of people who seemed far too old to be possible successors. He concluded:

> The death in 1978 of Kulakov eliminated the only possible successor who combined characteristics associated with previous successions to leadership: an age over ten years junior to the incumbent, close association with him, and long tenure in both the central party Secretariat and the Politburo.[18]

Although Kulakov's death had removed the most likely successor, the problem was still only theoretical. Brezhnev was alive and in full control. But the death created several vacancies: Politburo membership, Central Committee secretaryship, head of the Central Committee agricultural department, Supreme Soviet deputy and several lesser posts. It was decided not to have a by-election in the Petrovsky electoral constituency, since the next elections were due in 1979. The Politburo vacancy could be filled in November, when there would be a regular Plenum. The election of a Central Committee secretary also required a full Plenum. But it seemed important to elect someone to head the agricultural department of the Central Committee immediately. A competent person should be in charge at the peak of the harvesting season and the appointment could be made by the Politburo and Secretariat. However, the decision was delayed for several months, and it seems reasonable to suppose that there was no consensus on a candidate acceptable to the various groups that made up the leadership. It was an important position, particularly because the incumbent might later become a secretary of the Central Committee and be promoted to the Politburo.

It is almost certain that Brezhnev's choice for the position was Bodyl, whom he wanted to bring to Moscow (he finally succeeded in 1980, when Bodyl was put in charge of agriculture in the Council of Ministers). But there were two other likely candidates – Gorbachev's North Caucasus rivals, Bondarenko and Medunov. They were both agronomists and long serving secretaries in the best agricultural areas. In fact, it was Gorbachev who was given the position, but the choice was not easy and it took several months before agreement was reached.

Since Gorbachev was not Brezhnev's choice, there was speculation in the West that it must have been Suslov, a former Stavropol secretary and a patron of the area, who recommended Gorbachev for promotion. Suslov apparently knew Gorbachev rather better than other members of the Politburo did. But Andropov and Kosygin both knew him as well and had a high opinion of his integrity and qualifications. They probably also realized that both Medunov and Bodyl presented problems (this only became public knowledge rather later). In August and September 1978, Suslov, Kosygin and Andropov all spent some time in Stavropol *krai*. They had official *dachas* in the Sochi area of Krasnodar *krai*, but in the 1970s they often stayed in special sections of the sanatoria in Kislovodsk belonging to the Central Committee, the USSR Council of Ministers and the KGB respectively. Although the three were not particularly close friends, they had several things in common. For one thing, they were independent and did not belong to Brezhnev's group. For another they were not corrupt and as 'true believers', they adhered firmly to certain Communist Party principles. From a medical point of view all three had kidney problems and diabetes and had been prescribed the hot water spas and mineral waters of Kislovodsk.

According to protocol, the *kraikom* secretary, Gorbachev, would have met Politburo members at the airport or station when they arrived and escorted them to their residences, returning a few days later to enquire about their health and whether conditions in their sanatoria were satisfactory. Kosygin was probably the best known of the three in the area, not only because he was head of government, but because he did not like the closed environment of the sanatorium and often went walking, watched from a distance by his bodyguards. (One of his favourite footpaths has officially been named Kosygin Walk and has become a tourist attraction). Andropov, by contrast, did not like leaving the KGB sanatorium and very few people (but they included the former Soviet diplomat and UN official, A. Shevchenko, who defected later) knew when he was in the area.[19] Suslov, second-in-command and the Party ideologist, was a very private person and little is known of his hobbies. He had suffered a heart attack in 1976 and was not allowed much exercise. It is extremely likely that these three men would have met to discuss Politburo and government problems and that they would have seen Gorbachev, who would have seemed a suitable replacement for Kulakov. In 1978 Stavropol *krai* was doing very well and the Ipatovsky method of harvesting seemed very successful. Gorbachev was a decent man, well-educated, confident, young and energetic. Although his Party record was less impressive than those of Brezhnev's favourites, Brezhnev was not yet strong enough to put somebody in charge of a Central Committee department in the face of objections from Suslov, Kosygin and Andropov. In any case, a compromise suited Brezhnev – he was about to move his old friend and personal chief-of-staff, Chernenko, up to full membership of the Politburo (although he had only been a candidate member since 1977). He also wanted to make Tikhonov a candidate member of the Politburo, in preparation for eventually becoming Prime Minister. He was thus in a weak position to insist on his own candidate for Kulakov's job. Gorbachev must have seemed too young to represent a serious challenge and the possibility of promoting him to Politburo status was not an immediate problem. It had taken Kulakov seven years to move from the Secretariat to the Politburo. Nonetheless, Brezhnev seemed in no hurry to agree to the appointment.

In September 1978 Brezhnev and Chernenko (who now accompanied Brezhnev everywhere) visited Baku at the invitation of Aliyev. They travelled by special train via Rostov, where they were met by local officials who reported on the affairs of the area. The next stop, on September 19, was Krasnodar *krai*. There they were met by Medunov and the chairman of the *ispolkom*, Rasumovsky, who reported that Krasnodar *krai* had already sold 3.3 million tons of grain to the state (this was less than the 4.2

million tons which Medunov had promised in his XXVth Party Congress speech). On the same day the special train reached Mineralnye Vody, in the Stavropol resort area. Gorbachev and *ispolkom* chairman I. Taranov were waiting to report to Brezhnev. Stavropol *krai* had gathered a record harvest and had already sold 2.5 million tons of grain to the state, 750,000 tons above the official state plan for the area. Brezhnev and Chernenko may not have paid much attention to this success, but Andropov, who just happened to be on holiday here, was also present. The central newspapers gave front page prominence to Brezhnev's meeting with both Medunov and Gorbachev.[20] But even this was not enough. In October, the second most important of Brezhnev's men in the Politburo, Kirilenko, also arrived in Stavropol to meet Gorbachev and to make a tour of the *krai*. Gorbachev accompanied Kirilenko everywhere. This visit did not figure prominently in the Moscow newspapers but was extensively reported in the local press.

It often happens that appointments to certain positions in Moscow are made well before the formal official announcement at the regular Central Committee plenum. However, this was not the case with the agricultural secretaryship. Gorbachev was in Stavropol at least until the middle of November, when he took part in the local conference.

When the regular November Plenum of the Central Committee met in Moscow on November 27, many changes were announced in the top level of the hierarchy. Chernenko became a full member of the Politburo and his picture and biography appeared on the front page of all Soviet newspapers.[21] Tikhonov, despite his advanced age (73), was elected candidate member, and so was Shevarnadze, secretary of the Georgian Party. Kirill Mazurov retired from the Politburo 'for reasons of health'. He had been Kosygin's first deputy and possible successor. Clearly, Brezhnev intended Tikhonov for this position, but he needed first to remove Mazurov, Tikhonov's junior by nine years and already a full member of the Politburo. Mazurov, together with Suslov and Shelepin, was known to have criticized some aspects of Brezhnev's economic policy at Central Committee meetings.[22] The last in the list of reported promotions was Gorbachev. He had been appointed secretary of the Central Committee, and although his responsibilities were not specified, it was clear that he had inherited Kulakov's position.

Kulakov's grand design to reach the top had failed, but at least he had been replaced by his young friend and protegé. Podgorny's dismissal in 1977 and Kulakov's death, Mazurov's retirement and the promotion of Chernenko and Tikhonov in 1978 made Brezhnev's intentions unmistakable. Party *apparatchiki*, Moscow intellectuals and Western Kremlin watchers did not miss the signs. Chernenko had become Brezhnev's choice for his 'heir apparent' and Tikhonov was being prepared to replace Kosygin, who was in poor health and incapable of working full-time. It had taken until 1978, 14 years after Brezhnev's appointment as General Secretary, for the Brezhnev faction to achieve dominance in the Politburo. Brezhnev and his henchmen could now rule the Soviet Union without challenge. This was the beginning of a serious economic and political decline. The following four years of the Brezhnev era have become known as years of crisis.

5
In charge of agriculture in the Politburo

At the beginning of December 1978 Gorbachev moved to Moscow. His old friend, Murakhovsky, was elected first *kraikom* secretary in Stavropol. Since he was not an agronomist, he had been transferred in 1975 from being Gorbachev's deputy in Stavropol to the position of first secretary of the Karachai-Circassian region, a less important job less concerned with agriculture (the secretary of this region, which is merely part of a *krai*, has lower status than other *obkom* secretaries. Murakhovsky was not a member of the Central Committee, for example, and his rank in the Stavropol *kraikom* was only fifth or sixth). He was not the obvious successor to Gorbachev's first secretaryship and Gorbachev presumably supported him so that he could keep the *krai* under his personal supervision from Moscow. Conditions in Stavropol were very good. The number of tractors, combine harvesters and other agricultural machinery per 100 hectares of land was higher there than in any other area of the Soviet Union. The proportion of irrigated fields (370,000 hectares in 1978, about a tenth of the total) was higher than anywhere else in European Russia. The *krai* was also in a privileged situation in terms of the number of graduates per 1,000 of population. Kulakov's patronage had paid handsome dividends.

Raisa, Gorbachev's wife, was appointed to a readership (*dotsent*) in the Faculty of Philosophy of Moscow State University. Their daughter Irina was already in Moscow, studying medicine. She married a fellow doctor in 1978 and was expecting a baby. (Gorbachev's granddaughter was born in 1979 and was given a very rare Russian name, Ksenia.) Thus the transfer to Moscow went very smoothly from a domestic point of view. However, Gorbachev's new job in the Central Committee secretariat presented many difficult problems. The delay in reorganizing the top agricultural administration after Kulakov's death and the weakness of a very fragmented governmental agricultural network had meant that the crucial period in the agricultural season, from July to October, had proceeded without proper supervision and coordination. Local officials struggling with the task of collecting a bumper harvest of 237 million tons had not paid sufficient attention to preparing for the next agricultural season. As a result, although the annual plan for grain production was overfulfilled, the production of silage and haylage (which takes place in August and September) was well below the planned level. The consequent shortage of fodder promised a poor winter for livestock. The sowing of winter crops was also below the normal level. These crops, sown in August and September, were particularly important in the North Caucasus and the Ukraine, where winter cereals yield about twice as much as spring cereals. In colder regions the main winter crop, rye, is also more productive than spring wheat. However, instead of the planned 40 million hectares, only 26 million hectares had been sown in the autumn of 1978, the lowest amount since 1917.[1] Moreover, the plans for applying fertilizer during the autumn ploughing had not been met. This was particularly serious because the higher yields of 1978 had reduced the amount of nutritional elements in the topsoil in most parts of the country. By December it was too late to improve the situation. It must have been clear to Gorbachev that through no fault of his own, his first agricultural campaign was bound to be a failure. All he could do was to try to prevent a disaster, since it was too late to save the plan.

Soviet agriculture has often been the political graveyard of leaders who have been made responsible for it. Kulakov had been the only agricultural boss in Soviet history to be honoured with a Red Square funeral. Gorbachev would have to work very hard to fare as well. He soon discovered, however, that the financial situation of the *kolkhozy* and *sovkhozy* had not improved in 1978, despite the higher sales to the state of grain products and other food. The number of farms which were approaching the end of the financial year (which coincides with the calendar year in the Soviet Union) with profits was decreasing. Although more than 10 billion roubles of debt had been written off by a decision of the July Plenum of the Central Committee, long and short-term agricultural debts remained at the extremely high level of 70 billion roubles. At the beginning of 1979 they began to rise as farms requested credits for the spring.

Gorbachev was not really fully in charge of agriculture to begin with. His position was that of co-ordinator rather than manager. The dualism of Party and governmental management which, as we have seen, was an anachronism at the regional level, made effective and dynamic management from Moscow extremely difficult. After the revolution it had been a necessary expedient to appoint Bolshevik watchdogs over the professional experts who staffed the newly created People's Commissariats. When it became urgent to have a united and consolidated administration just before the war with Germany, Stalin assumed the role of chairman of government as well as leader of the Party. Khrushchev did the same thing in 1958, when Bulganin was forced to resign. This combination of political and executive power only becomes dangerous when there is no tolerance of opposition and the head of government becomes a *de facto* dictator. In Western democracies, for example, it is normal for the leader of the party which has won an election to assume executive power. Khrushchev, however, did not use his consolidated power wisely and, in reaction, the separation of Party and government systems was institutionalized in 1964 by a special decision (never published) of the Central Committee. Unfortunately, ever since then both systems have hypertrophied and shifted apart. This has had a negative effect on economic development and efficiency. The Party apparatus has tended to be more bureaucratic and conservative than the government system. There has thus been a reversal in the role of the Party. In the post-revolutionary period the institution of political commissars was intended to stimulate revolutionary transformation in the more conservative professional strata, whereas by the 1970s the Party *apparatchiki* tended to support the status quo.

The Central Committee department of agriculture which Gorbachev headed was not only responsible for agricultural production. In fact *production* problems represented a minor part of its work. The task of co-ordinating and supervising the work of similar departments in 14 other republics and the agricultural departments at *obkom* and *kraikom* level was far more onerous. All important appointments at those levels had to be approved by the Central Committee agricultural department in Moscow. Gorbachev and his staff also had to consent to important appointments in the government agricultural sector and the field of agricultural education and science. It published the influential Moscow newspaper *Sel'skaya zhizn'* (Rural Life), an official organ of the Central Committee with a circulation of 7 million, to reflect Party attitudes. This newspaper was allowed to criticize the government system, the Ministries of Agriculture, Procurements, Tractors and Agricultural Machinery, Meat and Milk Production, the All-Union network of *Soyuzselkhoztekhnika* (the system of repair and service stations which replaced the MTS when they were abolished in 1958) and other administrative bodies. Gorbachev's department was also in charge of the agricultural sections of *Pravda*, *Izvestiya*, *Ekonomicheskaya gazeta*, the agricultural publishing house Kolos, the agricultural department of the Komsomol, the rural broadcasting sections of Moscow radio and television, the agricultural sections of the Exhibition of Economic Achievements in Moscow and dozens of similar institutions and activities. It also had to approve the nominations at *obkom* and *kraikom* level of *kolkhozniki* and *sovkhoz* workers for medals, orders and titles before they were forwarded to the Presidium of the Supreme Soviet. Any book on agriculture published anywhere in the country had first to pass the censorship of the department of agriculture (a similar system operates for all other books – they must first be approved by the relevant Central Committee department). Before 1964 books in related fields, for example medicine, would also be examined by the agricultural department in case they contained direct or indirect criticism of Lysenko. Central Committee instructors also have the right to inspect the KGB files of individuals who have been nominated for promotion or awards or whose academic degrees have to be confirmed (the files are not open to lower officials, but can be seen by Central Committee *apparatchiki*). All candidates for election to the Academy of Agricultural Sciences must be approved by the Central Committee agricultural department. Many of these functions are unnecessary and represent a duplication of effort and a waste of human and material resources. Moreover, this is not an exhaustive list. The department has several hundred instructors to fulfil these tasks, organized into sections and subsections. There are also regional sections, supervising the agriculture of particular areas. Thus the apparatus over which Gorbachev now presided acted as final arbiter and super-instructor. It was formidable in size and power.

Agriculture was not the only activity with which Gorbachev was now concerned, however. As a secretary of the Central Committee he also participated in the work of the central Secretariat, the Party organ second in importance only to the Politburo in political matters, and more important in terms of administration. The General Secretary, the most powerful position in the Soviet Union, is, in fact, a post in the Secretariat, not the Politburo. There is no official chairman of the Politburo. The General Secretary heads the Secretariat (in Khrushchev's time it was called First Secretary), which meets weekly at least, usually on Wednesdays before the Politburo meeting on Thursdays, to approve the agenda for the Politburo meeting and to recommend immediate implementation of matters which do not require Politburo approval. In between Central Committee Plenums, decisions which emanate from the Politburo and Secretariat are considered to be decisions of the entire Committee. In 1978 the Secretariat consisted of 11 secretaries, each of whom supervised a particular field of activity (for example, heavy and military industry, light and food industry, Party organizations and cadres, ideology, foreign affairs, agriculture, etc.).[2] Thus Gorbachev's new position involved him in decision-making over a broad range of issues. He required the co-operation of other members of the Secretariat to implement decisions which went beyond the sphere of competence of his department – for example, mobilizing industrial workers and soldiers for the harvest, importing food and fodder products, etc.

Supreme Soviet elections took place in 1979 (they are held every five years). Election day was Sunday March 4. Members and candidate members of the Politburo and Central Committee secretaries had been nominated as candidates for several constituencies (the number was in direct proportion to their rank in the Party hierarchy) and had to choose which constituency they wished to represent in the Supreme Soviet. At the end of the nomination period, Party leaders traditionally publish an 'Open Letter' to all constituencies stating their choice. Although they often choose the constituency they have represented since the last election, this is the moment which allows for change. In 1979 Gorbachev transferred his candidature from the central Stavropol constituency (it was inherited by his successor in the *kraikom*, Vsevolod Murakhovsky).

It would have been normal for Gorbachev to inherit Kulakov's old constituency, Petrovsky. Since it was in Stavropol *krai*, he would have retained his power base. The way Gorbachev has changed the name and the borders of the Kulakov's constituency represents an interesting example of how electoral affairs can be manipulated to suit the political and propaganda requirements of particular leaders. Traditionally, the first secretary of an *obkom* or *kraikom* represented the city centre and it was, therefore, natural for Murakhovsky to take over the central Stavropol constituency. However, in 1974 the Krasnogvardeisky district, together with Gorbachev's native village of Privol'noye had been attached to the Stavropol city constituency. Gorbachev must have been pleased to represent his own village in the Supreme Soviet and to visit it not just as a son, but as a deputy to whom villagers could legitimately bring their requests and grievances. Murakhovsky probably recognized the problem. During a routine reconsideration of the borders of the *krai* constituencies, Krasnogvardeisky district was removed from Stavropol city centre and added to the Petrovsky constituency. The population of Stavropol had increased from 230,000 to 260,000 between 1974 and 1979 and this, together with the decrease in rural population, made the change legitimate. However, there was another, less natural change. Ipatovsky district had been part of Petrovsky constituency. Since 1974 it had achieved national fame. Although Petrovsky district was larger and contained a larger district centre, the constituency centre was moved to Ipatovo village and the constituency was renamed Ipatovksy. Clearly Gorbachev had decided to associate his name with Ipatovsky district, as well as to continue representing his own village.

When the Kremlin leaders published their Open Letter on January 27, 1979, Gorbachev's name was last in the list of leaders who had the privilege of choosing which area they would represent. This meant that he was 28th in the Party hierarchy. But it also meant that he would be the first to give his election speech. He met his constituency on February 2, leaving 30 days for his more senior colleagues to complete their campaigns and make their speeches in the traditional sequence. A condensed version of his speech was published in *Pravda*, *Izvestiya* and other central newspapers.[3] This was the first time that any major speech that he had made was published in the central press. The meeting took place in the House of Culture of Ipatovo village. The *raikom* secretary, Kalyagin, now a Hero of Socialist Labour, opened the meeting. The director of a local state sheep-breeding plant spoke about Gorbachev's life and achievements and appealed to the audience to vote for him. Other speakers made similar appeals. Gorbachev's speech followed. It was routine and rather boring. He praised the country's agricultural success in general and that of Stavropol *krai* in 1978 and since the previous election in particular. He mentioned the importance of Brezhnev's report and the decisions of the July 1978 Central Committee Plenum, praised the new 1977 constitution, and referred to problems of peace and security. He also talked about the tasks of agriculture in 1979 and about the specific problems of Stavropol *krai*. What was interesting about his speech, however, was that he gave rather muted support to the Ipatovsky method of harvesting. He did not suggest that it should be implemented in other parts of the country (which had been the message in the 1977 Central Committee resolution and in Brezhnev's letter to the Ipatovsky *raikom*), but merely praised the 'initiative', mentioning that it had been approved by the Central Committee and had spread well beyond the borders of Stavropol *krai*.[4]

Gorbachev clearly already realized that the Ipatovsky method did not enjoy universal popularity. It could not be used universally in its original form and required modification. For one thing, it was incompatible with the widely used contract brigade system and with the move which was then in vogue towards giving individual *kolkhozy*, brigades and smaller units (*zveno*) more independence and greater responsibility and paying them in accordance with the results of their work. For another, few regions had sufficient machinery and qualified combine operators and mechanics to harvest an entire area simultaneously. Furthermore, some *kolkhozy* and *sovkhozy* were reluctant to share their machinery with other farms while still retaining responsibility for any damage or poor maintenance which may have occurred. It was an essential feature of the method that all the combines, trucks and tractors in the area were pooled and used under the direction of the central operational headquarters of the district. Another important factor was that some agronomists had reservations about the method, believing, firstly, that it made it difficult to harvest the fields of 'hard' or 'strong' wheat individually (and this wheat was more valuable and brought in higher procurement prices). Secondly, the speed of the method made it impossible to control the quality of grain from individual field brigades or *kolkhozy*. Thirdly, the spring cereals which predominated in Kazakhstan, Siberia and the non-*chernozem* areas required individual assessment and were unsuitable for large mechanized complexes. Fourthly, large concentrations of machinery could not be used in the forest and forest-steppe areas of the country. Finally, another problem occurred because a significant proportion of the work-force during harvesting was mobilized from the towns. These temporary workers were unwilling to work round the clock.

The election campaign followed its usual pattern without any surprises. Suslov was still clearly second-in-command with Kirilenko behind him. Election day on Sunday 4, 1979 was a complete success. The proportion of registered voters who participated rose from 99.98 per cent in 1974 to 99.99 per cent. Of these, 99.89 per cent gave their support to the nominated candidates. Some dissent was registered in Estonia, where only 99.56 per cent of the electorate voted for the candidates, and in the Kalmyk Autonomous Republic, where the figure was 99.52 per cent. To make up for this, for the first time in Soviet history one area returned a 100 per cent vote in favour of the nominated candidates: in the Nakhichevan Autonomous Republic in Azerbaijan the entire electorate of 115,465 voted for the official candidates and there were no spoilt ballot papers.[5]

I followed this particular election very closely from London, not because of Gorbachev, of whom I knew very little at the time, but because of the appearance of a small dissident group in Moscow, called 'Election 1979' which had tried to nominate my brother, Roy Medvedev, as a second, unofficial candidate for the Sverdlovsk district of Moscow. The episode attracted the attention of foreign journalists in Moscow and my brother later wrote a brief article which was published in Britain describing his experiences as a possible second candidate.[6] There was nothing illegal about the activities of 'Election 1979' and the support it received from other dissidents. Both the constitution and the electoral regulations theoretically allow for two or more candidates from one district. The instructions on the ballot papers are phrased in a way that suggests that a choice is available: 'Leave the name of the candidate for whom you are voting on the ballot. Cross out other names'. In practice, however, only one name appears on the ballot paper so the choice remains theoretical. The attempt by 'Election 1979' to propose its own candidate did not succeed. Roy's name was not registered or included on the ballot paper. Clearly, the electoral authorities believed that Roy Medvedev, an historian and a graduate of Leningrad University, was not as well qualified to stand for election as the ballerina, Bessmertova, who was the official candidate for the district. Soon after the election the chairman of 'Election 1979', Vladimir Sychev, and his deputy and secretary, Vladimir Baranov, were forced to emigrate. But the publicity given to 'Election 1979' in the West and broadcast back to the Soviet Union led to a rash of attempts to nominate second candidates. Similar groups formed in Sochi, in Vladimir region and in Lithuania. None of their nominations were accepted. The chairman of the Sochi group was put in a mental hospital, but nothing is known about the fate of the other groups.

After the election Gorbachev was very busy supervising the sowing season. The winter of 1979 was extremely severe and the winter crops which were sown too late were damaged. May and June were far drier than usual. The early summer drought reduced the harvests of sown crops and the productivity of meadows and pastures, particularly in the European part of the Soviet Union. As a result, the production of hay in June and July was well below expectations. Hay, straw and other coarse fodder products normally produced in the western part of the country would have to be transported from the east. Although this would be expensive, it was essential. In addition, the Central Committee ordered the immediate mobilization of students and schoolchildren to collect vegetation from forests, bush areas and hills where mowing machines could not be used. This measure resembled the emergency campaigns of the war and immediate post-war period and it indicated that the situation was disastrous. Importing feed grain would not help, since there was an acute shortage of the coarse fodder which was required to feed the cattle. Newspapers published urgent appeals to everybody to take part in the collection of fodder to save the livestock population from slaughter.

By July it was already clear that the 1979 harvest was very poor. The government began purchasing extra grain from the USA while the international prices were low (they rise later in the summer) and without waiting for the results of the harvest in the eastern part of the country. In fact, when the harvest was gathered in Kazakhstan and Siberia it saved the Soviet Union, as it often had in the past, from total humiliation. These lands (part of Khrushchev's massive virgin land programme in the 1950s) were no longer virgin, but when the weather was good in that part of the country, they yielded a good harvest. Traditionally the Central Statistical Bureau publishes weekly reports on the harvesting campaign, covering all crops and all the main agricultural areas. The reports are usually supplemented by comments from the agricultural editor of the newspaper which reflect the position of the Central Committee department of agriculture. Regional authorities are often criticized and demands are made for improved performance. In September and October 1979 the criticism of local officials was particularly harsh. The agricultural season was almost over and there were too many unfulfilled targets. The harvesting of silage crops was not on target, the collection of potatoes and sugar beet had been delayed and the sowing of winter crops was so far behind schedule that the most favourable time had been missed. Autumn ploughing was also late. In the Soviet 'command economy', pressure from Moscow is an important element of local mobilization (but it can also lead to local falsifications of results). The final official figure given for the 1979 grain harvest was 179 million metric tons, about 60 million metric tons less than in 1978.[7] The harvest of other crops was also lower than in 1978 and the production of meat and milk did not rise, despite the large imports of feed and food grain. The amount of grain imported was 31 million metric tons, more than had ever been imported in a single year.[8] The only area which did well was Kazakhstan, which produced a record harvest of 34.5 million tons, 20.5 million tons of which was delivered to the state.[9] But the credit for this was given to Kunayev, not to Gorbachev. As a full member of the Politburo, Kunayev was independent, even in matters of agriculture. Jubilantly, he reported the 'great victory' to Brezhnev on the eve of the October Revolution anniversary celebrations.

Gorbachev's first year in charge of agriculture had been a failure. Fortunately, it was realized that it was a predictable failure and nobody tried to connect it to his performance. On the contrary, it helped his early promotion, since it was thought that a higher position would give him more authority to deal with local Party officials. At the regular Plenum of the Central Committee on November 17, 1979 he became a candidate member of the Politburo. (This was the Plenum that elected Tikhonov to full membership of the Politburo). But the poor harvest in 1979 had other serious implications. Amongst the measures taken by President Carter to punish the Soviet Union for its occupation of Afghanistan was a grain embargo. The White House expected that the Soviet Union would be unable to find alternative sources for grain and that the population would soon begin to feel the price of intervention. In fact, the embargo failed, the Soviet Union bought more grain in 1980 than in 1979 (although at higher prices) and diversified its sources to include Canada, Australia, Argentina and France. There were strange speculations in the West that the invasion of Afghanistan had been decided by Gromyko, Andropov and Gorbachev and that the other members of the Politburo 'were apparently notified after the fact'.[10] However, a knowledge of how the Soviet system operates (and of the requirements of a military manouevre on that scale) makes it obvious that long and careful preparations were required and that there must have been a consensus of the Politburo, Secretariat and the Military Council.

In 1980 the election campaign was launched for the elections to the Supreme Soviets of the RSFSR and the other republics and autonomous republics which form the Union of Soviet Socialist Republics on February 24. Observers who followed the pattern of election speeches found confirmation of Chernenko's new prominence. He had been elected a full member of the Politburo a year previously and he had already moved to Kulakov's place in the order of speeches. Shcherbitsky, Ustinov, Andropov, Pel'she, Romanov and Grishin, all of whom had served in the Politburo for far longer, spoke before him from February 5 to 14 (he met his constituency on February 15) and were clearly now less important. Moreover, Chernenko was to represent an important constituency in Moscow. Gorbachev was also a candidate for the Supreme Soviet of the RSFSR for the first time. As Central Committee secretary for agriculture, he was advised to choose an important agricultural district. He stood for the central electoral district of the Siberian Altai *krai* (he did not inherit this constituency from Kulakov, who had represented Pensa, where he had been chairman of the *ispolkom* from 1950 to 1955). Altai *krai*, five times larger than Stavropol *krai* but with the same size population, had been prominent in Khrushchev's virgin land programme. In 1979 it had produced a very good harvest and this was acknowledged by Gorbachev's decision to become the delegate from Barnaul, the capital of the area. He met his constituents on January 31 and praised the great efforts of the local *kolkhozniki* and *sovkhoz* workers. The agricultural problems which had been encountered in other parts of the country in 1979 were, he said, accidental and temporary. There was nothing particularly interesting or new in his speech. He did not propose the Ipatovsky method of harvesting for the area, despite the notorious reputation of Altai *krai* for long delays in harvesting.[11] He knew that the delays were not the fault of the local farmers. The combine harvesters for Siberia were specially produced in a plant at Kranoyarsk. They proudly bore the name 'Sibiryak' (strong Siberian), but they had a very bad reputation for constantly breaking down. Moreover, they were produced in insufficient quantities and there were shortages not only in Altai, but in Siberia as a whole. The Siberian economist, A. G. Aganbegyan (later to be one of Gorbachev's close advisers), calculated in 1979 that the amount of grain lost in Siberia because of late and delayed harvesting cost the state much more each year than it would have cost to construct an additional combine plant.[12]

Because of the American grain embargo, it became a matter of prestige for the Soviet leadership to make 1980 an agricultural success. The Central Committee tried very hard to stimulate a 'battle for the harvest' attitude throughout the country. At the same time preliminary decisions were made which would later be proclaimed as Brezhnev's ten year Food Programme for 1981–1990, designed to make the Soviet Union fully self-sufficient in the main agricultural products. Preparing these and other decisions to do with agriculture became Gorbachev's chief task. In April a Central Committee and government decree was published 'About additional measures for higher harvests, procurements of all agricultural products and preparation of cattle livestock for the winter of 1980/81'.[13] It was more practical than previous decisions, allocating more resources (trucks, lorries, machinery, petrol, repair and construction materials) to agriculture. What was even more important, the salaries of almost all groups of *kolkhozniki* and other agricultural workers were raised by 30 to 50 per cent and linked to productivity. Temporary seasonal workers drafted in for the harvest were also to be paid more. In return for overfulfilling their plans, many groups of farmers would be able to get free farm produce to supplement their incomes.

In May Gorbachev published his first major (but not very interesting) article on agriculture in *Kommunist*, the main theoretical journal of the Party.[14] He concentrated on previous successes rather than on current problems and quoted Lenin and Brezhnev three times each and Marx once. The few critical comments (about the inadequate production of groat crops and soybean, the shortage of fodder and the delay in introducing high yield varieties) were mild. The Ipatovsky method was mentioned only briefly as one of the 'patriotic initiatives' which had been undertaken. The main message of the article was optimistic – things were good, though they could be even better. It was in this article, however, that the idea of an agro-industrial linkage (linking agricultural industry, agriculture, food processing and food trade under the same management) was expressed in theoretical form for the first time.

The weather in 1980, however, was very bad again. This time the problem was not drought, but an unprecedented amount of rain combined with a cold, late spring. There were bad floods in some regions. The number of people mobilized from the towns to assist with the harvest was extremely high, 15.6 million, about 8 million of whom were workers from the productive sector of the economy. The rest were students, office workers, soldiers and schoolchildren.[15] The overall grain harvest was 189.1 million tons, slightly better than in 1979, but still very low. In financial terms, however, the production of 1980 was more than 3 billion roubles lower than in 1979. The potato harvest was 40 million tons short of the target, the lowest harvest since the 1930s. The production of oilseed, flax and other crops also declined. The production of milk and meat was well below the level of 1979. It was lower even than in 1975.[16] But there were other alarming phenomena in 1980: the tension of work, pressure from central and local authorities and the persistent instruction to produce as much as possible irrespective of cost, caused serious damage to the most important agricultural resource – the topsoil. In 1980 soil erosion accelerated in almost every part of the country. Equally serious was the fact that the great effort to increase the harvest in 1980 vastly increased the production costs of all agricultural produce.

Food imports in 1980 were higher than in 1979. 35 million metric tons of grain were purchased and almost a million tons of meat. However, once again the failure affected Gorbachev's standing favourably. At the regular Central Committee Plenum at the end of October 1980 he was promoted from candidate member to full member of the Politburo.[17] His photograph and a brief biography were published in *Pravda* and other newspapers. His colleagues must clearly have thought that he had done a good job under difficult circumstances. It was probably also thought that the person responsible for agriculture should be a full member of the Politburo. Brezhnev's speech at the Plenum reflected some of the ideas which had been expressed by Gorbachev in his *Kommunist* article. He announced that the Politburo had decided to prepare a special ten year Food Programme which would unite various branches of agricultural industry with agricultural production, transport, food processing and food trade.

The management of agriculture in the Soviet Union in 1980 was extremely complicated. There were 13 ministries and State Committees directly involved in one way or another. This fragmentation of administration made it difficult for the Central Committee department of agriculture to supervise and co-ordinate the various aspects of work. Gorbachev hoped that if all the ministries, committees and other networks (for machine servicing, fertilization, irrigation and land reclamation, etc.) were subsumed under a joint superstructure, the efficiency of the *kolkhoz*, *sovkhoz* and other sectors would be improved. The plan envisaged a new super-collectivization which would, in effect, eliminate the differences between collective and state farms.

Gorbachev was the youngest member of the Politburo and his power as agricultural boss of the country had been greatly increased. But this did not mean that Brezhnev gave him an entirely free hand in managing agriculture. At the Supreme Soviet session which was convened immediately after the Central Committee Plenum in October (the official business was to approve the state budget), it was announced that Kosygin was to retire because of ill health. Tikhonov was appointed the new Chairman of the Council of Ministers of the Soviet Union. The changes in the government included the appointment of Ivan Bodyl as First Deputy Prime Minister in charge of agriculture. Bodyl, 58 years old and the first secretary of the Moldavian Republic, had been Gorbachev's rival for the Central Committee job in 1978. Moldavia, like Dnepropetrovsk and Kazakhstan, was Brezhnev's power base. He had been first secretary of Moldavia from 1950–52, moving there from Dnepropetrovsk. Later he had gradually moved many of the colleagues with whom he had worked in Moldavia to Moscow (Chernenko, for example, as well as Shchelokov, the Minister of Internal Affairs, Tsvigun, the first deputy chairman of the KGB, and others). The appointment of Bodyl, who was a close friend of Chernenko and Shchelokov, as well as of the Brezhnev family, was likely to complicate Gorbachev's work and endanger his future. For one thing, Bodyl was unlikely to be docile in following Gorbachev's orders. For another, if the time should come when Gorbachev was held responsible for a poor harvest, Bodyl would be ready and waiting to replace him in his Central Committee job.

At the end of 1980 the Politburo was divided roughly into two groups. The Brezhnev faction consisted of men who had worked with Brezhnev in Dnepropetrovsk, Moldavia or Kazakhstan and whose promotion then or earlier had depended entirely on his patronage. Before Kosygin's retirement and death, he had not always agreed with Brezhnev on matters of the economy and appointments (or even, sometimes, principles). He had not interfered in Party matters, but he wanted more independence for the government and the economic reforms he envisaged would reduce the managerial power of the Party apparatus. He was supported by the governmental faction in the Politburo – Ustinov, Minister of Defence, Gromyko, Minister of Foreign Affairs and Andropov, Chairman of the KGB. Suslov was an independent. Like Kosygin and Ustinov, he had achieved prominence in Stalin's time and did not owe his promotion to Brezhnev. However, in 1975–80 he was already seriously ill and he rarely challenged Brezhnev's authority. Romanov was popular with neither faction, although it seemed that Andropov knew enough about his background to keep him under control. Gorbachev could be in no doubt that he owed his promotion to Andropov and Suslov, but it was only in 1982 that he came out openly in favour of Andropov. In 1981 he had no choice but to work closely with Brezhnev, because Brezhnev considered agriculture to be his own special field.

Although Gorbachev prepared all the important reports on agriculture, including the Food Programme, it was Brezhnev who was the spokesman, and who delivered the reports and took the credit. In some respects Gorbachev was little more than Brezhnev's speech-writer on agriculture. But even here his power was limited, since Brezhnev sent drafts of his speeches and reports to other departments and ministries for their comments and incorporated their suggestions into the text. There was no sign of any disagreement between Gorbachev and Brezhnev, however, on agricultural matters. Gorbachev's own ideas accorded with Brezhnev's (and with Kulakov's previous policies). Moreover, Brezhnev was always ready to support Gorbachev's proposals and to take credit for them when they were successful. Both men believed that the principles on which Soviet agriculture was based were sound. All that was required was better administration. Both were worried by the poor performance of agriculture, the exodus of the rural population, the low quality of Soviet agricultural machinery, etc., but neither could think of any remedy, except to increase investments and subsidies. They also had similar working styles, believing in well prepared resolutions which listed all the tasks and targets. They also shared a belief in plans and administrative measures, rather than real reform. Neither of them had the dynamic style of leadership which had been typical of Khrushchev. Khrushchev enjoyed travelling from one part of the country to another during the summer, supervising everything personally. Gorbachev, like Brezhnev, preferred to rule from Moscow. He did, however, keep a close personal eye on Stavropol *krai* and he visited it personally every harvesting season. Not that it helped very much – Stavropol *krai* did not fulfil its plan in either 1979 or 1980.

It has been argued that Gorbachev favoured the encouragement of private plots more than Brezhnev did, and that he was impressed by the higher productivity from these plots. In fact, the strong support of private 'subsidiary small-holdings' was very much part of Brezhnev's programme. The Central Committee decision which abolished Khrushchev's restrictions on private plots was taken in November 1964. By a decree of September 14, 1977, the permitted size of private plots was increased from 0.25 hectares to 0.5 hectares. The right to use plots of land for subsidiary small-holdings was enshrined in the Brezhnev constitution of 1977 and the important role of private agriculture featured more prominently in his speeches and reports (particularly in July 1978) than in Gorbachev's speeches.

1981 was the year of the XXVIth Party Congress, at which the new Five Year Plan would be adopted. All Central Committee departments were occupied in preparing the plan and despite his ill health, Brezhnev was expected to deliver the long, main report. Suslov was also ill and the main organization of the Congress fell to Chernenko's general department in the Central Committee. The Congress began its work on February 23, 1981. In the main report, which took almost six hours to deliver, Brezhnev spent less than five minutes (three paragraphs of text) on agricultural performance since the last Congress. This was the briefest discussion of agriculture at a Party Congress since the beginning of collectivization. Once it became clear that the Politburo had decided not to discuss agriculture, other speakers were discouraged from talking about it. It was a sign of how serious the situation was. The 1976–80 Five Year Plan had set a target of an annual average production of 215–220 million metric tons of grain. It had not been fulfilled and there was a reluctance to discuss the failure and find the causes. Despite the failure, the new Plan increased the target to an annual average of 238–243 million tons of grain. This was the amount of grain that was required to achieve self-sufficiency. The targets for meat were more modest. The previous target of 16 million tons had not been met and the new target was set at 17.0–17.5 million tons.

All efforts were now directed towards making the first year of the plan a success. However, there was a drought again in the European part of the Soviet Union. June was unusually hot and there was little rain. Haymaking was relatively easy in June, but the plans for silage and haylage were not fulfilled. The excessive rains the previous year had leached the nitrogen and potassium from many fields and plants suffered from a nitrogen deficiency. The sown area was increased, but it made little difference. Gorbachev could at least find comfort in the fact that Stavropol *krai* performed better in 1981 than it had in 1980. The *kraikom* had made the bold promise to produce 5 million tons of grain and sell 2.1 million tons to the state. By the middle of August this promise had been overfulfilled and 2.4 million tons had been sold to the state.[18] However, the campaign was led by Krasnodar *krai*, which fulfilled its planned deliveries ten days earlier. The general situation was very poor, however, and few other regions could report fulfillment of the plan. Kazakhstan sold 15.7 million tons to the state, less than the previous year, although still a good harvest.

The weekly statistical reports at the end of October indicated that the year was a disaster. The Ukraine, Don basin and Volga areas all produced far less than their plans. The total harvest was so poor that it was reported neither in Soviet statistical reports nor in the official records at the end of the year. Grain production statistics have been classified ever since then and no explanation has ever been offered about why they have ceased to appear. The gross agricultural output expressed in roubles was below the poor levels of 1980 and 1979. The production of other crops was also low and the production of oilseeds dropped below the average of 20 years previously in 1961–65. Meat and milk production were also below the 1980 level. The US Department of Agriculture estimated that the total grain harvest in the Soviet Union in 1981 was 155 million metric tons.[19] This would probably be about 160 million metric tons in Soviet figures (Soviet statistics usually give the 'bunker weight', that is the weight when the moisture level is higher than is required for storage). It was the lowest harvest since the disastrous season of 1975 and on a per capita basis, it was the worst harvest since 1965. Grain purchases abroad reached the all time record of 46 million metric tons.[20]

This time the poor harvest had a serious impact on Gorbachev's department. The much vaunted Food Programme could not be launched in 1981 because some of the target figures would have to be reconsidered. The huge project consisting of about 12 separate documents would have to be adjusted and rewritten. Once again, the poor harvest was blamed on the weather, but after three bad harvests in a row, the weather arguments were wearing a bit thin. There were serious food shortages in most industrial cities and a kind of rationing system operated for meat and milk products which were in particularly short supply. The food situation was very bad in Poland as well, resulting in discontent and the introduction of martial law. Fortunately, President Reagan lifted

Carter's grain embargo and this made it easier to purchase food abroad.

There is a complex interaction between agriculture and the rest of the economy. The light and consumer oriented economy suffers directly from a shortage of raw materials. Other branches of the economy suffer from the fact that too high a proportion of investment capital is absorbed by agriculture and food imports reduce the foreign currency reserves. Food shortages also have a deleterious effect on the morale of workers. Three years of bad harvests thus had very negative consequences for Soviet industry as a whole. The growth rate began to decline, productivity rose less than was expected and the production of high quality consumer goods was well below expectations. Nothing, however, could be done to improve the situation, except for waiting to see whether the weather would be better in 1982 and whether the Party and government resolutions and the decisions of the Party Congress would begin to pay off. It was decided to launch the Food Programme in the spring of 1982. It had to be announced in March if it was to have any influence on the beginning of the agricultural season. Brezhnev, however, was ill in March and the launch had to postponed until May. It was particularly important that 1982 should be successful, since it was the year in which the 60th anniversary of the formation of the Union of Soviet Socialist Republics was to be celebrated.

Gorbachev became very involved in preparing the Food Programme Plenum. Brezhnev was expected to deliver the main report, but all the documents had to be prepared and published separately as joint decrees of the Central Committee and Council of Ministers. The volume of work was enormous, since the decrees included target figures for various crops for ten years ahead, as well as figures for the whole agro-industrial complex. This involved all types of machinery, food processing, sales, exports and imports, procurement prices and other financial arrangements, science, education, demographic trends and a multitude of other factors. The future per capita consumption of all the main food products had to be calculated. The population was to be promised that the *scientific norms of nutrition* would be available by 1990. The credibility of the whole Brezhnev leadership was linked to the promise of better food supplies. Gorbachev's own credibility was even more at risk, however. If the 1982 harvest proved as disastrous as that of 1981, the leadership would almost certainly need a scapegoat.

On January 25, 1982 Mikhail Suslov died after having a stroke. He was 79 years old and had been in poor health, so his death was not unexpected. For Gorbachev, however, it meant the loss of a strong supporter. It also increased the Brezhnev faction's majority and Chernenko's prominence. It became clear that a power struggle was taking place between Chernenko and Andropov. Kirilenko was 76 and his health was also deteriorating. He was not considered a possible successor, but nor was it thought that he supported Andropov. Gorbachev supported Andropov strongly, but this aggravated his agricultural problems. Andropov's 'offensive' against the Brezhnev faction was based on charges of corruption and incompetence. Not surprisingly, the failures in agriculture were linked in public opinion with corruption and incompetence at the top. In this situation it was in Gorbachev's interest to keep a low profile and give the ailing Brezhnev the 'honour' of presenting the Food Programme.

Although Ustinov and Gromyko seemed to be fond of Gorbachev, they would be unlikely to try to save him if the failure of agriculture made it necessary to raise the question of 'strengthening' the leadership (a euphemism for replacing someone). They were well aware how damaging the dismal state of Soviet agriculture was to the Soviet international position and for Soviet military capabilities. But they did not understand what the problems were and could not be sure that Gorbachev was not responsible. Only Andropov, as head of the KGB, really understood the causes of the failures in agriculture. Or at least, he thought that he understood. He did not challenge the system, but linked the failures to the widespread corruption of officials, the lack of discipline and the decline in the quality of Party and state cadres. A new 'Andropov purge' was necessary to improve the situation. Gorbachev was not, apparently, on the list Andropov began to construct of people who would be removed from the leadership if he succeeded in replacing Brezhnev.

The Food Programme received so much advance publicity that people in the Soviet Union and abroad expected radical change and real reform. Their hopes were dashed as soon as the special Central Committee Plenum began to discuss the project. The Programme consisted of a a number of individual documents with a centrepiece which tried to cover the development plans of agricultural industry (machinery, fertilizers, irrigation technology, animal farm technology, etc.), agricultural production, reconstruction of rural settlements, the development of food processing and dozens of other tasks. There were separate documents dealing with the problems of manpower, rural services, payments, organizational structures, new forms of administration, etc. Every aspect of agriculture and the agriculture-related industries was mentioned. For every branch of agriculture there was a detailed, regional set of targets for each constituent republic. The amount of effort which had gone into preparing these documents was enormous and they had clearly taken the full-time work of thousands of experts. Nonetheless, there was not a single change which could be classified as a *reform*. The programme was reproduced in journals and newspapers and later published as a book.[21] But it did not excite anyone.

A careful perusal of the Programme makes it clear that while the Soviet agricultural leadership knew exactly what it wanted, it did not know how to achieve the targets, and it had very little idea of which targets were realistic and which impossible. Huge investments were allocated to agriculture, most of the debts which had been accumulated by the *kolkhozy* and *sovkhozy* were written off, procurement prices were increased and state subsidies were authorized to underwrite the low food prices. But it was obvious that these enormous funds would be wasted, because there was to be no liberalization of the decision-making process at the bottom level and no freedom of choice for individual collective and state farms. Once again, everything was prescribed from the top. Far from being more independent, the *kolkhozy* and *sovkhozy* were to be less free, locked into the complex and cumbersome superstructure of the 'agro-industrial complex', represented at the district or regional level by a large bureaucratic agro-industrial council, called RAPO or APO, which resembled a parallel governmental network. The entire government system was now divided into two parts, one for heavy industry and machine tools and other industries (for example, computers, atomic energy, transport, etc.) unrelated to agriculture and the other, uniting about 20 ministries and state committees which, in one way or another, were involved in agriculture (the tractor and combine industry, animal farm and fodder mechanization, chemical fertilizers and other chemical industries, rural construction, irrigation and land reclamation, repairs and servicing, meat and milk, food processing, light industry, trade industry, procurements, forestry, microbial industry, etc.). The second group was to be coordinated by a special governmental 'Agro-industrial Commission' (*Agroprom*). The peasant households, the farmers who did the real work, would gain little in this great new system, which represented the ultimate bureaucratic creation. There was little in the Food Programme to suggest a reform based on sound economic principles.

What was even more surprising was that there seemed to be no intention of discussing the Programme seriously. The draft, for example, was not published before the Plenum. The meeting, the most important agricultural Plenum for years, lasted only one day. The day after it met on May 24, 1982, a report was published, listing 21 speakers (including Shcherbitsky, Kunayev, Aliyev, Shevarnadze, Grishin, Romanov, Rashidov, Mesyats, and others).[22] Brezhnev's long report seems to have been delivered verbally, without being distributed as a transcript. It was published punctuated with 'applause', 'long applause' (for example, when he claimed that the Soviet Union should be self-sufficient in food and that it would stop importing produce which some foreign powers use a means of political pressure). No changes were made to the drafts at the Plenum. It took several days for the newspapers to publish different parts of the programme which had been recommended by the Central Committee with such speed.

With or without discussion, it was obvious that the targets of the Programme were unrealistic. Despite the previous three successive poor harvests and a grain harvest of 160 million tons in 1981, the programme set a target of an average of 238–243 million metric tons for 1982–85 and 250–255 million tons for 1986–90. The targets for meat production were more modest: per capita consumption was to rise from 58 kg. per person per year in 1981 to 70 kg. in 1990. The idea of reaching the American level in per capita food consumption which had been part of the twenty year Party Programme introduced in 1961 had, apparently, been abandoned. About 35 per cent of the state budget was to be invested in agriculture.

Western experts were not very impressed by the Food Programme. It was clear that Brezhnev had not participated actively in preparing it and that Gorbachev was the main person behind the project. In later years Gorbachev never criticized the Programme, always stressing that it was essentially right and had to be followed. Even though the targets were unrealistic, he insisted that they had to be met. The industrial part of the 'agro-industrial complex' did develop more or less as planned, but there was little progress in agriculture. In many cases, the increase of industrial investment actually led to a decrease in agricultural production. The main flaws were the absence of any real economic mechanisms of development and the reluctance to give farms any independence. The philosophy behind the programme relied on resolutions, rather than reforms.

In June Gorbachev published a long article in *Kommunist*, 'The Food Programme and the Task of its Realization'.[23] He maintained that the programme was scientifically based and acknowledged that it had taken many months and the efforts of thousands of Party and state experts and the experience of many regions, districts, ministries and research institutes to prepare it. He promised that the new mechanism of economic administration would work, as Lenin had demanded, with 'the precision and fidelity of the mechanism of a clock'. The workers of the agro-industrial complex were, he believed, 'inspired by the decision of the May Plenum and were making every effort to make a good start this year in realizing the Food Programme'.[24]

Unfortunately, neither weather nor enthusiasm respond to resolutions and programmes like clockwork. By July the harvesting of crops and haymaking were running behind and below schedule. By the middle of August, the foreign press had begun commenting on the poor harvest. Estimates put the harvest at 175 million tons and possible Soviet imports at nearly 50 million tons. The final figures were not reported, but it is now known that the Western estimates were correct. The harvest was slightly better than the disastrous 1981 level, but it was nonetheless a failure. 32 million tons of grain were imported. Few regions fulfilled their state delivery plans and Stavropol *krai* was not one of them. It was a bad sign for Gorbachev. The situation in Moscow was rather tense. At the end of September, for reasons which have never been made explicit, Kirilenko was sent into retirement (it was formally announced only two months later, during the Party Plenum, but he had not been seen since September and his portraits had been removed). It was rumoured that his son had tried to defect, but it is difficult to find confirmation of the rumour. At the same time Aliyev was promised promotion to full membership of the Politburo. He had proved himself a loyal and trusted friend to Brezhnev during the latter's visit to Baku. Brezhnev was treated extremely well and he returned to Moscow very pleased.

Murakhovsky, Stavropol *kraikom* secretary, recognized Gorbachev's problem and tried very hard to fulfil the plan. It was not easy and when the harvest was over at the end of August, extra grain had to be taken from the seed and feed grain reserves by coercive means. Gorbachev visited the *krai* and apparently gave Murakhovsky a deadline to report fulfilment before the November 6 Anniversary meeting in the Kremlin and the November 7 parade. The deadline was met just in time. The Central Statistical Board published a report from Stavropol *krai* on November 6, 1982, claiming that it had sold 1.9 million tons of grain to the state. The production figures were not reported and were probably lower than usual. According to the local newspapers, 1.5 million tons of grain were delivered to the state in Stavropol *krai* on August 16, 1982.[25] The harvesting season was over at the end of August. To meet the official plan of 1.9 million tons, the extra 0.4 million tons could not have been taken from the fields. They must therefore have come from the feed and seed grain reserves of the farms. There was no other source in September and October, except for modest amounts of corn. These efforts to extract extra grain from the peasants for clearly political purposes show how useful it was to have a friend in charge of one's native *krai*. But Murakhovsky knew that he was fighting for his own future as well.

It was, however, unlikely that Brezhnev would treat the general agricultural disaster in 1982 as lightly as he had treated the problem in 1979–81. In 1982 he suffered a double humiliation. It was the first year of the much publicized Food Programme and it was also the jubilee year of the creation of the Soviet Union. The huge Soviet propaganda machine had worked hard all year to appeal to everybody to mark the anniversary by their economic achievements. In May and September, during discussions about the successor to Suslov's ideology portfolio and about Kirilenko's fate, Gorbachev had been on Andropov's side in the Politburo. If a scapegoat were to be required, Gorbachev realized that there would be no escape. There was nobody but him to take the blame.

There is an old Soviet tradition that decisions which have negative consequences are avoided during the celebrations of the anniversary of the October Revolution. Even in 1937, at the height of Stalin's Great Terror, executions had been halted in Moscow on November 4 and resumed only on November 17 (when the backlog which had accumulated of people who had already been condemned was taken care of in a record number of executions). The regular Plenum had been set for November 16, 1982, when organizational questions would inevitably be discussed. Aliyev's promotion had already been agreed and Kirilenko's portraits were not visible in the traditional display of the Politburo members during the November celebrations. Gorbachev's tremendous efforts to get a report on the Stavropol grain deliveries before November 7 indicate that he was aware that his future would be discussed at the Plenum. To dispel the rumours about his poor health, Brezhnev spent several hours standing on the Mausoleum during the parade and demonstration on November 7, with Chernenko at his side. The weather was extremely cold. Gorbachev was saved by fate. The effort was too much for Brezhnev and he died suddenly on November 10 from a heart attack. It became more natural to make the deceased responsible for the agricultural and economic failures than to blame those who were still alive and well.

6
Andropov's ally

Since the end of 1981 there had been signs of a power struggle in the Kremlin. In the first half of 1982 it centred around the powerful position of 'chief ideologue', which had been vacant since Suslov's death. When Andropov was confirmed in this position at the May Central Committee Plenum, it became clear that he was now Chernenko's main rival for Brezhnev's job. His most senior supporters were Gromyko and Ustinov. Gorbachev and Romanov also both supported him, but for different reasons. Gorbachev knew that if Andropov became the leader, he could save his political career, whereas Romanov knew that Andropov could destroy his political future at any time if he chose to.

Power struggles have been a feature of every political succession in the Soviet Union. In every case they have not just been personality clashes, but have concerned principles and policies. In 1922–4, when Stalin and Trotsky were rivals during Lenin's protracted illness, Stalin won the succession struggle despite his obviously inferior qualities as leader, thinker and revolutionary. At that time he was a moderate who supported NEP and advocated stability and the consolidation of the power of the Party. Trotsky, on the other hand, was more left-wing, an internationalist who favoured the continuation of revolution. In the conditions of an impoverished Russia which had just emerged from a long and bloody Civil War, Stalin's victory was relatively easily achieved. The issues which accompanied Khrushchev's succession were more complex and conditions were very different. Khrushchev promised a modicum of liberalization, the end of the Stalin terror, particularly against Party cadres, and the supremacy of the Party over the security apparatus. This made it possible for him to defeat Beria in 1953 and all Stalin's other men in 1956–7.

But his later reforms and reorganizations were unpopular with Party professionals and Brezhnev seemed the only person who could offer a lasting stability to the government and Party apparatus.

Stalin had begun by working with the Party *apparatchiki* in the 1920s. But later he placed himself above the Party and state apparatus and became a dictator. No Russian tsar, Western king, or European dictator (including Hitler, Mussolini and Franco) has ever concentrated as much power and personal control over the economy, press, internal and external policy as Stalin did. Khrushchev also tried to place himself above the Party and state apparatus in the early 1960s, but he lost his struggle with the powerful bureaucracy. Brezhnev was the true representative of a bureaucracy which had grown tired of strong leaders. By the late 1960s and early 1970s the economic and political infrastructure of the Soviet Union had become very complex. It was impossible to rule the country on the basis of the decisions of a single individual. Brezhnev never attempted to become a dictator, enjoying the prestige and opportunities of leadership more than the power of decision-making. He transferred more power to the Party and government apparatus than any of his predecessors and he gave the functionaries of these organizations stability of tenure, confidence and many privileges and benefits. Some Western experts on Soviet affairs concluded in the 1970s and 1980s that the Soviet Union was 'no longer a leader-dominated political system'.[1] However, the stability of the Party elite, the absence of a critical press and legitimate channels for expressing public opinion, together with the non-existence of an independent legal system created ideal opportunities for corruption, favouritism and mediocrity.

The gap between the bureaucracy and the people widened. It had previously been possible to argue against Milovan Djilas' theory that a 'new class' had developed in the 1950s[2] by pointing out that the new elite in communist societies did not satisfy the definition of a class because it did not enjoy the life-long stability of its privileges, wealth and power and could not transfer elite status to its children and relatives, as the bourgeoisie or aristocracy could. However, Brezhnev went a long way towards making Djilas' theory valid. He made possible the *de facto* inheritance of the special opportunities and privileges of the elite, setting an example himself by making his alcoholic son Yuri a member of the Central Committee and a Deputy Minister of Foreign Trade, and his notorious daughter a high official in the Intourist organization and an influential figure in Moscow artistic circles. His other relatives were given important posts in the Ministry of Internal Affairs, KGB and other powerful and privileged institutions. Not surprisingly this new trend had an extremely negative impact on the Soviet economy, discipline, public morale, intellectual life, science and other aspects of the life of society. The divorce rate began to approach 50 per cent, life-expectancy declined for all age groups of the population, heavy drinking reached epidemic proportions, economic development stagnated and the production of food began to decline.

This situation made it natural for Andropov to declare the battle against corruption and incompetence a priority in the power struggle before and after Brezhnev's death. But Andropov wished to (or was forced to) 'clean the house without opening the doors or windows' (as Khrushchev had done in his treatment of Stalin). He tried to find and promote a few more competent and honest officials inside the Central Committee and the government. This was essential if the credibility of the Central Committee and government was to be preserved. When Medunov was dismissed from his post as secretary of the Krasnodar *kraikom*, Vorotnikov, already a member of the Central Committee, was brought back from his ambassadorial post in Cuba to replace him. When incompetent or old ministers were dismissed or retired, their positions were normally filled by one or other of their younger deputies. Really new blood could be brought into the top Party echelons during the periodic Party congresses which took place every five years, but the strict Party rules introduced by Brezhnev made it difficult for even very able people to bypass the normal hierarchy of promotion between congresses. Andropov had to follow these rules, even though it was clear that he was a man in a hurry.

Gorbachev enjoyed Andropov's full confidence and he probably hoped that Andropov would move him from agriculture to a safer sector of Politburo responsibility. But there were no reliable people amongst the high agricultural officials in either the Party apparatus or the government to whom Andropov was prepared to entrust the secretaryship of this high risk area. The new agro-industrial administration was introduced in December 1982.[3] It consisted of councils of the agro-industrial complex at district, regional and republican levels. The chairmen were not elected, but appointed by local Soviets or by the Supreme Soviets of autonomous republics. The agricultural department of the Central Committee and the Secretariat was expected to supervise the appointments in the key agricultural areas. Brezhnev's death had increased Gorbachev's power in the agricultural sector considerably and he now had the opportunity to make changes in the local administration which previously would have been blocked by Brezhnev and his faction. However, it was important to him that at the same time he should acquire broader responsibilities in the work of the Secretariat and the Politburo as a whole, so that agriculture could become only one of several areas he controlled, rather than his sole field of personal responsibility. This strategy did not necessarily reflect any particular ambition for the top job: it was merely a technique for survival at the Politburo level.

At the beginning of 1983 Andropov was the undisputed boss of the Soviet Union. His ultimate authority was obvious and nobody expected his tenure of office to be as brief as it turned out to be. It had taken Stalin, Khrushchev and Brezhnev years after their promotion to the top position in the Party to establish a confident personal supremacy over the other members of the Politburo and to become more than 'first among equals'. Andropov had managed to do this in a matter of weeks. This unusual phenomenon created an immediate interest in his personality and was reflected in the West in several 'instant' biographies.[4] But the unusually rapid acceptance of Andropov as supreme leader was related less to his personal qualities than to the mediocrity of most of the other members of the Politburo, particularly those who belonged to the Brezhnev faction. There had been a certain visible decline in the calibre of Party leaders from Lenin's to Khrushchev's generation, but in previous times it would have been impossible for men like Kirilenko, Grishin, Romanov, Shcherbitsky, Kunayev, Tikhonov and Chernenko to reach Politburo and Secretariat status. It was clear that they had reached this level through patronage and favouritism rather than on the basis of their own previous performance. They were people of the stature of district or regional leaders, rather than the super-elite of a great country. Andropov, Ustinov and Gromyko were far more impressive and this simple fact made them an extremely powerful group in the Politburo. Gorbachev was the only relatively young man in the Politburo. He was brighter and more competent than most of the other Central Committee secretaries, but he had not yet had the opportunity to prove himself. Agriculture was unlikely to be the field in which he would be able to make an impact.

Andropov's priority was to move younger and more competent people into the Politburo and the government but it was a difficult task that would take time. A Party Congress would create the ideal opportunity, but the next regular congress was not due to be held until 1986. In the first four months of the brief Andropov era there was no sign that he had decided to make Gorbachev his second-in-command. He introduced a new energetic and very personal style of leadership, but at the end of February his health suddenly began to deteriorate and from March 1983 he was already dependent on kidney dialysis. His walking was affected and it became essential for him to have a reliable deputy to represent him and his policy. Gorbachev was the only possible choice. Although Gorbachev's official rank in the Party did not change, he became an influential figure within the Party apparatus as Andropov's closest ally and spokesman at various meetings. It was not, however, a diumvirate. Gorbachev was the junior member of a group in which Andropov, Ustinov and Gromyko were the real masters. But his influence in Party organizational matters was very great because he was a member of the Secretariat, whereas Gromyko and Ustinov were members of the government.

In April 1983 Andropov's health problems were still being kept secret from the Party. However, Gorbachev's new prominence became obvious when he was selected to give the traditional speech to mark Lenin's birthday on April 22. Andropov's selection for that task a year previously had been interpreted as a sign of his rising status. In general there are no strict rules about who makes this annual speech. In periods of leadership stability any member or candidate member of the Politburo may be given the opportunity. Andropov had given the speech twice, the first time in 1964, when he was a junior secretary of the Central Committee, but not a candidate or full member of the Politburo. In transitional periods, however, the selection of speaker is not accidental since the task involves formulating the new policy line and giving an example of how certain sensitive subjects should be treated. Gorbachev's speech in 1983 followed this pattern.[5] It was designed to show that everything that had happened in the Soviet Union during the previous year had been done in accordance with Lenin's teaching and that everything which had happened in the world had fulfilled his basic predictions. The 'Lenin speech', however, also gave Gorbachev the opportunity to discuss theoretical and international problems, achievements in industry, culture and other spheres of activity and to show off his own ability in formulating the general political line. Agriculture was mentioned only briefly and in the context of the development of the Food Programme, as if the Programme rather than real success in agricultural production was significant. Andropov's name and prescriptions were mentioned at least twice in each of the three sections of the speech, second in frequency only to Lenin. Brezhnev's name was mentioned only once, in the section on Soviet peace policy. This was in sharp contrast to the previous speeches in the series, including the immediately preceding one delivered by Andropov in 1982. Although Brezhnev had not yet become a 'non-person' his legacy had become much reduced and restricted to international relations. The Andropov line was the only important aspect of domestic policy.

In May 1983 Gorbachev made his first extensive official trip abroad, leading a Supreme Soviet delegation to Canada. Since he was not yet considered a possible future leader, his trip did not receive much attention or publicity in the Western press. However, the trip, his first since he had become a member of the Politburo, was an important test. The schedule was rather varied, including talks about agriculture and visits to farms as well as political discussions with members of the Canadian parliament.[6] There were no press conferences or any other open exposure to the Western media, but Canadian MPs were free to ask all sorts of questions. Gorbachev also had a working meeting with Prime Minister Trudeau. The central event, however, was a meeting on May 17 with the Standing Committee of the Canadian House of Commons and Senate on external affairs and national defence. A number of difficult and hostile questions were asked during this meeting about Poland, Afghanistan and human rights. Gorbachev turned out to be well prepared. He discussed the problems in a seemingly uninhibited way, provoking many favourable comments in the Canadian press. The full account of the discussion published in the Minutes of the Standing Committee show that the Canadian MPs were not very well informed, however, about the details of Soviet foreign policy or the problems of the arms race. They did not know many figures, for example, or the circumstances of the events in Poland or Afghanistan. When Gorbachev insisted that Soviet troops were in Afghanistan 'at the request of the legitimate government', none of the Canadian MPs pointed out that the Karmal government had been installed in Kabul only *after* the arrival of the Soviet troops.[7]

Gorbachev naturally expressed a keen interest in Canadian agriculture. Since 1963 Canada had been a very important source of Soviet grain imports. Accompanied by Eugene Whalen, the Canadian Minister of Agriculture, he spent several days touring the main farming areas. He also paid the standard tourist visit to the Niagara Falls and took a boat ride to see the most attractive tourist spots shared by Canada and the United States.

He left Canada two days earlier than scheduled, which gave rise to speculation that changes in the leadership were imminent. In fact, his unexpected departure seems to have been connected with preparations for the 'ideological' Central Committee Plenum which had been postponed several times since March because of the illness of Chernenko, the main speaker. Chernenko had not been seen in Moscow for about three months and there were rumours that he was about to retire. But he reappeared and delivered a long report to the Plenum on June 18.[8] The Plenum also considered organizational matters and it was expected that Andropov might try to rejuvenate the composition of the Politburo. In fact, the changes turned out to be modest. Solomentsev was promoted to full membership (a long overdue promotion: he had been a candidate member since 1971), and there was only one new face – Vorotnikov – who became a candidate member of the Politburo and was expected to be made Prime Minister of the RSFSR. It had also been expected that Nikolai Ryzhkov, an able technocrat whom Andropov had promoted to the Secretariat in November 1982, or Yegor Ligachev, who had been elected to the influential post of head of the organizational department of the Central Committee in April, would also become candidate members of the Politburo. They clearly enjoyed strong support from Andropov, but their promotion was opposed by Chernenko and Tikhonov. Andropov had the power to move new people comparatively freely into the Party apparatus, but promotion to the Politburo still required consensus and the newcomers had to wait until it could be obtained.

The June Plenum made Andropov's strategy in the Party and government apparatus apparent. His team of 'heavyweights' now included Solomentsev as chairman of the Central Committee Control Commission to supplement Gromyko and Ustinov. He also formed a more dynamic operational team for internal and economic changes. Gorbachev seems to have been in charge of this team which included Vorotnikov, Ligachev, Ryzhkov and Chebrikov, the new head of the KGB. Most of the team members already had significant power and it became possible to guess what was intended for their future destinations. Vorotnikov was regarded as Tikhonov's probable successor. Ryzhkov, former deputy chairman of Gosplan, would probably be given full control over the powerful State Planning Committee in due course, as well as overall control of economic reform. His position in the Secretariat was concerned with supervision of the wider use of computers and high technology in various branches of the Soviet economy. Ligachev, a tough disciplinarian with puritanical tastes, had been brought to Moscow from the Tomsk region of Siberia. He was ideally suited for the position of chief ideologue, Suslov's former job, currently held by Chernenko. Gorbachev, who was in charge of this unofficial *orgburo*, became Andropov's most likely choice as his own successor. Andropov's intentions must have been obvious to the other members of the Politburo and Central Committee. The effect was to strengthen their powers of resistance.

In an effort to weaken the resistance, Andropov prepared a comprehensive description of the corruption cases against Shchelokov, former Minister of Internal Affairs, and Medunov (both still members of the Central Committee) for the Plenum. The many criminal charges which had been prepared by the investigation systems of the KGB, MVD and General Procuracy were included in the description. According to the rules introduced by Khrushchev and strictly followed by Brezhnev, any case against a Party official had to be discussed and decided upon by the Party organization before formal charges could be made through the legal system. The Central Committee Plenum was obliged to expel Shchelokov and Medunov for their 'errors', but this was as much as Andropov could achieve. The Central Committee was still composed, for the most part, of Brezhnev loyalists of quite senior age. When there is no consensus in the Politburo (for example, about rapidly promoting someone) Politburo members or large groups of Central Committee members may insist on a secret ballot. But Andropov knew that he would be unlikely to get majority support with a secret ballot in cases like these. He had, therefore, to content himself with the actions he could get through the Central Committee openly. But many important appointments could be made in the government and Party apparatus via the Secretariat and Presidium of the Supreme Soviet. From the way in which these appointments were made, it became evident that Gorbachev had been given the task of supervising personnel changes in the Party apparatus and government.

At the Supreme Soviet session on June 16, Andropov was elected Chairman of the Presidium. The nomination speech for this position is traditionally made by the second-in-command in the Party. It was Chernenko, therefore, who proposed Andropov. At the session of the Supreme Soviet of the RSFSR which convened in Moscow a few days later, however, the main task was to elect a new Prime Minister to replace Solomentsev. This time it was Gorbachev who made the speech to propose Vorotnikov. But the clearest indication of Gorbachev's responsibility for supervising crucial appointments came from his chairmanship of the Plenum of the Leningrad regional committee on the occasion of the election of a new first secretary when Romanov was transferred to Moscow.

Solomentsev's promotion to the Politburo filled the vacancy left by Pel'she, who had died in May 1983. But there was an urgent need to fill the senior secretaryship vacated by Kirilenko. The responsibilities of this post included supervision of the heavy, nuclear and military industries. The only person qualified to do the job in the existing Politburo was Romanov (he was probably better qualified than Kirilenko had been). He was an unpopular man, abrasive, orthodox and by no means puritanical. But he was also efficient and his authoritarian methods would be better employed in the military industry than in the Leningrad Party organization. He had a technical education (shipbuilding) and he had acquired some experience in the naval design bureau in the early 1950s. He had also served in the Soviet army during the war. Leningrad was an important centre of the military, heavy, machine and high technology industries and, judging from its industrial performance, Romanov's record was good. Thus, despite his unpopularity, he was appointed to the Central Committee Secretariat to fill Kirilenko's post. He had been a member of the Politburo since 1976 and this meant that he immediately became a more senior figure in the Secretariat than Gorbachev.

Romanov's promotion attracted the attention of all 'Kremlin watchers'. But it was a side-effect of his promotion – the election of the new Leningrad first secretary – which was probably a better indication of Andropov's shrewdness and far-reaching intentions. It is usually important that local Party officials choose their own successors when they are transferred to a higher position in Moscow. If successors are not the 'clients' of previous incumbents, unexpected and embarrassing discoveries can come to light. One reason why Suslov always kept a watch over the appointment of senior Party officials in Stavropol, for example, was to ensure that the local files and archives of the 1939–44 period would be considered in a favourable light. The same consideration was important to Brezhnev, to Kulakov and to Gorbachev as well. This method of keeping a regional power base is essential to all Party leaders. Very few *obkom* secretaries manage their regions without some resort to arbitrary methods, favouritism, covering up fraudulent information, gifts to higher officials visiting the region, etc. In the case of Romanov, however, Andropov promoted him to a higher position based in Moscow without allowing him to select his successor and to preserve a power base in Leningrad.

In 1970, when Vasilii Tolstikov, first secretary of Leningrad *obkom*, had been dismissed, Romanov had been promoted from being a second *obkom* secretary to replace him. It was not a popular choice, but it was not unusual, particularly considering that Tolstikov had been dismissed on charges of corruption which emerged because of an accident.[9] *Obkom* secretaries, when promoted, usually have the privilege of suggesting their own replacements. But if they are dismissed in disgrace, someone more independent is recommended for the job. For important regions like Leningrad, both decisions are made at Politburo and Secretariat levels. In the case of Romanov's promotion, the

Politburo did not offer him the privilege of choosing a close colleague. Instead it recommended Lev Zaikov, Chairman of the Leningrad City Soviet, who was only sixth in the regional Party hierarchy and who had no previous experience of Party work. Born in 1923, Zaikov was an industrial manager until 1976, and only then was he elected to the Leningrad City Soviet. His immediate boss, Ratmir Bobovnikov, chairman of the Leningrad Regional Soviet, was younger and more prominent, with considerable experience in Party work (as Leningrad *gorkom* and *obkom* secretary). Their mutual boss, Yuri Solovyov, also younger than Zaikov, formerly chairman of the Leningrad city and regional Soviet and now first *gorkom* secretary, was also more prominent. But for some reason Zaikov, who was known not to be a client of Romanov, was promoted over their heads. He was popular in Leningrad because he was said to be the only honest person in the leadership. Gorbachev was sent to Leningrad to chair the Plenum on June 22 and to recommend Zaikov on behalf of the Politburo.[10] This episode, more than any other, was a message to the Party apparatus that Gorbachev had become the Politburo member responsible for cadre policy.

The performance of the agricultural sector was a little better in 1983, partly due to Andropov's measures to improve work discipline, and partly because the weather was good. After a mild winter, the spring rains were plentiful. In July the United States Department of Agriculture predicted that the Soviet harvest would be 200 million tons.[11] This was still short of the target, but it represented a 10 per cent improvement on the 1982 harvest. Foreign observers realized that a good harvest would improve Gorbachev's chances for succession. In the middle of June discussions began about Andropov's failing health. At the Supreme Soviet session on June 16 he was unable to walk to the podium and had to make his acceptance speech from his usual seat. He also needed help walking when he met the Finnish President, Mauno Koivisto. When he went on his official holiday at the end of August, he left Gorbachev in charge of the day-to-day running of the Secretariat. Chernenko chaired the Politburo meetings, but the Secretariat is more important for effective management of the country.

The preference shown to Gorbachev in August and during the autumn was justified by the importance of mobilizing people for a successful harvest. If the top executive in the country was also the person responsible for agriculture, local officials would take his instructions more seriously. However, Gorbachev's priority in September turned out to be far removed from worrying about a bumper harvest. The management of an international crisis took precedence. A Korean Boeing 747 passenger airliner was shot down by a Soviet fighter plane on September 1 over Sakhalin. The consequences of the tragedy were extremely serious. Andropov's health prevented him from returning to Moscow to deal with the situation. Ustinov was a party to the initial cover-up of the extent of the disaster (this later resulted in the first personal clash between Andropov and Ustinov). It was Gorbachev who chaired the crisis management group and who put Marshal Ogarkov forward to explain the incident at a press conference on September 9, 1983. As it happened, Andropov was never seen publicly again. He remained bedridden until the end of his life in February 1984.

In September and October Gorbachev worked very hard to show that his almost supreme power in agriculture could make a difference. The maturing harvest was, indeed, good, but the most difficult problem in the Soviet Union was, as always, to reap it in good time and with minimal loss. The news of the big Soviet harvest did not give anyone in America anything to cheer about. American farmers suffered a severe drought in 1983, but the huge surpluses which had accumulated from the record harvest the previous year had still not been sold. American farmers were pressing Washington to promote grain sales to the Soviet Union, but the usual large end-of-summer import orders from Moscow were delayed in anticipation of a successful Soviet harvest. In the end, however, the success did not materialize. In the period July–September Soviet grain imports (4.7 million tons) were well below the purchases during the same three months in 1981 (10.8 million metric tons) and a little below the 1982 level (5.1 million tons). But in October–December the import orders began to rise sharply, reaching 8.6 million tons, more than a million tons more than the 1982 level in the same months. A further 20 million tons of grain were imported during the subsequent winter and spring to cover the domestic deficit.[12] For the first time the American estimate (200 million tons) was higher than the real bunker harvest (190 million tons) later reported by Chernenko to have been a success.[13]

The Politburo discussed the problems of agriculture frequently in 1983. This became clear from Andropov's innovation of publishing weekly summaries of Politburo meetings. There were also several special high level conferences in the Central Committee during the spring and summer to mobilize Party cadres for new initiatives at which Gorbachev was the main speaker. Agricultural workers in the livestock and agro-industrial sectors were awarded salary increases which were particularly high if they fulfilled the plan.[14] But real success evaded Gorbachev and the report of the harvest was not published. At the end of September *Izvestiya*, in an official commentary for the weekly statistical report about the progress of the harvest, unexpectedly criticized the Ipatovsky method.[15] It is possible that Gorbachev's new prominence had made many local officials attempt to use the method, hoping to please him, perhaps in conditions where it was likely to be counter-productive. In September only spring grain crops are normally reaped and in most places conditions for using large concentrations of machinery in one place do not exist. Selective assessment of the fields and their maturity would give far better results. This was the message published by *Izvestiya*. The comment described ironically how the combines and other machinery in some regions were organized in 'armadas' which moved, often without much effect, through large fields, while small fields in which the crops were ready to be harvested were bypassed. The author of the article expressed himself in favour of the Ipatovsky method as such, but only in areas where its use could be justified. *Izvestiya* is the organ of the government and the Soviets, unlike *Pravda* or *Sel'skaya zhizn'* (*Rural Life*), which are official organs of the Central Committee. It is possible that government officials or the Ministry of Agriculture had decided that the time had come to make it clear that they did not endorse the universal application of the Ipatovsky method and that it could, in some cases, actually cause damage.

At the end of September newspapers began publishing alarm signals. Harvesting should have been almost complete, but in the Urals and Siberia it was behind schedule and grain was being lost. The supplies of coarse fodder and silage were better than in 1982, but the harvesting of fodder beet and other livestock food crops was delayed. The Central Statistical Bureau's report of the harvesting campaign on October 10 (by which time the frosts have usually begun in the eastern, central and north-western regions) listed many unfulfilled tasks. Few regions and republics reported fulfillment of the state procurement plans. At the end of October Gorbachev travelled to Stavropol *krai* where he visited several districts and many collective and state farms.[16] He spent four days in the area and made a speech at a constituency meeting in Ipatovo village. At a conference in Stavropol he discussed general and local problems and ways of fulfilling the plan. Stavropol *krai* was not doing as well as Gorbachev would have liked, but his position was more secure now and he did not need to put pressure on the area to deliver extra grain before the October revolution anniversary celebrations. The traditional annual 'October Revolution' report of the Central Committee on November 6 was made by Romanov.[17] The choice does not seem to have been accidental – it underlined the fact that the two senior secretaries had been given equal status.

The substance of the 'October Revolution' report is usually different from the Lenin birthday speech in April. In April the speaker talks less about current economic performance and more about the Party line in matters of ideology and theory. In the November report it has become traditional to mention the preliminary results of the economic performance in the current year, to show that the fruits of the October Revolution have been material, as well as ideological and political. It is necessary to show that life has improved in the past year as a result of the efforts of the Party leaders. The economic performance in 1983 was, in fact, better than the performance of 1982 and Romanov had no difficulty in giving credit to Andropov for his policy and his personal interference. Agriculture had also improved, but Romanov mentioned it only briefly. Half of the report was devoted to international problems and Romanov's approach was clearly that of a hard-line hawk, since he used blunt language and a great deal of demagoguery. Andropov's absence from the events marking the anniversary celebrations once again stimulated speculation about his poor health and his possible successor. The main attention was now focused on the two relatively young leaders – Gorbachev and Romanov. Nobody expected the successor to be an aged and infirm interim figure.

The regular November Plenum of the Central Committee was postponed. There were rumours that important changes in the

Politburo and in internal policy were being considered for the Plenum and that Andropov's health might improve sufficiently to allow him to attend the meeting. When the Plenum was finally convened at the end of December, however, no important changes were made in the Politburo, but the effect of the few changes which were introduced was to consolidate Andropov's influence, despite his absence. Vorotnikov was promoted to full membership of the Politburo and this seemed to signal unmistakably that he was to be Tikhonov's successor. His rise in the Party ranks had been meteoric, since he had spent only a few months as a candidate member and was then given priority over most of the other candidates who had been waiting for promotion for years. Chebrikov, the new chairman of the KGB, became a candidate member of the Politburo, while Ligachev, head of the cadre department of the Central Committee, was elected to the Secretariat, thereby significantly increasing his power over appointments in the Party apparatus. The Central Committee also confirmed the instructions for the election campaign at district and regional levels. These elections presented Andropov with an opportunity to alter the composition of the local bureaucracy and thus to influence the composition of the delegates to the next Party Congress. Gorbachev and Ligachev were given the crucially important task of supervising the regional elections and recommending younger and more able Party officials in regions where the economic performance was poor and plans were underfulfilled, or where corruption was evident.

In December and January election conferences were held in more than 140 regions, *krai* and autonomous republics. But local Party officials failed to be re-elected in only 20 regions. Although it was the highest turnover of local officials since the beginning of the Brezhnev period, it represented a rather modest shake-up.[18] The highest percentage of dismissals was in the Ukraine and Kazakhstan and the commonest cause was corruption and the falsification of local statistical data. Kunayev and Shcherbitsky could hardly have been pleased at the purge of their domains.

The annual budgetary session of the Supreme Soviet had also been postponed from November. It finally took place on December 28, later than ever before. Once again Andropov was absent. Gorbachev's position in the Party ranks seemed to have been enhanced. The Supreme Soviet session is the second best (after the sequence of speakers during an election campaign) index of the comparative standing of Politburo members. Since it takes place more frequently than elections, it is the best way of detecting change within a particular year. The seating arrangements of the Presidium during the joint session of the two chambers are strictly ordered. Members of the Presidium of the Supreme Soviet and the senior members of the government sit in separate wings. The Chairman and Deputy Chairmen of the session have a special row of seats in front in the centre. On the left behind them, visible to the photographers, there is a 'Politburo section', consisting of three rows of five seats each. The front row is occupied by the General Secretary, the Prime Minister, the Chief Ideologue or second secretary and two other senior members. In the last session before Brezhnev's death, on November 17 1981, these seats were occupied by Brezhnev, Tikhonov, Suslov, Kirilenko and Chernenko.[19] In the November session in 1982 the 'front benchers' were Andropov, Tikhonov, Chernenko, Ustinov and Gromyko. Behind them, in strict order of importance, were Shcherbitsky, Kunayev, Pel'she and Grishin, with Gorbachev, Romanov and Aliyev in the back row.[20] At the June session in 1983, Gorbachev had moved forward slightly, to the last place in the second row after Shcherbitsky, Kunayev, Grishin and Romanov.[21] In December 1983 his move was more dramatic. Shcherbitsky and Kunayev had moved back to the third row, Andropov's seat was vacant and Gorbachev sat behind it, in the first place in the second row. Next to him were Grishin, Romanov and Vorotnikov.

Gorbachev's seniority was confirmed by the large number of constituencies which named him as their alternative candidate for the Supreme Soviet elections in March 1984. 'Kremlin watchers' have long since discovered that the number of nominations received by Politburo members is not accidental. The General Secretary always receives the most, and the rest are nominated according to seniority. The public which nominates candidates seems to know how many times it is permitted to nominate someone as second candidate. Politburo members usually finally agree to stand for election in districts where they are not opposed by local celebrities. In other constituencies, where local candidates are likely to emerge, the nomination of Politburo members, candidate members and Central Committee secretaries usually serves a political and symbolic purpose. Everyone knows that they will not accept the nomination and the function is to show that the local public knows the leaders and is enthusiastic about seeing that they get elected. The degree of enthusiasm and the number of nominations can be measured to rank the leaders. Some foreign research agencies (for example, the research department of Radio Liberty which is owned by the US Information Agency) carefully screen all the reports in Soviet newspapers of the thousands of nomination meetings held by farmers, workers, clerks, etc., and count the total number of nominations for each member of the leadership group. Research on the electoral campaign in January 1984 showed that by number of nominations, Gorbachev was fourth in the Party hierarchy, after Andropov, Chernenko and Tikhonov.[22]

The newly elected Supreme Soviet traditionally accepts the resignation of the Prime Minister and forms a new government. This is usually a constitutional formality, since the joint session requests the Prime Minister to carry on. But in 1984 there were strong indications that the formation of the new government would be entrusted to Vorotnikov who would propose a new and younger list of ministers. If that had happened it would have represented a truly historic (and perhaps irreversible) change in Soviet politics. Andropov knew that his anti-corruption campaign had scratched little more than the surface of the establishment. There was a very close patron–client relationship between the Party apparatus and the government system. Until it was broken, corruption, the abuse of power and the growth of elite privileges would remain inevitable. If a more independent government was formed, and if it included a high proportion of younger, more competent and technocratic people, the vicious circle of corruption, incompetence and the formation and renewal of a 'new class' might be broken.

Andropov realized that his life was drawing to a close. As the longest serving head of the KGB, he knew better than anyone else in the world how extensive the corruption was in a large part of the super-elite formed during Brezhnev's long tenure. He had become a leader by his own efforts, not through Brezhnev's patronage. His only chance of making a lasting contribution to the history of the Soviet Union was by creating a more independent government. The regular Party Congress was still two years away.

If he had lived another two months, the history of the Soviet Union might have taken a different course. Since the invention of kidney dialysis, people have been known to live for five or seven years with kidney failure. But in the absence of real international co-operation, dialysis and kidney transplant surgery were introduced into Soviet medicine ten years later than these techniques were introduced in the West. At the end of the 1960s, for example, when there were more than 100 'artificial kidney centres' in the United States which could serve about 20 to 30 per cent of all patients with acute kidney deficiency, there was only one such centre in the Soviet Union, at the kidney clinic of the Moscow Medical Institute (a close friend of mine, Valery Pavlinchuk, who suffered, like Andropov, from acute nephritis, was refused treatment because of the absence of facilities and died in 1968). Kidney dialysis was considered too expensive in the Soviet Union to be introduced widely. Although the Kremlin hospital had the necessary equipment (imported from Japan and West Germany), when a patient appeared who at last was considered worth the expense, there was insufficient experience to treat him successfully. At the very end of January Andropov's health began to deteriorate and late in the afternoon of February 9 he died.

7
Second-in-command

Andropov's death was reported on Soviet radio and television on Friday, February 10, 1984. Everyone expected that the same procedure would be followed as after Brezhnev's death and that the name of the new General Secretary would be announced the following day. There was, however, no report of a Central Committee Plenum on February 11. Foreign leaders were invited to attend the funeral on February 14. But when the heads of state and foreign ministers of more than seventy countries were advised not to arrive until late on February 13, it became clear that proper arrangements to meet them at the airport could not be made immediately and that the choice of successor was not going smoothly.

Although Chernenko had chaired Politburo meetings in Andropov's absence, he had not really been considered a serious contender for the position of General Secretary. After all, he had been defeated in 1982, after Brezhnev's death. In any case, it seemed irrational for the Politburo to consider appointing someone three years older than Andropov and in obvious ill health. It was generally understood that Andropov had been grooming Gorbachev to replace him, but Romanov also seemed to have a strong claim to the supreme position. When Chernenko was appointed chairman of the Funeral Commission, it was clear that he had entered the race. But it was equally clear from the embarrassingly long delay before any announcement was made that there was no consensus and that some hard bargaining must be taking place within the Politburo. Chernenko's main liability was his age. After Andropov's death the handicap of being Brezhnev's close associate disappeared. The position of all Brezhnev's friends improved immediately as the fear of Andropov's anti-corruption campaign subsided. They knew that they could rely on the majority of the Central Committee. Gorbachev also found that his age was a problem, but in his case the handicap was his 'political age'. His lack of substantial successes and his relatively short and narrow experience would make it difficult to present him to the Party, nation and world as an obvious leader.

In their search for the rationale behind communist succession practices, Western experts have produced an optimal 'profile' of the front runner. He should be about 60 years of age, Russian, with a higher technical education. He should have been promoted to full membership of the Politburo after being First Secretary of an important *oblast'* or republic. He should have spent several years in the Central Committee Secretariat and have a range of experience in industrial, agricultural, nationality and foreign affairs, with contacts in the KGB and the military and he should be acceptable to the majority of Politburo members. Neither a conservative, nor a reformer, he should appear to be centrist. He should also be an effective administrator with some leadership qualities.[1] It was perfectly obvious in 1983 that nobody possessed all these qualities. Any such well-qualified potential leader would have been destroyed by Stalin, dismissed by Khrushchev, and sent as ambassador to a foreign country by Brezhnev. However, it was also obvious that Gorbachev approximated to the profile more closely than Chernenko did. Chernenko did not have a proper education, had never served as First Secretary in an important *oblast'* and had no experience in industry or agriculture. His only experience was in the field of propaganda and ideology. He was a pure *agitprop* man, an *apparatchik* whose administrative talents had never been tested. The only criterion which he met was his acceptability to the majority of the Politburo.

It is improbable that it was just the question of *who* was to succeed that took so much time to settle. More difficult decisions probably concerned the question of whether Andropov's policy was to be continued. It is likely that people like Ustinov, Gromyko and Gorbachev agreed to Chernenko's succession as General Secretary only on condition that he did not have a free hand in rehabilitating Brezhnev and possibly turning Andropov into a non-person in revenge. Given Chernenko's infirmity and age, a formal decision had to be made about who was to act as second secretary and how to increase his role in Party affairs. The extraordinary Plenum of the Central Committee finally took place on Monday, February 13 in the Kremlin. Chernenko was elected as the new ruler and in his long acceptance speech he expressed the intention of following Andropov's lines without reservation. There was no mention of Brezhnev's name. Gorbachev also made a brief concluding speech at the Plenum. It was a signal to the Party that he was now a strong second secretary.

I watched Andropov's funeral on February 14, 1984 on television in London. It was a copy of Brezhnev's funeral in all essential details. Chernenko, who had seemed quite fit in November 1982, was now quite obviously rather weak. The long debates in the Kremlin on the previous day had affected him. Nonetheless, he had to make the first speech from the podium in the bitter cold of that February day. Moreover, it was his first speech as leader, addressed not only to the Soviet people, but to a large world television audience. It was a great disappointment and embarrassment to his fellow countrymen and women. It was incomprehensible how this obviously sick man would be able to do the job for which he had been chosen. He could hardly get through his speech, running out of breath in the middle of a sentence or even in the middle of a word. After the speeches, when the brisk military parade began, he tried, like Ustinov who was standing beside him, to salute. But he could not keep his hand up for more than a few seconds. He tried to raise it again and failed, observed by the millions watching him on television. When the time came to step down from the mausoleum and escort the coffin on its last few dozen feet to the grave near the Kremlin wall, Chernenko still could not raise his arm to pretend that he was carrying the coffin. His fellow Politburo members followed suit and the coffin went to the grave carried by military officers, with Politburo members walking between them. The procession showed unambiguously that Gorbachev was second in the Party and state hierarchy, since he led the procession with Chernenko (at Brezhnev's funeral the procession had been led by Andropov and Tikhonov, the General Secretary and Prime Minister).

Although Western 'Kremlinologists' understood the significance of this protocol, many of them failed to recognize it as a sign of Gorbachev's power. Instead they interpreted his second place in the hierarchy as a compromise between the old and the young. There was some truth in this conclusion. Both Ustinov and

Gromyko were apparently still more senior. But in any possible future scenario they could only be 'kingmakers', never kings. It is also true that being second-in-command does not guarantee the succession. Bukharin in the late 1920s, Molotov in the 1930s, Malenkov in the 1940s, Kirichenko in the 1950s, Kozlov in the early 1960s, and Suslov and Kirilenko in the 1970s had all been second in the Party hierarchy and in official ceremonies. But none of them had retained the position for long enough to inherit the leadership position. When Andropov moved into Suslov's job in May 1982, he created a better jumping off point for himself than Gorbachev had in 1984. The secretary in charge of the ideological portfolio also controlled most of the appointments in the Party apparatus. Gorbachev's role in the Party cadre nominations in 1983 resulted from Andropov's delegation of his own responsibilities, rather than from Gorbachev's formal position in the Secretariat. Chernenko had no intention of delegating this kind of power to Gorbachev. The position of ideological secretary was vacant and Gorbachev would certainly have liked to move from agriculture, but Chernenko decided to retain supervision of ideology. Being a professional ideologist and propagandist himself, he had no need for a chief ideologue. Neither Stalin nor Khrushchev had required the position (since they themselves wanted to be recognized in this field). It had been created by Brezhnev. Chernenko returned to the previous tradition and immediately began to try to inculcate a 'Chernenko cult'. Since he controlled the press, he encouraged it to build up his image by publishing the full texts of the congratulatory telegrams which he had received from all over the world. In November 1982 Moscow newspapers had published only a brief list of the foreign leaders and prominent figures who had sent congratulatory telegrams to Andropov.[2] In February 1984 the office of the General Secretary released the full texts of hundreds of telegrams, most of them highly flattering. Day after day they were published on the first and second pages of the central newspapers and millions of people read the inflated praise of Chernenko's exceptional qualities from the leaders of Bulgaria, Poland, Czechoslovakia, Vietnam, Nicaragua, Cuba, Gabon, Lesotho, Angola, the Seychelles, Jordan, Egypt, Yemen, Malta, Mozambique, Zambia and dozens of other countries. The publication ceased after ten days, probably only because room had to be given to the Supreme Soviet election campaign which had been interrupted by Andropov's death.

Some Central Committee secretaries (including Ligachev) had made their election speeches before Andropov's death, naturally without mentioning Chernenko's name. But as soon as the campaign was resumed, his name and quotations from his works and speeches became mandatory. The sequence of speeches, ending with that of the General Secretary on the eve of the election, confirmed Gorbachev's position as second in the hierarchy. In the 1979 election campaign Gorbachev's meeting had started the campaign. This time his speech was one of the last, on Wednesday, February 29, the day before the Prime Minister spoke to his constituents. Ustinov's speech had been on February 28, and Gromyko's on February 27. Grishin and Romanov had both spoken on February 25, not because they were equal, but because the interruption caused by Andropov's death and funeral had delayed the schedule. Chernenko was called variously 'the outstanding figure of the Leninist Party', 'a talented organizer of the masses', 'an innovator' and 'a realist' with 'high principles' and 'a Leninist style' who had made a 'great contribution'. But the flattering phrases did not deceive the general public.

Gorbachev once again met his constituents in the Ipatovsky district which he had represented in the 1979 elections. This time the meeting was presided over by the First Secretary of the Stavropol *kraikom*, Murakhovsky (in 1979 the chairman had been *raikom* secretary Kalyagin). In his speech, Gorbachev spent more time than his colleagues speaking about both Andropov and Chernenko. Unlike his fellow Politburo members, he brought personal greetings to his constituents from Konstantin Ustinovich Chernenko who, according to Gorbachev, wished all those who lived in Stavropol *krai* 'success, well being and happiness'.[3] This special message was intended to indicate that there was full harmony rather than rivalry in the Politburo. In the business part of his speech, Gorbachev did not talk much about agriculture. Instead he concentrated on the more general problems of the economy, scientific and technical progress and the need to improve the quality of industrial production. He also made a special point about the fight against corruption, crime, hooliganism and the falsification by officials of statistical information about agricultural and industrial production. He talked of international problems with the confidence of a man who deals with these problems himself. Like all the other candidates standing for election, he made several remarks about local matters, but he did not mention the Ipatovsky method.

This speech was clearly not the report of the agricultural secretary, but of a leader with a broad range of responsibilities. And it is true that he now supervised many different fields, in addition to agriculture. He would probably have been extremely pleased to hand over responsibility for agriculture to some other reliable official, but Chernenko seems to have blocked any change which would affect the balance of power. During the whole of Chernenko's rule there were no promotions to the Politburo, or even to candidate membership or to the Secretariat. There was also little change in the composition of the government.

The new Supreme Soviet was duly elected on March 4 by an overwhelming majority and, in accordance with the constitution, its first session took place in April. The first priority of the session of a new Supreme Soviet is to elect the government for the next five-year period. The nomination of the Prime Minister is traditionally the privilege of the General Secretary. Before Andropov died it had seemed certain that Tikhonov would not be re-appointed. He was 79 years old and it would have been unnatural to ask him to serve for a five-year period during which there were to be reorganizations and reforms. It was known in Moscow that Andropov had given the task of preparing the list of the new government to Vorotnikov and that various ministerial positions were under review. It was also rumoured that Chernenko had confirmed Andropov's promise to Vorotnikov, thus securing his support during the Politburo meetings on February 11 and 12. A second important task for the new Supreme Soviet was to elect a new Chairman of the Presidium of the Supreme Soviet, the nominal head of state. The tradition established by Brezhnev and Andropov indicated that the post would be given to Chernenko.

The first session of the Supreme Soviet started as usual with brief separate meetings of the two chambers to approve the credentials of the deputies and to elect the Standing Commissions which would consider any new legislation. Gorbachev was elected chairman of the Foreign Affairs Commission, a position which had previously been held by Suslov and then Chernenko and was thus considered the preserve of the second secretary. Although the position has little influence on foreign policy, it gives the incumbent the advantage of foreign trips on behalf of the Supreme Soviet. It was in the capacity of chairman of this commission that Gorbachev made his much publicized trip to Great Britain later in 1984.

The two chambers meet in a joint sitting to elect the Presidium of the Supreme Soviet consisting of 39 members, and its chairman, as well as to make other important decisions. In April 1984 the chairman of the joint session, deputy L. Tolkunov (the director of Novosti Press Agency), gave the floor to Gorbachev to make the nomination. This was another acknowledgement that he held the number two position in the Party. In June 1983 Chernenko had been given the privilege of nominating Andropov as Chairman of the Presidium. The combination of two posts – General Secretary of the Central Committee of the CPSU and Chairman of the Presidium of the Supreme Soviet – had been introduced by Brezhnev in 1977 and was interpreted as a final device to consolidate his power. From the beginning of the Soviet state in 1917 until 1977 these two posts had always been separate, held by two different people. Each was considered a full time job. Although the General Secretary was a member of the Presidium, he was not its Chairman. It had not been obvious that Andropov would want to continue Brezhnev's new tradition, particularly since he was already too ill by 1983 to be able to fill both positions. He might, indeed, have lived longer if he had not had to sign innumerable decrees and fulfil the symbolic duties of the President of the Soviet Union, duties which had little real political importance. But having decided to become President, the only person who could have signed the decrees in his place was the first deputy chairman of the Presidium of the Supreme Soviet, Vasilii Kuznetsov, who was 82 years old and not much more able-bodied. Chernenko, too, was obviously not a well man and it seemed absurd for him to add a new position to the difficult job of being General Secretary. But he apparently wanted to continue the Brezhnev tradition and to have the prestige of being President as well as General Secretary.

Gorbachev's nomination speech was longer than Chernenko's had been the previous year. The combination of the two posts had previously been explained to the general public as having certain advantages for Soviet international activity. Gorbachev, however, offered new explanations about why the two posts should be combined. He suggested that there were special constitutional provisions for the combination:

> This decision is indissolubly connected with the leading role of the Communist Party in our society, a role which is confirmed in the constitution of the USSR, and with the fact that the Party has defined and continues to define the main directions of the activity of all sections of the political system, and particularly of the Soviet government. Long practical experience has proved convincingly that the embodiment of the policy of the Party in the activity of the state has been and remains the most important condition . . . for widening and deepening socialist democracy.[4]

This is a rather loose interpretation of the constitution. If the same logic were to be used lower down the hierarchy, it would mean that *obkom* secretaries and other Party officials should also combine Party and local legislative and government positions. It is one thing to maintain that the Chairman of the Presidium of the Supreme Soviet should belong to the Party, but to claim that the constitution specifically provides for the combination of the two top positions is to read something into the constitution which does not exist. The combination of the two posts is not permitted at the union and autonomous republican level and their constitutions are modelled on the constitution of the USSR.

Once the Chairman of the Presidium had been elected, the next task of the joint session was to proceed to elect the government. According to the constitution, the 'Council of Ministers shall tender its resignation to a newly elected Supreme Soviet of the USSR at its first session'.[5] This was duly observed in 1984 and the chairman of the session read Tikhonov's letter of resignation. In line with the usual tradition, the new nomination was made by the General Secretary who was now also Chairman of the Presidium. Chernenko's speech was very brief. He nominated Tikhonov to become Prime Minister again. The nomination was greeted with applause and Tikhonov was reappointed. Vorotnikov would have to wait for a General Secretary who would honour Andropov's promise. On the following day Tikhonov presented the Supreme Soviet with his list of ministers. Their photographs were published in *Izvestiya* and *Pravda* on April 13. There was not a single new face. The large government, probably the largest in the world (3 first deputy chairmen, 11 deputy chairmen, 62 ministers, 23 chairman of state committees and 15 chairmen of the Councils of Ministers of the constituent republics), consisting of 114 men (there were no women in the Council of Ministers of the USSR), was exactly the same as it had been before the elections. The oldest minister was E. P. Slavsky, Minister of Medium Machine Construction (a euphemism for the nuclear industry), who had been born in the 19th century and was now 86 years old. He was probably the oldest active minister in the world.

The joint session of the Supreme Soviet also discussed briefly the reform of general and vocational education. Six speakers expressed themselves in favour of the controversial reform which then became law. A few other decisions were made and within two days the annual legislative load had been dealt with. The deputies to the most democratic parliament in the world were now free of their legislative duties until November, when they would meet for another two-day session to approve the budget for 1985. Between sessions, i.e. for 361 days a year, the 39 members of the Presidium of the Supreme Soviet would have the full power and authority of the two chambers to introduce new laws, ratify international treaties, declare war and peace and make changes in the membership of the government.

On Sunday April 15 the full texts of the congratulations received by Chernenko as the newly elected Chairman of the Presidium began appearing in the newspapers. He had become Mr President and telegrams were published from heads of state, presidents, kings and queens. When he became Chairman of the Supreme Military Council, his succession was complete – he had acquired the full panoply of power possessed by Brezhnev and Andropov. The anti-corruption campaign slowed down and members of Brezhnev's family and his retired assistants began reappearing at high level receptions. Chernenko took over the chairmanship of the commission which had been set up some time before to prepare a draft of the new Party programme to be adopted by the next Party Congress. Some of the liberal figures who had been appointed by Andropov were replaced. Andropov's short tenure had, in general, been far from liberal and the number of restrictive instructions and laws had increased in 1983. Chernenko continued this trend. Molotov, Stalin's ally and Foreign Minister, was rehabilitated and his Party membership was restored. The decision was made to boycott the Olympic Games in Los Angeles. Emigration, already at an extremely low level, practically ceased. A new law was passed in May which introduced additional restrictions on contacts between Soviet citizens and foreign visitors. Repressive measures against dissidents increased. Those who were in prison camps or exile began receiving additional sentences to prevent them from returning when they had completed their original terms. My brother, Roy Medvedev, was isolated by a round-the-clock police watch which prevented foreigners and all but the boldest Soviet citizens from visiting him. Those who wanted to see him had to identify themselves by showing their passports and when he went out he was followed openly. Western correspondents in Moscow ridiculed the measure,[6] but it was in force for over a year and the uniformed policemen only disappeared from his door in June 1985. There were more serious concerns about Andrei Sakharov. He was taken to hospital and his wife, Yelena Bonner, was sentenced to exile in Gorky. All contact between them and the outside world ceased and for more than a year there was no information about their whereabouts or their health. Chernenko was obviously not solely responsible for these measures. The KGB, MVD and ideological sectors of the Central Committee were equally responsible.

Chernenko's attempts to slow down the anti-corruption campaign were probably supported by Tikhonov, Kunayev, Shcherbitsky and Grishin. Romanov was probably also on their side, primarily because he was Gorbachev's bitter rival, but also because he had a great deal to lose if the eradication of corruption remained an important goal. The position taken by Aliyev and Solomentsev was unclear. Ustinov, Gromyko and Vorotnikov probably continued supporting Gorbachev. Brezhnev's old proteges occupied powerful positions in the Secretariat. Of the ten secretaries only Ryzhkov and Ligachev belonged to Gorbachev's team. Ponomarev, Zimyanin, Kapitonov, Rusakov, and Romanov were Chernenko's supporters. Dolgikh's position was uncertain. As a technocrat and a candidate member of the Politburo he had previously been considered as Brezhnev's possible choice for the Prime Ministerial position, if Tikhonov had to retire for health reasons. The possibility of promotion had receded, but not disappeared. There was no particular reason to restore the membership of the Politburo to 14 in 1984. Each new voice in the Politburo could have made a difference, and Chernenko seems to have preferred to play safe by keeping the existing balance.

There were no specific rules about how many members the Politburo should contain. There had been 15 members before and 14 members after the XXVIth Congress in 1981, but only ten after the XXIIIth Congress in 1966. In Khrushchev's time the size of the Presidium had varied from 11 members after the XXth Congress, to 15 in 1957 and then 11 again after the XXIIth Congress in 1961. Thus if the 12 members were managing to supervise the most important sectors of national and international affairs, there was no particular reasons to restore the membership to 14. The people in the front line for promotion were not those who had been candidate members or secretaries for longest, but those who occupied powerful, Politburo-linked positions – Chebrikov, chairman of the KGB, and Ligachev or Ryzhkov. But they had all been promoted by Andropov and were now perceived to be in Gorbachev's team. That Chernenko made a deliberate decision to exclude them is indicated by the fact that two of them moved into the Politburo in April 1985 without serving as candidate members for an interim period. Within the existing Politburo, however, there were policy differences and hidden personal antagonisms which were deep enough to have a negative impact on the efficiency of the administration. In any case, the fact that the three highest posts in the country – General Secretary, Prime Minister and Chairman of the Presidium of the Supreme Soviet of the USSR – were occupied by two very old, ill, unpopular, dull and uninspiring men affected the Soviet command economy. The momentum of 1983, when economic performance had shown signs of improvement and productivity had risen above the planned level, was lost. Industrial output began to decline, discipline was poor, public morale was low and appeals for efficiency and increased productivity became empty gestures.

It was, however, crucially important for Gorbachev to show that the agricultural improvement of 1983 would continue in 1984. As the official second-in-command he now had more power, but failure in agriculture would inevitably be linked to his performance as an administrator. The succession, the election campaign in March and the Supreme Soviet session in April had interfered with the important period when preparations were made for the sowing season. The mobilization of *kolkhozy*, *sovkhozy* and the agro-industrial administration for sowing or harvesting required an intensive publicity campaign. All newspapers in the Soviet Union from *Pravda*, *Izvestiya*, *Komsomol'skaya Pravda*, *Sovetskaya Rossiya* to republican, regional and district papers carry agricultural news on their front pages, bombard their readers with agricultural editorials, praise the achievements and criticize the shortcomings of farms and managers. Reports from the field are rather like war reports. There are 'heroes', 'strategists', 'offensives', 'retreats', 'failures', 'mobilizations', etc. Television and radio stations treat agriculture equally seriously and news bulletins normally begin with reports about the sown acreage in various regions rather than with news of kidnappings, terrorism and earthquakes which is kept for the end of the programme. In 1984 the newspaper space which was devoted to the election and to Chernenko's congratulatory messages had been borrowed from the normal annual spring reporting of agriculture. This must have been extremely irritating for the Central Committee agricultural department. But Gorbachev had been working hard to mobilize agricultural cadres for a quick and efficient sowing campaign. Sowing is a vital stage of the agricultural season and Gorbachev knew that any delay would be transformed into harvest losses. This is an unavoidable law of nature.

At the end of March a top level two-day All-Union Conference on the agricultural economy and the agro-industrial complex was convened in the Kremlin Palace in Moscow, attended by all the high level officials and administrators of the central and local 'agro-system' (agricultural ministers, secretaries of the constituent and autonomous republics, *obkom* and *kraikom* secretaries, chairmen of local Soviets and local agro-industrial councils). Gorbachev delivered the key report on March 26.[7] He stated that the negative trends of 1979–82 had been checked and partially reversed in 1983. Total agricultural production was 5 per cent higher in 1983 than in 1982 and Byelorussia, Latvia, Estonia and Kazakhstan had done even better. The plans for livestock production had been fulfilled for the first time in nine years. Gorbachev pointed out that the general situation, however, was still not satisfactory and that other targets had not been met.[8] He analysed the performance in various agricultural regions, making it clear that the Altai *krai*, an important Siberian region, was doing very badly. This must have been a particular disappointment to him, since he represented the central district of the *krai* in the Supreme Soviet of the Russian Federation. But he particularly stressed the importance of a continuing and even faster improvement of economic performance and the unfailing fulfilment of all targets for production and deliveries by every farm, district, region and republic in 1984 and 1985. Reaching this goal required better co-ordination between different sectors of the agro-industrial complex and urgent measures to sow more high quality seed material and to complete agricultural machinery repairs in good time. All sectors should be intensified, but this applied particularly to livestock and milk production. It was clear from Gorbachev's speech that the Central Committee would no longer tolerate delays and mismanagement. Procurement prices had already been increased from the beginning of 1983 and the Central Committee now expected results.

Not even the agricultural newspapers and magazines printed Gorbachev's report in its entirety, a sure sign that he had spoken too bluntly at times, making personal criticisms in a plainer language than was considered suitable for open publication. He had insisted that the target figures of the Food Programme were still valid and that the new administrative agro-industrial councils and the new ways in which farmers were organized for agricultural work (in semi-independent 'contract brigades') could and should make a difference. During the debate most speakers praised both approaches as being very progressive. They were clearly considered to be Gorbachev's initiatives. The main view which emerged was that the link between production and the real income of members of the contract brigades would stimulate collective farmers and state farm workers into working harder and increasing their productivity. The conference also appealed to farmers to use what was called 'intensive technology'. In practice this meant applying larger amounts of fertilizer, making better use of herbicides, pesticides and irrigation and finishing the various tasks in the optimal time.

For some reason Western observers considered the formation of the semi-autonomous contract brigades to be a new, liberal, market-oriented reform. In fact, experiments with 'independent' brigades (groups of 30 to 100 workers under a chairman who has a degree of independence in deciding who is to undertake which aspects of the work, who sign a contract with the state or collective farm under which their income rises in proportion to the harvest) had been undertaken previously both with brigades and with the smaller unit called a *zveno*. The idea was simple: if the cash profit was linked to total output, there would be an incentive for fewer workers to produce the same output, since each would receive a larger share of the profit. Moreover, each worker would press his colleagues to work harder and better, since a poor worker could reduce the income of the whole group. But the method required young and fit brigade members, and crops which relied on human labour (for example, vegetables and cash crops). In reality, however, the peasant workforce in the Soviet Union consists mainly of old people, widows, women with children and temporary workers mobilized from urban areas. Contract brigades did not suit them very well and nor were they suitable for grain crops, for which most of the work is done by machine. Various types of contract brigades had also been tested successfully in industrial plants in the 1970s, but industrial workers are usually easier to organize than peasants.

Gorbachev's second initiative – the creation of district and regional agro-industrial administrative units (called RAPO and APO) – also received the warm support of the conference participants. The only criticism which was voiced was by G. D. Mgeladze, from Georgia. He pointed out that the system of agro-industrial councils was no more than a complex bureaucratic exercise, a new superstructure which made the lines of responsibility even less clear. The ministries which, in the normal planning of agricultural work, had the responsibility of providing supplies and services (the Ministry of Chemical Fertilizers, the Ministry of Tractors and Combines, the Ministry of Agricultural Machinery, the Ministry of Livestock Machinery, the Ministry of Irrigation and Land Reclamation, *Selkhoztekhnika*, which was responsible for the servicing and repair stations, etc.) had, in fact, become the masters and they made the decisions about which services should be provided to farms. As a result, the authority of farm directors and chairmen was reduced and not enhanced by the agro-industrial councils. Other delegates failed to support this criticism and none of them chose to follow the Georgian example of trying to simplify the administration (in Georgia all the ministries of the agro-industrial complex had been abolished and replaced by a single state committee of agriculture, which was chaired by Mgeladze).

The beginning of the agricultural season was no better than usual, despite the numerous appeals from the top and the equally numerous organizational changes and programmes. In March and April complaints were published about the shortage of high quality seed materials in many regions, particularly in Siberia. This 'seed shortage' is a traditional feature of almost every spring sowing season. It is the result of an absurd practice initiated by Stalin which obliges the farms to deliver their first harvested grain to the state. In fact, prudent farmers who think about the future rather than about fulfilling procurement quotas should keep the first harvest in reserve as seed grain. But Stalin's practice had been retained and the first priority remained the state procurement of early harvests. Creating seed grain reserves was the second priority and, as a result, they were usually made from later harvests with poorer quality grain. The higher the pressure for larger procurements, the poorer the quality of the seed grain kept for the following season. In 1983 the pressure on *kolkhozy* and *sovkhozy* to meet their procurement quotas had been particularly heavy. As a result, in 1984 some Siberian farms reported that their seed grain was only 30 to 40 per cent viable and that they urgently needed to exchange it for better seed material from the state reserves. This was a formidable task during the spring, requiring the delivery of more than one million metric tons of grain to farms over roads which, after the thaw, were unpassable. Inevitably, the sowing programme was delayed. The Central Statistical Bureau, which publishes weekly reports on sowing, only reported the completion of the season on June 11. In May the Politburo discussed the problems of sowing twice, and the Central Committee and Council of Ministers of the USSR passed the usual 'emergency' resolution on agriculture which allowed the mobilization of the urban population for agricultural work as a 'temporary measure'.[9]

The weather was fine in 1984 and there was no drought. August was dry, which was good for the harvest. The organization of the harvest was poor, however, and the work was delayed. Combine harvesters were not ready everywhere and complaints were received from various regions, including Stavropol *krai* which was not doing well. By the end of September and beginning of October the work had still not been completed and the Central Statistical

Bureau reports became alarming. In October, when the first frosts had begun making agricultural work difficult, 9 per cent of all the fields in the country had not yet been harvested and the sowing of winter crops was well behind schedule.[10] According to the plan, more than 40 million hectares should have been sown with winter cereals (which give the best yields), but only 34 million, 80 per cent of the plan, had been sown. It makes no sense to continue sowing in October. Autumn ploughing was also less extensive than expected (58 per cent of the plan) and supplies of hay, silage, haylage, grass flour and other fodder crops were lower than in 1983. The harvest was very poor indeed. No grain production figures were disclosed in 1984 and 1985, but reliable American estimates put the 1984 grain level at 170 million tons, 70 million tons short of the targets of the Food Programme and the Five Year Plan.[11] This was a disaster. It would have been considered a normal harvest in 1964–66, but by 1984 the population of the Soviet Union had grown by 40 million compared to 1965 (and the urban population had grown by 45 million). Grain imports had to be increased.

These agricultural problems did not have an immediate impact on Gorbachev's power and position. He was even more visibly prominent, since Chernenko had become seriously ill again. The burden of the top position is extremely heavy, and it seemed as if Andropov's fate was repeating itself. To demonstrate that he could cope with his position, Chernenko had engaged in intensive diplomatic activity, meeting and talking to the foreign leaders whose visits had been postponed in 1983. There was a change of policy regarding the Geneva arms negotiations, and the Soviet negotiating position had to be prepared. Numerous other events required his personal involvement, either in the capacity of General Secretary or as Chairman of the Presidium of the Supreme Soviet or as Chairman of the Supreme Military Council. This intense activity exhausted him even more quickly than it had affected Andropov in 1983. In July he had to leave Moscow and go to the south to rest. His doctors advised him to stay in the North Caucasus. A special new *dacha* had been built high in the mountain area (3,300 feet above sea level) where the air, enriched by pine forests and the evaporation from the hot spas, was considered particularly healthy. His previous *dacha* had been situated near Brezhnev's, on the Black Sea coast. The new one was in Stavropol *krai*, near Pyatigorsk and the Mashuk mountain where the great romantic poet, Mikhail Lermontov, had been killed in a duel in 1841. Lermontov is an extremely popular poet (second only to Pushkin) and the area is a great tourist attraction. Millions of people visit it each year. Once Chernenko's *dacha* had been built, however, the hills were covered by security patrols and it was forbidden to carry cameras and take pictures.

The weather was unusually wet in the North Caucasus in July. Since the harvest is gathered in July in this area, this was serious trouble. But it was also serious for Chernenko, since it made him spend his time indoors. His doctors decided to move him to the Crimea, where the weather was better. Once again there were elaborate security arrangements around the *dacha*, far more elaborate than for Stalin, Khrushchev or Brezhnev, all of whom had liked to stay in the Crimea. On August 10 the security measures were suddenly lifted – Chernenko had been flown to Moscow and admitted to a special hospital on Granovsky Street, near the Kremlin. This exclusive hospital is reserved for Politburo members. Brezhnev had been treated there, and Suslov had often spent the night there rather than being driven home when he was ill. The street is rather like an extension of the Kremlin. When the old houses were confiscated from former aristocrats and rich merchants, they were transformed into apartments for high officials. Molotov still lives in Number 14 and Khrushchev's family still has an apartment there. The 'closed shop' reserved for Central Committee members is situated opposite Molotov's house, invisible from the outside. The hospital is only a block away from the building which houses the official reception office of the Presidium of the Supreme Soviet, the office to which hundreds of people from all parts of the country come each day to present complaints, petitions, requests or statements of their grievances and problems to the Chairman of the Presidium of the Supreme Soviet. Kalinin, official head of state before 1946, occupied this building and was genuinely popular because he used to meet some of the visitors, listen to their complaints and try to help them (or so legend has it). The practice of personal communication between the head of state and his people only ceased in 1977, when Brezhnev took over the position and was too busy to continue it. Neither Andropov nor Chernenko restored the practice or revived the legend of the top official helping to solve the problems of ordinary folk.

Gorbachev's former rival for the secretaryship of agriculture, Medunov, had been dismissed from his *kraikom* position in 1982 and expelled from the Central Committee in June 1983. Although it was rumoured that a criminal case had been prepared against him, nothing was known about his fate. In 1984 a special investigation began into corruption in the Rostov region (this is an important agricultural area in the North Caucasus). The investigation seemed to be directed against Ivan Bondarenko, a protege of Brezhnev, secretary of the region and Gorbachev's rival. Rostov had very good official economic and agricultural records and Bondarenko, an agronomist, had been made a Hero of Socialist Labour. But the area was known for its corruption, particularly in the trade system. Many high-ranking local officials had been arrested by the anti-fraud department of the MVD and the investigations had gone so far that it was impossible to halt them. The day after Chernenko's departure to the south *Izvestiya* published a long article about the criminal activity of trade officials in the Rostov region and the arrest of 76 officials from the regional trade system and their contacts in the RSFSR Ministry of Trade.[12] Bondarenko shared Medunov's fate: he was dismissed from his post for his 'errors'. In July and August *Pravda* published several strongly critical articles about corruption in Kazakhstan and Uzbekistan. It seemed as if Chernenko's absence was being used to revive the anti-corruption campaign, at least at the regional level. This was confirmed by an article, '*Rasplata*'(retribution), published in *Izvestiya* in August, which reported details of the case against the director of the largest foodstore in Moscow, Yu. K. Sokolov.[13] He had been arrested in 1983 and sentenced to death in November of that year, but an appeal for clemency had been pending in the Presidium of the Supreme Soviet. The article reported that the appeal had been dismissed and that Sokolov had been executed. Other executions for economic crimes were carried out in August when Gorbachev was left in Moscow as acting leader.

Chernenko stayed in hospital for more than three weeks. He then resumed his duties and was shown on television on September 5 awarding gold Hero's medals to the spaceship crew. This ceremony was long overdue. At the time that he went back to work another event occurred which attracted the attention of

Western observers – Marshal Ogarkov, the Chief-of-Staff, was suddenly dismissed. The dismissal was first reported on Moscow radio very late on Thursday, September 6 and it was assumed that the announcement was made immediately after a Politburo meeting. It was issued, however, as a decision of the Council of Ministers, signed by Tikhonov. Since Politburo meetings start at 11 am (the tradition was introduced by Lenin in 1922), the dismissal was generally considered to have indicated the beginning of a power struggle, in particular to prevent Ogarkov from being appointed Minister of Defence. Ustinov was known to be in poor health.

The sudden dismissal of a senior military professional is a rare occurrence in the Soviet Union. The last man to meet this fate was Marshal Zhukov in October 1957. Since Marshal Ustinov was not a member of the professional military, Ogarkov, his First Deputy Minister, was thought to be the most influential person in the army. In other countries dismissals like this are usually signs of weakness, uncertainty or a power struggle. The Kremlin leadership certainly showed signs of a temporary weakness, with Chernenko just discharged from hospital and Ustinov ill. Western observers linked the demotion variously to a disagreement between Ustinov and Ogarkov or between Romanov and Ogarkov or, conversely, to a strong connection between Romanov and Ogarkov.[14] The real reasons have not been disclosed, but Ogarkov was known to have been close to Andropov. They had known one another since the Karelian military campaign in 1942–44, when Ogarkov began his military career as a captain, reaching the rank of colonel at the front headquarters. At that time Andropov was Komsomol secretary of Karelia and in charge of the partisan movement there.

Gorbachev was due to go to Bulgaria on September 7 to participate in the celebrations of the 40th anniversary of the liberation of Sofia. Ryzhkov was a member of the delegation. Romanov was also leaving on September 7 for Ethiopia to take part in the official declaration of the formation of a Marxist-Leninist party. This was a huge and expensive celebration in the capital of a country where millions were starving to death (the Soviet press reported the speeches made about the victories of socialism in Ethiopia without mentioning a word about the famine). Gorbachev's speech in Sofia on September 9 was not very interesting. Soviet speeches made at jubilee celebrations like this are normally prepared by a group of speech-writers from the international department of the Central Committee. They are formal and follow a set pattern, without any personal touch.

Chernenko tried to resume his normal duties, but his health had clearly deteriorated and his breathing had become so bad that he had difficulty making a full speech. At the 50th anniversary celebrations of the Union of Writers on September 25 at the Kremlin Palace, he read the introduction to his speech and the rest of the text was given to those present in printed form. Gorbachev was in Moscow in September and October, presiding over the co-ordination of the completion of the agricultural season. On October 18 he was present at the official ceremony to present the Order of Lenin to Gromyko on his 75th birthday. The official photographs published the following day showed Romanov closer to the central group (Gromyko, Chernenko, Tikhonov) than Gorbachev. This was probably accidental, but it was sufficient to make 'Kremlin-watchers' suggest that 'Gorbachev is under a cloud' because of the poor harvest.[15] An agricultural Plenum of the Central Committee was due to meet in Moscow on October 23 to discuss the long-term irrigation and land reclamation programme and the construction of a great canal to divert the waters of the Irtysh river in Siberia to Kazakhstan and the Central Asian republics. This new programme was to be added to the Food Programme, which was faltering. Although Gorbachev was the most senior person concerned with agriculture at the Plenum, the main report was delivered by Tikhonov and Gorbachev was not even mentioned as one of the speakers.[16] This again seemed to indicate that he was in trouble, although some foreign commentators suggested that the real reason was that he was opposed to such expensive programmes and favoured private initiatives. There were other rumours that he had not attended the Plenum and had instead taken a holiday. In fact, the rumours were groundless. The programme was certainly prepared in the Central Committee with his full support. He was a great believer in irrigation and had done a great deal to provide more of it in Stavropol *krai*. Major reports of this kind are traditionally presented by the General Secretary. Chernenko had introduced the report, but could not deliver all of it. It was, in any case, more suitable for Tikhonov to present it on behalf of the government –

it concerned construction and was to absorb very large investments. The discussion of the project was very brief and the Plenum ended after one day.

The regular Plenum to discuss the budget and the annual plan was due in the middle of November. Organizational matters, promotions and dismissals are also usually considered then. There were some long overdue promotions. There had been no change in the Politburo for about a year and the pressure to move some secretaries (for example, Ligachev and Ryzhkov) and Chebrikov up to the Politburo was strong. Chernenko was no longer able to deal with urgent matters in the field of ideology and there were many unresolved questions. A new member of the Politburo was urgently needed to take care of this sector and Ligachev seemed ideally suited for the job. In November it was confirmed that Ustinov's illness was serious – he was unable to review the military parade on November 7 and his place was taken by his deputy, Marshal Sokolov. The November Plenum was cancelled and replaced instead by an extended Politburo meeting on November 15 which considered the budget and the 1985 plan.[17] Some observers considered this normal, in light of the extraordinary agricultural Plenum in October. In fact it was designed to avoid changing the composition of the Politburo. Chernenko believed that any alteration would shift the balance of power against him. Neither the KGB nor the army supported him strongly. Postponing the Plenum would prevent any possible challenge to his position. The economic results of that year were poor and an open discussion of the 1984 performance (much reduced from 1983) would have been embarrassing.

It is unlikely that Gorbachev pressed for the regular Plenum to be held, since agriculture was the weakest section of the economy. In August and September, while Chernenko was ill, the Politburo had discussed agricultural problems and the progress of the harvest almost every week. The weather was fairly good, but the administrative structures and economic incentives which Gorbachev had promised would improve the situation seemed to be having no effect. The fact that Chernenko and Tikhonov were prominent at the agricultural Plenum in October and at the enlarged 'budget' Politburo meeting in November was seen in the West as a sign that 'Chernenko and his older-generation colleagues, such as Tikhonov, still can command a majority in the

Politburo, especially when the younger generation fails as spectacularly as Gorbachov & Co. did with this year's harvest'.[18] Nonetheless, these commentators did not think that Gorbachev's chances should be entirely written off.[19]

Winter was late in 1984 and until the beginning of November the agricultural administration in Moscow tried to salvage as much as possible from the autumn fields. An *Izvestiya* editorial on October 30 listed the many tasks which had yet to be completed and acknowledged that harvesting was still continuing in some regions. Potatoes and vegetables were being collected from under the snow. After the budget meeting of the enlarged Politburo in the middle of November, Gorbachev took a brief holiday. His Politburo *dacha* was situated at Pitsunda, near Sochi, in the Georgian part of the Black Sea Coast. He must have been greeted upon arrival by the First Secretary of Georgia, Shevarnadze. Gorbachev probably combined his holiday with preparations for his forthcoming trip to Britain. He must have welcomed the opportunity to improve his image provided by this official trip, which was to last for a week from December 15. A delegation from the Supreme Soviet had been invited by the British Parliament (a group of British MPs had visited the Soviet Union previously and this was the reciprocal visit) and Gorbachev was leading the delegation as Chairman of the Supreme Soviet Standing Commission on Foreign Affairs. Since he was known to be second-in-command in the Soviet Union and Chernenko's probable successor, the interest in his visit to Britain was very high. As a result the amount of publicity accorded to the trip was incomparably more than that which his visit to Canada in a similar capacity had aroused the previous year. Moreover, Soviet–American arms negotiations were due to be resumed at that time, and this provoked even more interest in his trip.

Before departing for Britain Gorbachev was the main speaker at a conference on ideology in Moscow on December 10. The purpose of the conference was to discuss the changes in ideological work implied by the ideological Plenum held in June 1983. Chernenko had been the main speaker at the Plenum and would have presided over this conference, but he was too ill. Gorbachev conveyed his greetings and gave the main report. His co-speaker was Mikhail Zimyanin, the Central Committee secretary responsible for the press and the official Soviet spokesman on international affairs. Gorbachev's report kept to traditional orthodox lines, which was natural given that he was a contender for the succession. But many intellectuals in Moscow were encouraged by his statement that 'openness is a compulsory condition of socialist democracy and a norm of public life'.[20] In fact, the Russian word which he used for 'openness', *glasnost'*, is rather ambiguous. It conveys the idea of publicity rather than of frankness. The publication of selective reports about the weekly Politburo meeting is an example of *glasnost'*, but the very fact that the reports are selective and brief show the limits of the meaning and how far it is from open government.

Gorbachev arrived in London on December 15 and it immediately became clear that his visit would be a resounding success. The British press, which had taken to describing him as the 'leader-in-waiting', gave him enormous publicity. Everyone who met him found him charming, with a good sense of humour and his wife, Raisa, captured the British imagination. Mrs Thatcher had a long talk with him and made the famous statement: she liked him and found that 'we can do business together'. He also met senior MPs and peers at the Houses of Parliament, leaders of the Labour Party, representatives of the business community and other officials. His charm was such that Denis Healey became quite lyrical:

> He is a man of exceptional charm with a relaxed, self-deprecating sense of humour. Emotions flicker over a face of unusual sensitivity like summer breezes on a pond. In discussion he was frank and flexible with a composure full of inner strength. He was fierce but courteous in argument, raising Northern Ireland whenever we raised human rights with him.[21]

One thing puzzled Healey: 'How could someone so nice and human run the Soviet system?'[22]

In fact, despite his style and excellent sense of presentation, there was little in what Gorbachev said in Britain to suggest radical new policies in the future. He was uncompromising on human rights and equally adamant about Afghanistan and other current problems. Nonetheless, the very fact that he was relaxed, flexible in his programme and prepared to enter into some discussion augured well. If he was prepared to listen to alternative opinions he might learn to be more tolerant towards diverse views in his own country. One thing was clear: he was the best man in the Politburo.

It was important to Gorbachev that his visit to Britain should receive wide and positive coverage in the Soviet press and on Soviet television. It was the first time that a foreign trip undertaken by a high Party official was shown live on Soviet television. The Soviet public had never before seen its leaders in the glare of Western publicity and they liked what they saw. Television had been the enemy of Brezhnev, Andropov, Tikhonov and Chernenko, since they were too old and too ill to project an image of strength and ability. It was an image which could be superimposed on still photographs, but not before live television cameras. For Gorbachev, on the other hand, television was an ally, enhancing his popularity. The daily news of his British trip made him the most popular Soviet leader domestically. The television showed him as he really was (the large birthmark which runs from the top of his forehead and is prominent in Western photographs and television pictures disappears on the Soviet official still photographs).

There was a negative side to Gorbachev's new-found popularity at home and abroad. It reduced his standing in the Soviet bureaucracy. Probably even Gromyko resented the diplomatic success of Gorbachev's trip to Britain and the general approval of his relaxed style and the flexibility of his schedule. The Soviet diplomatic community, however, must have approved of it, since they did not like Gromyko's style and his insistence on the strict observance of protocol. The diplomats thought that they would have more freedom to enjoy life in the West when Gorbachev inherited the leadership. They must have been all the more disappointed when Gorbachev issued an order in 1985 that embassy receptions and parties should be alcohol-free.

Gorbachev's trip to Britain came to a sudden and unexpected end when a message was received that Ustinov had died. He flew to Moscow to attend the funeral, probably worrying about the change in the balance of power in the Politburo. His rival, Romanov, was chairman of the funeral commission and the main speaker at the funeral meeting at Red Square on December 24. Chernenko had been present the day before during the Politburo 'Guard of Honour' in the Hall of Columns, but it was too cold for him to be present outdoors at the final ceremony. Marshal Sergei Sokolov was appointed Minister of Defence. He had been commander of the Leningrad military district in the 1960s and it was therefore assumed that he was a supporter of Romanov. In fact, he was probably neutral. At 73 years of age, he was unlikely to inherit Ustinov's important political role of power-broker.

At the very end of 1984 Soviet television once again showed Chernenko to the public. On December 27 he awarded medals to a small group of prominent Soviet writers, making a brief speech.

1984 ended without any of George Orwell's predictions coming true. 'Big Brother', Orwell's high-tech version of Stalin, was nowhere to be seen. Neither Andropov, nor the weak and ailing Chernenko bore any resemblance to Big Brother. Soviet economic performance had deteriorated badly and the authority and popularity of the General Secretary had diminished with it. The country seemed to lack a leader, and to be functioning by sheer bureaucratic inertia. Chernenko was visibly dying and people began to wish that he would complete the process and be done with it. Instead they were forced to demonstrate yet again how fervently they supported him. The election campaign for the Supreme Soviets of the union republics began at the beginning of 1985. The Soviet electorate were given the opportunity of exercising their constitutional rights and showing how much they supported Konstantin Chernenko and appreciated his outstanding services to the Soviet people and the rest of the world.

Chernenko lived long enough to see this support in action, but he died soon after the election. As for Gorbachev, his real Soviet biography only began with Chernenko's death. If there was something which had occurred previously of which he was not very proud, he could be assured that it would now be written out of his biography by Soviet authors. But he was now also able to express his personality more freely and openly for the first time. Soviet leaders are no more free to speak their minds and act according to their true convictions and logic than are leaders anywhere. But they are a great deal more free to do so than their fellow countrymen and their colleagues. On March 10, 1985, Gorbachev became General Secretary of the Communist Party of the Soviet Union. The old and infirm had finally relinquished the future. But had a new era really begun?

TWO

Gorbachev in Power

8
Changing the Kremlin guard

As soon as Chernenko's funeral was over, Gorbachev must have realized that he was a popular leader, the favourite of domestic and foreign publics alike. In political systems like the United States, presidents can appear from nowhere. In the Soviet Union, where membership of the Politburo is the *sine qua non* for any potential General Secretary (a Party and not a government position), Gorbachev was clearly the best possible choice. The general public may not have known him well, but they knew enough to realize that he looked and spoke better than any of the other Politburo members. He had personality. He was a charismatic leader, a quality which was distinctly absent in Brezhnev, Andropov and Chernenko, none of whom benefited from television exposure or direct contact with the general public. The often mentioned secretive, closed style of Soviet government arises from the personality of the leader, rather than from the constitution. It is an acquired feature. Stalin, a short, unattractive man with a pitted complexion and Georgian accent so heavy that it sometimes made his Russian almost incomprehensible, never met his subjects face to face. Brezhnev was incapable of making even a short, simple speech without a written text. Of the post-Lenin leaders, only Khrushchev preferred a more open style of leadership and this was later thought of as an anomaly, rather than a permissible alternative.

Gorbachev must always have known that he could benefit from a more populist style, but he could not risk it before 1985. An *obkom* or *kraikom* secretary can afford to be a populist, but not a Central Committee secretary for agriculture, and particularly not when agriculture is doing badly. If he had travelled too much or spoken too often during his agriculture secretaryship, the poor performance of agriculture would have been attributed more directly to his administration rather than collectively to the Politburo and government. But as the newly elected General Secretary, Gorbachev could now afford to adopt a populist style. Chernenko's short and unremarkable tenure in office provided a perfect foil for Gorbachev. If he had inherited his position directly from Andropov, the general public would probably not have been as impressed by the contrast. Andropov remained an enigmatic figure to the end: a sophisticated intellectual who managed to present even KGB work as a romantic occupation. There was no Gorbachev enigma. He had to demonstrate his competence and good qualifications for the job and could not rely on a superman legend.

It was not only that he had inherited many difficult problems. His power base within the Central Committee was even narrower than the one which made Chernenko's emergence possible in 1984. The 'law of diminishing general secretaries' is the other side of the coin of Politburo consensus.[1] Stalin had put himself well above the Politburo. Khrushchev was forced to take account of the Politburo's opinion, but he did not always have to follow the advice of the majority. He knew that he could sometimes overrule Politburo decisions and get away with it, because he had the support of the Central Committee. In the end this method proved to be unsafe and he was forced to resign. As a result, Brezhnev could never afford to fight a majority decision. Gorbachev was entirely dependent on the Politburo, but he had a better opportunity than his immediate predecessors to make substantial changes in its composition. The Politburo had lost six members since 1982 (Suslov, Kirilenko, Brezhnev, Pel'she, Andropov, Ustinov, Chernenko) and only two new members had joined it in that period (Aliyev and Solomentsev). The vacancies were manifest. Since the Politburo is the top organ of power in the country and has to discuss and approve all major decrees and decisions in the political, economic, military, international, social, educational and other fields of activity, and since these decisions have become increasingly complex and sophisticated, Politburo membership has grown. In the Stalin period, and more particularly during Brezhnev's rule, it developed into an institution in which the major professional and economic interests had to be represented by the heads of the appropriate fields of endeavour.

Moreover, it had to reflect the multinational character of the Soviet Union by including some of the Party secretaries of the union republics at either candidate or full membership level. If this change had not taken place, it would have lost its role as the real government of the Soviet Union.

According to Party doctrine, the Politburo acts as a generator of ideas, but its role is not limited to this. It is more or less accepted in the West that the Politburo is 'the institutional apex of the Soviet political structure'.[2] The very fact that it now only had ten members and that it therefore failed to represent some traditional power or bureaucratic interests meant that it was functioning less efficiently as a decision-making system and that the solution of urgent problems had been delayed. The regular Central Committee Plenum offered an opportunity to restore its size. The changes which were made were predictable.

Gorbachev had kept a low profile before the Plenum. Only a short list of names of the foreign leaders who had sent congratulatory telegrams was published in the newspapers.[3] The very enthusiastic Western newspaper comments were not mentioned in the Soviet press, although they were numerous and extremely positive. Gorbachev was called, for example, a 'bright, incisive, brisk-mannered man',[4] with 'high intelligence, considerable organizational abilities, political acumen'.[5] When the newly elected Supreme Soviet of the Russian Federation met, only Gorbachev and Gromyko occupied the seats in the front Politburo bench. Tikhonov was absent, probably ill. He was expected to resign within a few weeks, when he celebrated his 80th birthday. But the problem of his replacement had probably not been sorted out, because his birthday came and went without any announcement of retirement. There were some signs that Gorbachev had resumed Andropov's 'housecleaning' operation, but it was confined to local officials whose fate could be decided at the level of regular Secretariat meetings. A few ministerial appointments were made which had probably been agreed previously. Although there were rumours that Romanov was in trouble, he led a delegation from the Soviet Communist Party to the XIIIth Congress of the Hungarian Communist Party at the end of March. Soviet newspapers gave more prominence to his speech at the congress than to that of Kadar, the Hungarian leader.[6] He made favourable comments about the Hungarian economy and this must have reflected the general opinion of the Politburo. The Hungarian press considered this an official endorsement of the Hungarian model. The annual Lenin birthday speech on April 22, made by Aliyev, was the first important policy speech since the succession. As was to be expected, Aliyev mentioned Gorbachev as a true Party leader, by implication on a par with Lenin. His critical comments about negative tendencies and economic problems related entirely to the Brezhnev and Chernenko periods. 1983 had been a year in which progress had significantly accelerated, but the momentum had unfortunately not been preserved in 1984 and the first quarter of 1985.[7]

The Central Committee Plenum took place on the day after the speech. In addition to deciding on the date for the XXVIIth Party Congress, the Central Committee promoted Chebrikov, Ligachev and Ryzhkov to full membership of the Politburo. The latter two men had not served the traditional candidate membership period. Marshal Sokolov became a candidate member of the Politburo and Viktor Nikonov was made Central Committee secretary for agriculture. It was assumed in the Western press that these appointments increased Gorbachev's personal authority. It was even suggested that Gorbachev now had 'more power than anyone since Stalin',[8] and that he had 'surrounded himself with reformers of the Andropovian school'.[9] It is true that the three new Politburo members were all Andropov men and that they had supported Gorbachev in the crucial period of the succession. But they were independent figures, and their promotion did not mean that Gorbachev had sole power. This was the beginning of his collective leadership and the formation of a reliable team, rather than a sign that he had imposed his own individual rule. Moreover, there was nothing yet to suggest that these men were really reform-minded. On the contrary, they were all rather orthodox and could even be called hard-liners. It was Andropov who had originally intended promoting Ligachev, Chebrikov and Ryzhkov to full Politburo membership and there was no reason to suppose that they would accept Gorbachev's superiority unquestioningly in the way they might have accepted Andropov's authority. In the closed circle of the Politburo they were likely to treat him as an equal, rather than as the boss. It was he who had to thank them for their support, not they who were beholden to him for their promotion. They were all three older than Gorbachev and they had wider Party and state experience.

After the April Plenum Ligachev assumed the position of second-in-command and took on the ideological portfolio. He became the Party watchdog, responsible for the final version of the Party programme and statutes and the organizational work for the Congress. He was known to be uncompromising, with a strong character and unfaltering convictions, and not reluctant to express his views. During and after Andropov's anti-corruption campaign he had often clashed with higher ranking *obkom* and republican secretaries like Shcherbitsky, Kunayev or Grishin on the question of dismissing corrupt officials in their domains. He tried, for example, to expel some Moscow *raikom* secretaries who were linked with corruption cases in trade, the allocation of apartments, etc. without getting Grishin's permission.

At this point Ligachev was 65 years old and had joined the Party during the war in 1944. A graduate of the Moscow Aviation Engineering Institute, he later attended the Higher Party School of the Central Committee. After the war he had worked as an engineer at the Novosibirsk Aviation Plant. In the early 1950s he became a professional Komsomol worker, going up through the ranks of the Novosibirsk Komsomol *obkom*. He then became secretary of the Party *gorkom* in Novosibirsk, transferring into the state system to become chairman of the *ispolkom* from 1955–8 and back again to the position of secretary of the Novosibirsk *obkom*. Although the Novosibirsk region is no larger than Stavropol *krai*, it has a larger population. The city is a very important industrial and research centre, with a population of over 1 million. In 1961 Ligachev was transferred to Moscow to work in the Central Committee apparatus, first in the propaganda department and then in the department of Party organs. At this stage he was far more prominent than Gorbachev, who was still head of the Party organs section of Stavropol *kraikom*. He fell out of favour in 1965, when Brezhnev reorganized the Party central apparatus. Kapitonov, who had been dismissed from his position as Moscow *gorkom* secretary and sent to Ivanovo region by Khrushchev a few years previously, was brought back by Brezhnev and put in charge of the department of Party organs in 1965. He transferred Ligachev back to Siberia, this time as first secretary of Tomsk region, a smaller and much less important region than Novosibirsk. Here Ligachev spent 18 years. He was known as a tough but popular and accessible leader. Although his record was very good, he probably never expected to be promoted again. When Andropov brought him back to Moscow in 1983, Kapitonov was a secretary of the Central Committee and head of the enlarged department of Party organs. He and Ligachev clearly would find it difficult to co-operate, so Kapitonov was transferred from this crucial department to head the department of light industry, probably to pave the way to his eventual retirement. As a seasoned Party veteran, Ligachev probably considered some of his Moscow colleagues, including Gorbachev, too soft and too willing to compromise. Although he was a good ally in the battle against corruption and incompetence, he could hardly be considered a Gorbachev client.

Ryzhkov was only two years older than Gorbachev, but he also had more administrative experience. His career had been extremely successful. A graduate of the Ural Polytechnic Institute in Sverdlovsk, he rose from being head of a brigade to being an engineer, then Chief Engineer and finally General Director of the Ural Machine Construction Plant, known as *Uralmash*, the largest industrial plant in the Soviet Union. As General Director from 1970–5 he transformed *Uralmash* into the key centre of Soviet heavy industry. It became a conglomerate of many plants which produced thousands of different items, from heavy turbines to missile parts and high technology. In 1975 he was appointed First Deputy Minister of Heavy and Transport Machine Building. In 1979 he became First Deputy Chairman of Gosplan, the state planning committee. Andropov made him a Central Committee secretary in 1982. When he joined the Politburo, he immediately became the most knowledgeable technocrat in that body. An undisputed authority in his field, he knew the strong and weak points of Soviet industry better than any of the long-standing Politburo members. Gorbachev had little industrial experience. His first visit to a big industrial plant seems to have been made in 1985, during the election campaign for the Supreme Soviet of the RSFSR, when he went to a plant in his Moscow Kiev electoral district. It was unlikely that Ryzhkov would need his advice about industrial and economic problems. Once Ryzhkov became a Politburo member, he was the strongest contender for the position of Prime Minister. Neither Vorotnikov nor Aliyev had his range of industrial experience and knowledge. They were good administrators, but could not really be called technocrats. Ryzhkov had proved himself on the shop floor, rather than in Party supervision. Like Ligachev, he could be considered Gorbachev's ally, but not his client.

The 62-year-old Chebrikov was also an independent figure. Promotion to full membership of the Politburo gave him the same kind of independence that Andropov had achieved in 1973. When the head of the security apparatus is not a full member of the Politburo, he is more likely to serve the General Secretary than the Party as a whole. Politburo promotion, however, makes the Chairman of the KGB answerable to the Politburo or Central Committee, not to the General Secretary. Thus Chebrikov's promotion reduced his dependence on Gorbachev. In any case, he had originally been promoted by Brezhnev, not Andropov, and this too made him more independent. He was the only Politburo member with genuine military experience, having joined the army as a private in 1941. By 1946 he was a major and commander of a battalion and had taken part in the fighting on many fronts both during the retreat of 1941–2 and during the offensive in 1943–5, including the famous battle for Stalingrad. After the war he graduated from the Dnepropetrovsk Metallurgical Institute (the institute which has provided the Soviet Union with so many of its leaders, including Brezhnev, Tikhonov and Shchelokov). When Andropov was made Chairman of the KGB in 1967, Chebrikov was promoted from second secretary of the Dnepropetrovsk *obkom* (Brezhnev's power base) to Moscow, to become head of the KGB cadre department. This decision was presumably made by Brezhnev. Brezhnev appointed Chebrikov, Tsinev (also from Dnepropetrovsk and a graduate of the same institute) and Semyon Tsvigun, a KGB man from Moldavia (another of Brezhnev's power bases), deputy chairmen of the KGB, probably to ensure that the KGB did not work against him. The effect was that these three men became rivals. Chebrikov, the youngest of the three, probably moved closer to Andropov.

When Andropov became Central Committee secretary in 1982, a new KGB chief, Vitalii Fedorchuk, was unexpectedly brought in from the Ukraine. Fedorchuk was not even a member of the Central Committee and in retrospect his appointment seems to have been an attempt to neutralize the KGB in the power struggle which was taking place over Brezhnev's successor. The fact that

Andropov later moved Fedorchuk to the Ministry of Internal Affairs to replace Shchelokov and promoted Chebrikov to Chairman of the KGB and candidate member of the Politburo suggests that Chebrikov was loyal to him. He had always been more of a political figure in the KGB, like Andropov himself and unlike Tsvigun and Tsinev, who were KGB professionals (both had moved into the KGB from the army). Tsvigun had been head of the KGB in Azerbaijan from 1963–7, where he had made a bright, ambitious KGB professional, Geidar Aliyev, his first deputy. This connection could not be ignored by either Andropov or Gorbachev. There was nothing in Chebrikov's background to suggest that he might be a reformer or that he was an intellectual. His political experience outside of the KGB had not been very wide.

It is thought to have been Chebrikov who blocked Grishin's candidature for the post of General Secretary during the crucial Politburo meeting on March 10. Rumours circulated later (probably deliberately leaked) that Chebrikov had played the 'Beria card' against Grishin, effectively silencing him. As so often with Kremlin rumours since 1981, the story seemed credible. It involved Grishin's son, who was about 40 years old and married to Marta Gal'perina, the daughter of Lyalya Gal'perina, well known in Moscow high society. Grishin's son, a graduate of the Moscow Institute of International Relations, worked in one of the research institutes of the international department of the Central Committee. Marta, an economics graduate from Moscow State University, worked in the Ministry of Foreign Trade. As a young and pretty schoolgirl her mother, Lyalya Gal'perina, had been one of Beria's many mistresses in the 1940s. She was said to have been his favourite girlfriend. Their affair was not kept secret and when Lyalya's daughter, Marta, was born in 1950, Beria is said not have objected to her patronymic being known as Lavrentyevna (from Lavrentii, Beria's name). Marta and Grishin's son were married in the early 1970s and they had two children.

But it was not only the fact that his daughter-in-law's father was Beria that compromised Grishin. Lyalya's later love life was infamous. One of her lovers was said to have been the famous underground currency speculator, Rokotov, who had been arrested and executed in 1962 (it was his case which had prompted Khrushchev to introduce a controversial article into the

Penal Code which provided for the death penalty in the case of serious economic crime). In April 1985 Grishin's son applied for a divorce, and Grishin's official connection with Beria and with Lyalya seemed to be over. In fact, the divorce merely fuelled the rumours. In any case, no divorce could change the fact that Beria was the other grandfather of Grishin's grandchildren.

Marta Lavrentyevna and Grishin's son had been members of the 'golden youth', a group of Kremlin children who considered themselves above the law. It is quite possible that Grishin himself knew very little of what went on in this group and that his Politburo colleagues did not care to dig too deeply. But Andropov was collecting dossiers on certain figures. All Beria's connections must certainly have been well known within Chebrikov's cadre section of the KGB. Andropov's relations with Grishin had been strained since the disastrous fire in the hotel Rossiya in 1980. Grishin and the Moscow Soviet supported the view that the fire had been caused by sabotage, while the KGB believed that the causes were an electrical fault, the violation of a number of safety regulations and the excessive use of inflammable plastic materials in the construction of the hotel. There were probably other black marks against Grishin and his political life was drawing to a close. He was unlikely to be co-operative, but there was no hurry to remove him from the Politburo. Romanov had to be dealt with first.

Of the other recent promotions, Marshal Sokolov's owed nothing to Gorbachev. It arose entirely from Sokolov's previous position. But he was already 74 years old and would therefore probably not be Minister of Defence for very long.

The only promotion that was entirely Gorbachev's choice (but still not his client) was that of his own successor in agriculture, Viktor Nikonov, the new Central Committee secretary for agriculture. The appointment presented a great problem. There were very few Central Committee members who were qualified for this extremely difficult job. The fragmentation of the agro-industrial complex among 13 ministries and state committees meant that most of the ministers and chairmen of these bodies were too specialized. In any case, many agricultural ministries had become scapegoats and were singled out for sharp criticism in Gorbachev's speeches. Ivan Bodyl, who was the deputy prime minister in charge of overall co-ordination of agriculture in the government system, was a client of Brezhnev and Chernenko. Gorbachev appeared to be waiting for the opportunity to retire him (this was done in May). The promotion of Mesyats, USSR Minister of Agriculture, was not considered appropriate and his political future depended upon the results of the 1985 harvest. It was difficult to give the agricultural secretaryship to a successful *obkom* or *kraikom* secretary, since there were no really successful agricultural regions in 1984. Six years of poor harvests had depleted not only the state reserves of food, but also the availability of good agricultural administrators at the national level. The traditional hierarchy of appointments made it impossible to offer such a high position to a young expert from the academic sector or from the lower echelons of the Party. It was thought that Gorbachev wanted to promote G. P. Razumovsky, who had become first secretary of the Krasnodar *krai* after Vorotnikov's short tenure of office. Previously chairman of the Krasnodar *ispolkom* and head of the *krai* agro-industrial council, Razumovsky had been Gorbachev's ally against Medunov. But he was neither a member nor a candidate member of the Central Committee and this made it impossible to make him Central Committee secretary. He may well be promoted rapidly after the Party Congress in 1986, though in May he was moved to Moscow to head the department of the Party organs vacated by Ligachev.

In the meantime, Nikonov became Central Committee secretary for agriculture. 56 years old, he is an agronomist by training, with eight years of practical experience in agriculture, including the directorship of a MTS. When the MTS were abolished in 1958 (this decision was one of Khrushchev's most serious errors), he moved into the Party system. In 1979, when he was first secretary of the Mariisky *obkom* in the central part of the RSFSR, Gorbachev selected him to head the newly created agro-chemical network, *Soyuzselkhozkhimiya*. The task of the network was to improve the use of organic and mineral fertilizers in agriculture. As the head of this large organization, Nikonov was also a deputy minister of agriculture of the USSR. In 1983 he was appointed Minister of Agriculture of the RSFSR. Although this was not obvious to outsiders, it was a demotion. The all-Union *Soyuzselkhozkhimiya* disposes of much larger funds (about 7–8 billion roubles per annum) than the Ministry of Agriculture of the RSFSR. Moreover, the director of *Soyuzselkhozkhimiya* is expected to be a member of the Central Committee, whereas this is not necessarily the case for ministers of the RSFSR. *Soyuzselkhozkhimiya* had failed to make the expected impact on crop yields and agricultural performance, despite a significant increase in the production of mineral fertilizers in 1979–83. Nikonov is probably not really strong enough to supervise agriculture in the Soviet Union as a whole, although professionally he is better qualified for the job of Central Committee secretary for agriculture than Gorbachev had been in 1978. He seems unlikely to be a reformer. His articles in the agricultural press in 1980–84 about the problems of Soviet agriculture are uncritical and suggest the traditional stereotypes of a hardline believer in the advantages of 'socialist agriculture'. While he seems to lack the qualities to make Soviet agriculture successful in the near future, he can be relied upon to ensure that the failures of 1979–84 do not feature prominently in any report in a way that might embarrass Gorbachev. He will, for example, probably not insist upon a serious discussion of agriculture at the Party Congress in 1986.

The time had come to deal with Romanov. The beginning of the anti-alcohol campaign was a good excuse to consider the matter at the very highest level. He was known to be a heavy drinker (this had not been a liability during the Brezhnev era). In Hungary in March he had often been drunk at official dinners. At the beginning of May he was mentioned amongst the various Politburo members who participated in the many events celebrating the 40th anniversary of the end of the war. He was in his usual place on the mausoleum during the May Day parade, standing between Grishin and Solomentsev.[10] On this occasion it became apparent that Ligachev was now more prominent than both Aliyev and Vorotnikov. The Party and state leaders stood in exactly the same order for the victory parade on Red Square on November 9 (the official anniversary of the end of the war is a day later in the Soviet Union than in the West).[11] This meant that Romanov was still fifth in the Party hierarchy. But as soon as the celebrations were over, the 'housecleaning' operation resumed.

The tough new anti-alcohol laws were published on Friday, May 17. The newspapers reported Gorbachev's departure for an inspection tour of Leningrad. Since Leningrad was still considered Romanov's domain, many observers found it strange that he was not amongst the Politburo members who accompanied him to the airport or met him in Leningrad. Gorbachev's speech to the Leningrad Party active on May 17 was broadcast on television (regular programmes were cancelled for the occasion). It was an impressive speech, the best Gorbachev had made to date. The official abbreviated version published in the newspapers did not do it justice. The version published later in *Kommunist* was more authentic, although there were still some omissions.[12] Only those people who followed the trip on television or who were there personally realized that Gorbachev's comments were directed against Romanov. He made ironic comments, for example, about officials who travelled in motorcades with more pomp and ceremony than the Tsars would have permitted themselves. Romanov was known to be the only leader apart from Brezhnev who had instructed the police to clear the streets of traffic when his driver drove him at very high speed, for example, through the streets of Leningrad to the Smolny Institute (Lenin's headquarters in October 1917 and now the *obkom* residence). His motorcade, with its noisy sirens, had long been a source of irritation to the Leningrad public. Brezhnev's motorcade had travelled in the same way from his apartment on Kutuzovsky Prospekt to the Kremlin, but the journey was shorter. Gorbachev was also driven to the Kremlin in an official ZIL, but without a motorcade and through normal traffic.

After Gorbachev's Leningrad trip, Romanov disappeared from public view. He was said to have gone on 'holiday' to his *dacha* not far from Sochi. His absence from the Central Committee conference on the acceleration of scientific and technical progress on June 11–12 was particularly noticeable, because the subject was relevant to his Politburo responsibilities.[13] The other 12 members of the Politburo were all present to discuss Gorbachev's key report. It seemed clear that a decision had already been made about Romanov by the Politburo and that it would be made public after it had been approved by the regular Central Committee Plenum at the beginning of July. This proved to be the case. Romanov's fall was confirmed on July 1, when it was reported that his request to be relieved of his duties for health reasons had been accepted.[14] He retired on a pension, but without honour or thanks. He was only 62 years old and, apart from his heavy drinking, he was not known to suffer from any health problems. The Plenum also promoted Shevarnadze to full Politburo membership and Boris Yel'tsin and Lev Zaikov secretaries of the Central Committee. Yel'tsin, a graduate of the Ural Polytechnic Institute and first secretary of Sverdlovsk *obkom*, was apparently Ryzhkov's protege and he was to take over supervision of heavy and military industry. Zaikov, also an engineer, had been Gorbachev's choice for Romanov's job in Leningrad in 1983. His background in Leningrad research and industry indicated that he would probably take responsibility for technological reconstruction.

Romanov's fall came as no surprise to Western observers or to people in the Soviet Union who knew or had heard about him. It is probable that many people in Leningrad greeted the news with satisfaction. But the Supreme Soviet session on July 2 produced more serious news, particularly for diplomatic circles. Gromyko was elected Chairman of the Presidium of the Supreme Soviet and he was replaced as Foreign Minister by Eduard Shevarnadze. Gromyko's new position was not a sign that he had been 'kicked upstairs', as some commentators suggested. He was approaching 76 years of age and the role of an active, travelling Foreign Minister had become too arduous. His great experience had made him indispensable to Andropov and Chernenko, neither of whom were well enough to travel abroad. With a young and energetic new General Secretary who wanted to practice an active, personal diplomacy, Gromyko's role became less important. The position of Chairman of the Presidium of the Supreme Soviet was the most suitable role to offer him and the general public would approve of the move. The Soviet public has always, accurately in terms of the distribution of power in the Soviet system, treated the position of Chairman of the Presidium of the Supreme Soviet as a more important position than that of Foreign Minister. Moreover, it can be and has been a position for life. After Chernenko's death, decrees of the Presidium had been signed by Vasilii Kuznetsov, who had been Gromyko's first deputy in the Ministry of Foreign Affairs for 22 years, from 1955 to 1977. He was a candidate member of the Politburo and he and his old friend, Gromyko, would now be able to advise the Politburo on foreign affairs and diplomatic problems.

Gorbachev could not have forgotten the arguments he had made in 1984 in favour of combining the post of General Secretary with that of Chairman of the Presidium of the Supreme Soviet. But he must also have known that the combination was absurd and unconstitutional. The absurdity lay in the fact that the same person who, as General Secretary, had to sign all *proposals* and drafts of legislation before they were put by the Secretariat to the Presidium, then, in his capacity of Chairman of the Presidium, had to go to another building to sign the proposals again to make them laws or operative decrees. In nominating Gromyko for the position in July 1985, Gorbachev explained that the combination had been necessary in 1977–84 in an attempt to activate the role of the Supreme Soviet. But it had now become more important to activate the work of the Central Committee and the Politburo. It would therefore be more rational to give the General Secretary the opportunity to concentrate his attention on the organization of the work of the central Party organs, the co-ordination of the efforts of all Party, state and social organizations with the aim of successfully implementing the contemplated course of policy'.[15] Gorbachev became one of the members of the Presidium of the Supreme Soviet, the traditional governmental position of the General Secretary for the 40 years preceding 1977.

Everybody expected that Tikhonov would finally retire at this session. He was 80 years old and too infirm to cope with the 'new tasks' and 'new methods' which Gorbachev had indicated would be the first priority of both Party and government. The election of Shevarnadze as Foreign Minister, however, indicated that the decision about Tikhonov's successor had once again been postponed. It also meant that Aliyev stood little chance of becoming Prime Minister. The Russian public greeted Shevarnadze's promotion with some disappointment: there was a feeling that the Foreign Minister should be Russian, not Georgian. It was unlikely that a second representative of an ethnic minority would be promoted to the post of Prime Minister. Apart from pure ethnic prejudice and the fact that Shevarnadze spoke Russian with a Georgian accent, he seemed poorly qualified for his new job. He had been a successful ruler of Georgia, but his background was in the police, not in diplomacy. He had graduated from the Teacher Training Institute in the small Georgian town of Kutaisi. After a period of Komsomol and Party work, he had become Georgian Minister of Internal Affairs.

Like Aliyev in Azerbaijan in 1969, Shevarnadze was given full control over the local Party and state system in 1972. These moves represented plans organized in Moscow to eradicate chronic local corruption. Both Aliyev and Shevarnadze used tough methods when necessary, including repression. They were both successful in improving the economic and general situation in their republics. In terms of economic performance, Azerbaijan and Georgia became the leading constituent republics. The black market economy was reduced and the activity of the local 'mafia' became less visible. However, both considered Brezhnev to be their benefactor and they competed in the praises they lavished on him in their speeches at the 1976 and 1981 Party Congresses and at Party Plenums. Although they were good friends, they were also rivals. They were both very clever, humorous and entertaining. Both came from proud, ancient nations of the Caucasus. The Azerbaijanis were Moslem and the Georgians had adopted Christianity in the 5th century, more than 400 years before Russia became Christian.

Although there are many people like me who know and like the distinctive Georgian traditions (I was born in Tbilisi, lived there in 1941–3 and my mother lived there until her death in 1963), there are some intellectual circles in Moscow who have never forgiven the Georgians for the fact that both Stalin and Beria were Georgian. As a result, Shevarnadze's promotion to Minister of Foreign Affairs was not met with universal enthusiasm in Moscow. It had to be admitted, though, that there were no other members or candidate members of the Politburo or senior government officials who seemed better suited. His speeches at Supreme Soviet sessions are often the only ones worth reading; and his speeches in Georgia are even more interesting. He has proved himself to be both bright and flexible, and to be an excellent advocate of the Soviet system. His appointment does not mean that Gorbachev wanted an inexperienced man so that his own influence over foreign affairs would be dominant. If that had been the case, one of Gromyko's deputies could have filled the job. Gromyko was Minister of Foreign Affairs for 16 years before he became a member of the Politburo in 1973. In those years he was very dependent on the General Secretary. Once he became a Politburo member, he was much more independent. The fact that Shevarnadze was elevated to Politburo membership before being made Foreign Minister indicates that the Central Committee wanted a Foreign Minister with some power and independence. It is more than likely that Western observers have underestimated his abilities and his influence in the Soviet system.

Although Tikhonov was not replaced at the July session of the Supreme Soviet, the reorganization of the rest of the government which had been going on since well before the session continued. More than 10 ministers had been replaced before July, retired because of advancing age or dismissed because of the poor performance of their respective branches of industry. The pace of this shake-up increased in July. On July 17 alone, for example, *Izvestiya* reported the appointment of three new ministers, two of industrial ministries and the third as the new Minister of Higher Education. In the majority of cases, the new ministers had previously been deputy ministers or ministers of the RSFSR and they were between 53 and 62 years of age. After consolidating his power at the April Plenum, Gorbachev had managed to replace more ministers by the summer than Andropov had during the entire 15 months of his tenure.

It became clear that Tikhonov was not taking an active part in the work of the government, although he was still Prime Minister. This probably meant that there was some disagreement within the Politburo or the Central Committee about his successor. Aliyev was certainly out of the race. At the July session of the Supreme Soviet, he sat in the third row of Politburo seats, while Vorotnikov and Ryzhkov sat together in front of him. They were the chief rivals for the top government position and they probably each had supporters in the Politburo and Central Committee. It is likely that the higher officials in the Council of Ministers would have been in favour of Vorotnikov, since he was a more traditional administrator with two years of experience as Chairman of the RSFSR Council of Ministers. Like Ryzhkov, he was more of a technocrat than a bureaucrat. A graduate of the Kuibyshev Aviation Institute, he had worked in industry until 1960. His later posts included work in the Kuibyshev *ispolkom* and *obkom* and he had served for five years as first secretary of Voronezh *obkom*, an important agricultural and industrial region. He also had considerable governmental experience and had spent four years as Soviet ambassador in Cuba. He was a modest, quiet man and foreign diplomats and journalists who met and talked to him were impressed by his competence and business-like attitude. These were the qualities which had attracted Andropov, who had seemed to want to make him Prime Minister.

Ryzhkov probably had the brighter personality, but he was unpredictable and rather authoritarian. He was known to be strict and sharp in his treatment of subordinates and he showed signs of enjoying power. In the final analysis, it was probably his past industrial success which tipped the balance in his favour. In Vorotnikov's two years as Prime Minister of the RSFSR, there had not been much economic improvement. The premiership of the USSR would be an even more difficult job. Gorbachev announced his decision unexpectedly. The delay in replacing Tikhonov had led to rumours that Gorbachev wanted to combine the premiership with being General Secretary. If there is any truth in this, it is clear that his Politburo colleagues would not have supported the ambition.

Tikhonov's resignation was finally announced on September 27 at a meeting of the Presidium of the Supreme Soviet. According to the general press and the report in the Supreme Soviet *Vedomosti*, Gromyko informed the Presidium that Tikhonov had sent a letter of resignation addressed to Gorbachev personally.[16] The letter stated that his health had deteriorated and that his doctors insisted on his retirement. His resignation was accepted and Gorbachev, on behalf of the Politburo, nominated Ryzhkov as the new Chairman of the Council of Ministers. The Presidium passed the appropriate decree. Vorotnikov was left with his Russian Federation and Aliyev with the job of improving Soviet transport of all types. Only time will tell whether Ryzhkov was the best choice or merely a gamble.

The time had also come to replace Nikolai Baibakov, Chairman of Gosplan since 1965. He was retired on a pension at the age of 74 and Nikolai Talyzin, a deputy prime minister, took over Gosplan. At a Central Committee Plenum on 15 October 1985 Talyzin was elected candidate member of the Politburo. This upgraded the post of Gosplan Chairman. The Gorbachev team seemed to be complete. Gorbachev was indisputably in command. His second-in-command was Ligachev. As Chairman of the Council of Ministers, Ryzhkov occupied the second most important post in the country. Gromyko, Chairman of the Presidium of the Supreme Soviet, was the constitutional head of state. The government apparatus had been rejuvenated and a modest purge had occurred in regional Party organizations. It seemed inevitable that there would be a radical rejuvenation of the Central

Committee at the XXVIIth Party Congress in February 1986.

It began to look as if Gorbachev had established a meritocracy and that the old system of patron–client relationships had ended. However, at the beginning of November the Presidium of the Supreme Soviet passed a decree about another change in the government. Vsevolod Murakhovsky was appointed a first deputy chairman of the Council of Ministers.[17] Until July there had been three first deputy chairmen, Aliyev, Gromyko and Arkhipov (there were a further 12 ordinary deputy chairmen). Because the Soviet government is so large, it is established practice that the first deputy chairmen can report direct to the Politburo, bypassing the Prime Minister and the Council of Ministers. It is also not unusual for first deputy chairmen to be members of the Politburo (both Aliyev and Gromyko, for example, were both first deputies and Politburo members). When Gromyko became Chairman of the Presidium, only two first deputy chairmen remained, and one of them, Arkhipov, was 78 and too old for active work. There was clearly a pressing need for another first deputy. Nonetheless, Murakhovsky's promotion was remarkably rapid. He had spent his entire life in Stavropol *krai* and had no experience of government work. Arkhipov was mainly in charge of Soviet external economic relations and Murakhovsky did not seem to have the expertise to take over these responsibilities. Gromyko's previous responsibilities as first deputy are unclear. He was probably given the position in 1983 so that he could act as Andropov's trusted aide in the government. Presumably this is one of the roles that Murakhovsky will fulfil for Gorbachev. He has also been appointed chairman of the new agro-industrial committee which has been formed to manage the five newly merged agricultural and food supply ministries and the State Committee which includes *Souzselkhoztechnika*.[18] Since as a first deputy prime minister he can report directly to the Politburo, this makes his position in agriculture senior to that of Nikonov's. It may be that his dramatic elevation is as good a choice as any. But it was a disappointing signal to give to the Party apparatus. It demonstrated either that Gorbachev did not, in fact, feel unassailable, or that he was not above the pleasure of giving high posts to personal friends.

At the end of 1985 it was Grishin's turn to step down – retired on pension, without thanks.

9
Getting the country moving

No previous Soviet leader had received so much immediate publicity or such an enthusiastic welcome from the general public. Gorbachev's popularity was closely linked to his energetic, charismatic, competent and obviously intelligent personality and with the new role of television rather than with the substance of his statements or speeches. There were both positive and negative aspects to this immediate acceptance of Gorbachev as leader. Many people began to feel that he could indeed be an inspiration and produce a psychological change comparable to the effect which great revolutionaries like Lenin, Trotsky or Mao Zedong had exercised on people. He might manage to unite people and inspire them to greater and more effective feats of work and endurance. Even the intellectual dissidents who understood that rising up through the Party apparatus, Central Committee and Politburo does not create liberals or revolutionaries enthusiastically expected rapid reforms. My brother, Roy, for example, was still hampered by a round-the-clock police watch, but he could talk to foreign journalists on the telephone. In March his favourable and positive comments about Gorbachev were published in the Western press.[1] A few months later, however, he could no longer offer his comments by telephone. The police watch had been removed, but instead the authorities disconnected his telephone in September. By then public opinion had begun to change.

Gorbachev's new style was popular, but some of his methods found less favour. Since they were often purely administrative, imposed from above without any discussion, they seemed coercive, disciplinarian and over-confident. To intellectuals this neither seemed to herald a new era, nor to be the liberalism they had been expecting. But Gorbachev's first decrees were not designed to impress intellectuals. They were aimed at improving a sick economy. The new style was perhaps designed to inspire, but 'shock treatment' was required to get rapid results. Many new resolutions, programmes and decrees were passed to prove what a bright outlook there was for the future.

The new style

While he was secretary for agriculture, Gorbachev showed little evidence of a populist style. Khrushchev's habit of mixing with the public was not popular with Brezhnev and his men. Andropov had begun to restore the practice of meeting ordinary people face-to-face, but his poor health soon made this impossible. Chernenko's meetings with the public were few, artificial and confined to political rallies. Gorbachev sought a middle way, not as direct and spontaneous as Khrushchev, and not as official as Brezhnev. During tours and visits, for example, he frequently diverged from his official programme.

His first excursion into real life in the Proletarskii district of Moscow in April produced an unexpected heated discussion. He visited plants, a local supermarket, a school and a hospital. Newspapers did not report the discussion which took place in the hospital in detail, mentioning only that he spoke about: 'problems which concerned medical workers and patients. The questions of supplying modern technology and drugs to medical institutions and the salaries of doctors and middle and junior medical personnel were raised.'[2] In fact, the discussion in Hospital No. 53 was very blunt. The chief surgeon took the opportunity of explaining the plight of the Soviet health service to the new General Secretary. He was the only surgeon in that big hospital with sufficient experience to treat serious surgical cases, he pointed out. Of his two surgical colleagues, one was too young, the other too bad at his work. He often had to do more than one complicated operation a day. He was paid 5 roubles for each operation, less than he had to pay the taxi driver who drove him home if he worked too late to go by public transport. Nursing sisters, who earned between 60 and 80 roubles per month, complained about their low salaries. He also pointed out that Soviet hospitals did not have the modern drugs which were freely available in other countries and that there were serious shortages of equipment.

Gorbachev must have been impressed because medical salaries were discussed at a Politburo meeting a few weeks later as part of a more general consideration of the salaries of engineers, technologists and scientists.[3] However, the outcome was merely a modest salary increase for surgeons and personnel working in intensive care units (from 130 to 200 roubles per month, still less than the average salary of a factory worker with far fewer qualifications[4]). In reporting the increase Burenkov, Minister of Health, said that it was temporary and would be reconsidered each year together with productivity.[5]

During the summer Gorbachev made a number of trips and was shown on television talking animatedly to people in the street. Once again the substance of the conversations was not disclosed. Other aspects of the new Gorbachev style which received publicity in the Western press (for example, the prominence given to Raisa Gorbacheva and her rather expensive tastes) remained unknown to the Soviet public. When he was not on tour, Gorbachev started his day very early. He was driven to the Kremlin in a single ZIL without any escort and he worked late, often till after 10 pm. He is said, on occasion, to have dropped into the restaurant 'Moscow' for lunch, where he was served like an ordinary customer. When he visited the theatre he did not use the special government box, but sat in the stalls with Raisa. There must, of course, have been security men around, but they were invisible.

Under Stalin the practice had developed that young girls presented the Party leader with large bunches of flowers on every possible occasion. Gorbachev seems to have reprimanded the Leningrad officials when this happened. The girls were embarrassed, but Gorbachev told them to keep the flowers for themselves. After that the practice was dropped from official protocol.

During official meetings with foreign leaders Gorbachev has usually spoken for himself without recourse to his assistants (Brezhnev and Chernenko often required help with an appropriate reply). Sometimes his assistants (often Alexandrov-Agnetov, who had worked for Brezhnev, Andropov and Chernenko) did not have the opportunity to say a word. Gorbachev also seemed to be able to talk without a prepared text. This simpler, less pompous style seemed to be both designed to win him popular support, and intended to be a model for other Party officials. The gap which had developed between the public and the Party elite in the Brezhnev era had to be bridged.

It was a change designed for public relations, however. It did not denote democracy. Despite the intensive decision-making during Gorbachev's first year in office, most of the new decisions and decrees were imposed on the country without either proper democratic discussion or serious analysis. There was no democratization or liberalization. Gorbachev's measures resembled those of previous leaderships.

The battle against the bottle

Successive Soviet leaders have identified particular social evils and fought against them, often merely to establish their 'revolutionary credentials' and to increase their own personal power. In the late 1920s, Stalin's *bete noire* was private agriculture, and the *kulaks* or well-to-do peasants who practised it most successfully. He collectivized agriculture and eliminated the *kulaks*. Khrushchev's was the phenomenon of Stalinism, which he blamed for the country's economic problems. For Brezhnev, the main evil was Khrushchev's 'voluntarism' and administrative blunders. Andropov saw the corruption of Brezhnev's men and lack of discipline as the causes of decline. Gorbachev was more specific. His 'public enemy number one' was vodka and he began to attack it immediately.

The drive against vodka was long overdue, but the history of the problem has not been explained in proper perspective. Drinking had indeed become a national calamity in the Soviet Union, as it was in Tsarist Russia. But the current problem can hardly be linked with Tsarist policy. At the beginning of the First World War the sale of vodka was prohibited and the productivity of workers rose by 7 to 10 per cent immediately. The new Bolshevik government did not legalize vodka and there was no drink problem during Lenin's lifetime. The production and sale of vodka and other spirits were introduced in 1927 for economic reasons. Stalin made no bones about it in an interview with a foreign workers' delegation. It was important: '. . . to introduce the vodka state monopoly in order to obtain the necessary working capital for developing our industry with our own resources and thus to avoid going into foreign bondage'.[6] He claimed that it would be a temporary measure. In 1927 the state received about 500 million roubles of revenue from vodka alone, 10 per cent of the 5 billion rouble state budget. In later years alcohol revenues increased. By 1972, when the decree to reduce drinking was passed, total purchases of vodka were at the level of 26 billion roubles, on which the net profit for the state was 19.2 billion roubles. (The total state budget was 175 billion roubles that year).[7] Between 1970 and 1983 the state production of vodka and wine increased by 35 per cent and 97 per cent respectively and the retail price of alcohol almost doubled.[8] Alcohol sales had reached 15 per cent of the total trade turnover. The sale of low quality wine was particularly high. The Food Programme envisaged further increases in the production of alcoholic drinks and in 1983 new cheap brands of vodka (known in popular slang as 'Andropovka') became available. Since population growth from 1970 to 1983 was only 12 per cent, alcohol sales were clearly becoming an increasingly important proportion of the state budget.

There comes a point, however, when the economic benefits of alcohol revenues are outweighed by the costs of heavy drinking. Increasing crime, poor productivity, absenteeism, an increasing number of problem children of alcoholic parents, reduced life expectancy and alcohol-related health problems all create a heavy burden on the national economy. A high proportion of road accidents are caused by drunkenness. Unofficial calculations indicated that state sales of alcohol (about 50 billion roubles in 1984[9]) no longer even covered the cost of the negative effects of drinking. The general public health was at risk and the time had come to tackle the problem seriously.

Previous attempts to reduce drinking had been half-hearted and had not included any curb on the production or sale of vodka. This time a press campaign against alcoholism and drinking began in April 1985, after an anti-alcohol decision of the Politburo had been reported. On May 17 three separate decrees were published, one in the name of the Central Committee, another in the name of the Council of Ministers and a third, listing the punishments and fines, signed by the Presidium of the Supreme Soviet.[10] The minimum age for purchasing alcohol was raised from 18 to 21 and alcohol would no longer be sold in ordinary food stores. Wine shops would not be permitted to sell any alcohol before 2 pm. Restaurants could no longer serve alcohol (including beer) with lunch or before 2 pm. Stiff sentences were introduced for private stills. Being drunk in a public place became punishable by fines ranging from 50 to 100 roubles or by imprisonment, while supplying drink to young people made the offender liable to a labour camp sentence. The production of alcoholic drinks from fruit and berries was to cease by 1988.

The new policy met with initial approval. But by the end of 1985 the predictable consequences had begun to appear. In most food stores alcohol had been the only profitable commodity on sale. Once it was removed, profits fell and the salaries and bonuses of the staff were affected. It has taken a while to establish special liquor stores (they are popularly known as 'the last pockets of resistance') and each day there are long queues (called 'Gorbachev's nooses') outside them. People often wait for hours in these queues to buy as many bottles as possible. Social drinkers who merely wish to obtain wine for parties and celebrations have as much difficulty buying it as alcoholics do. The black market sale of vodka and wine has proliferated and prices are often double or triple the official price. At the end of the last agricultural season millions of tons of fruit were left to rot in the country. Wine and vodka distilleries which had been instructed to change to the production of fruit juices, *kvas* and other soft drinks did not have the equipment to do so. Many fruit and vineyard collective farms in Azerbaijan and Moldavia were almost bankrupt by the end of the summer. The production of vodka was reduced by 30 to 35 per cent but, as a result of the loss of revenue and shortage of cash, many groups of workers failed to receive their usual end-of-year bonus. The courts have been filled with people who have been charged under the new laws. The total number of drink-related cases is not known, but a new penal network has been set up to supplement the existing vast number of prison labour camps. Presumably the idea behind the new 'colony-settlements' is that it is counterproductive to mix drunkards with common criminals. The decree which established them on September 17, 1985 made it possible to transfer people who had been tried and sentenced for drink offences before September and female first offenders under other laws.[11]

Increasing the minimum 'drinking age' to 21 was not a popular measure. People of 18 can get married (in the south the age is 16 for women) and a wedding without drinking is almost unthinkable. Other difficulties included the problem of separating food stores from wine shops in small towns and villages which often only have one small shop. No doubt the restrictions will have beneficial effects on public health and on labour discipline. But as with any restrictive measure imposed from above which puts all the blame on the people rather than on the state and its previous policies, the anti-alcohol campaign has become unpopular and it has created a degree of social tension.

The economy: resolutions without reforms

Since October 1917 each new Soviet administration has tried its own specific model of economic development. The Brezhnev–Kosygin administration, for example, restored the centralized planning and administration which Khrushchev had dismantled. Initially they also tried to introduce some elements of competition and market-oriented production. This was reflected in the 1965 Economic Reform, which was predominantly Kosygin's idea (he was influenced by the arguments of Liberman, who had published articles in *Pravda* in the early 1960s, critical of Khrushchev's methods). However, by the 1970s Kosygin's methods of placing consumer welfare before heavy and military industry, reducing the expenses of an expansionist foreign policy, developing trade with the West, reducing Party influence in the economy and increasing the power, decision-making role and independence of government agencies and local managers had fallen victim to Brezhnev's consolidation of power. The role of the Party apparatus and its domination of the government system was enhanced. Under the premiership of Tikhonov the government role in the economy was further reduced and the result was poor management, unrealistic planning, economic disproportion, poor quality manufactured goods and a slow and inflexible decision-making system which could not respond effectively to the economic challenge from the West or to the revolution in high technology. The Soviet economy continued developing extensively. Many industrial plants became obsolete and high technology was far too dependent upon imports in exchange for natural resources.

Andropov seems to have been open minded about possible long-term solutions. His statement at the November 1982 Plenum that he had 'no ready-made prescriptions' opened the way to a wide range of economic experiments including some which may lead to serious reform.[12] He also maintained that 'the experience of fraternal countries' was worth taking into consideration and assessing,[13] seeming to suggest the Hungarian model, since it was the most successful of the East European economies. His fierce criticism of the performance of the Soviet economy had immediate effects. The growth of production increased to 5 per cent in the first three months of 1983 (from 2 per cent in 1982) and labour productivity rose by 5 per cent.[14] However, this momentum was lost completely under Chernenko. In the first three months of 1985 the growth rate fell to 2 per cent and productivity was only 1.5 per cent higher than for the same period in 1984.[15]

Gorbachev's first priority was to deal with the economic decline. In March he met several prominent economists for consultations and established special commissions to investigate various urgent current problems. Two main schools of thought have emerged about the remedies required.

The first school, represented by Academician Abel Aganbegyan, sees the solution in better planning, better co-ordination and better administration. Aganbegyan is not, as has sometimes been suggested, a supporter of 'market socialism', or a new NEP in the form of a version of the Hungarian model. Director of the Siberian Institute of Economy, he is the author of many books on the use of mathematics in the economy, the role of mathematical economics models in planning, management and efficiency, etc. The second school, less prominent and less 'official', believes that economic problems are caused by social relations between people, between workers and administration, lack of work satisfaction, the price and salary systems, etc. While the 'planners' are in favour of better organization and more power for administrators, the 'social economists' advocate some liberalization and the legalization of freelance activity in some sectors. They understand that competition and the market can provide a stimulus. The 'planners', on the other hand, believe that modern computer technology can take millions of variables into account and perfect the economic plans. Free competition and market-oriented production will, they think, create waste and redundancy.

An article by Aganbegyan was published in *Izvestiya* on March 25 and it became known that he had been invited to serve as Gorbachev's adviser. He quotes many examples of poor management and waste, but his prescriptions are hardly revolutionary: the replacement of poor administrators by better educated managers. He offers a computerized version of the command economy:

> This process can and must operate. If we can quickly convey up-to-date management experience to an efficient, forward-looking director, teach him modern methods of 'commanding' production based on the skilful application of economic levers, then we will be able to improve the situation in a collective of many thousands.[16]

Aganbegyan's ideas can easily be recognized in Gorbachev's speeches in 1985 and in the economic plans for the future. They do not, however, take into account the basic fault of the Soviet administrative system: the primacy of Party administration over governmental and managerial administration. Mathematical models (like models of the biological transfer of information or commands) are based on the assumption that the top level generator of instructions (like DNA in cells) has the highest level of fidelity and is almost error free. Errors can be made at the next level, where the original instructions are 'translated', but they will easily be recognized and repaired. In the Soviet system, however, the Politburo cannot serve as the store of necessary information. It is the political intermediary between sources of information (research system, commissions, government agencies) and the executive branches. It is far from error free. In fact, more mismanagement and poor co-ordination results from the decisions of the Politburo and Central Committee than from government decisions. A market-oriented economy is far more flexible and can establish optimal co-ordination. The losses caused by error are smaller and far easier to repair than the errors produced in a centralized economy. Nonetheless, a better centralized management, closer co-operation between the government and the Politburo and a reduction in the influence of the Party apparatus, would certainly improve the Soviet economy.

Gorbachev began his leadership with impressive energy and

activity, planning and passing more resolutions than any previous leader in a comparable time and showing more expertise knowledge of the economy. At the beginning of April he and other leaders met a selected group of industrial plant directors, *kolkhoz* chairmen and scientists at a one day conference. A report of the conference was published under the title 'Initiative, Organization, Efficiency'.[17] In his speech Gorbachev called for better work and discipline, equal efforts from workers, managers and scientists, better quality production with penalties for plants which did not come up to standard, and an economic mechanism which would make income dependent on the quality and profit of the product. A few days later a Central Committee and government decision was published about the development of a service industry for house repairs, and the construction of garages, sheds and co-operative apartment blocks until 1990 (it could be extended to the year 2000).[18] In future private citizens would be allowed to buy cement and other building materials. The implication was that private activity would be allowed, at least for house repairs and improvement. Unfortunately, the state plans for cement, timber and other building materials were not fulfilled in 1985 and therefore the free sale of these commodities (previously strictly reserved for distribution amongst ministries) was impossible.

In a report to the Central Committee Plenum on April 23, Gorbachev stressed that the main strategic factor in intensifying industry and agriculture was the acceleration of scientific and technical progress. He was frank in criticizing the poor development of Soviet science and technology, particularly in modernizing and improving existing equipment. Ageing plants and factories required radical rejuvenation, but appropriate new technologies had not emerged from the Soviet research establishment. The task had become urgent and science and technology had to find new solutions which matched Western technology. It was decided to convene a special All-Union Conference on scientific and technological progress and the Central Committee and Council of Ministers also passed a decree 'On Measures to Develop Local Industry in 1986–1990 and until the year 2000'.[19] Local industry was to increase its output by 30 per cent in 1990 and 80 per cent in 2000. The hope that small private businesses in the service sector would be legalized was not fulfilled. Local factories would be permitted to employ people to work at home, but only where this work represented a second occupation. Thus women who worked as full time secretaries, for example, would be allowed to supplement their incomes by doing piece work at home for local industries.

There was a sensation when Gorbachev permitted the full television broadcast of his speech in Leningrad on May 17. It was unannounced and unexpected. There was a great deal of talk about the speech later. There were some omissions when the text was published.[20] The editors of *Kommunist* clearly found some of his criticisms too sharp. The speech had been delivered spontaneously, without a prepared text. It was emotional and extremely impressive. The public, which had long since lost interest in the public appearances of Party leaders, was captivated. In criticizing the performance of Soviet industry, Gorbachev included Leningrad industry, considered the best in the country. He made a particularly strong point about the need for technical reconstruction and the introduction of high technology into all branches of the economy. The cheap resources in the Western part of the country had been almost exhausted. Relocating industry in Siberia was difficult and costly. The production cost of Siberian oil was almost double the production cost of oil ten years previously. There was an energy shortage, in part caused by obsolete methods of transforming oil and coal into electricity.

The Central Committee conference on the problems of accelerating scientific and technical progress was held on June 11 and 12 in Moscow. Gorbachev's report was titled 'The Fundamental Question of the Economic Policy of the CPSU'.[21] It was a good speech, containing many examples of the uneconomic use of resources, poor returns for investments, poor quality industrial and consumer goods, etc. He did not waste time describing successes and, unusually in a Soviet speech, he criticized particular ministers by name. His emphasis was on the computerization of the economy and the development and use of modern technologies. Scientific research should be given priority and the links between science and industry should be strengthened. Although the discussion which followed was interesting, none of the speakers from the scientific establishment commented on the need for liberalization if science and technology were to develop properly. Industry can, perhaps, react to 'commands' from above, but real scientific progress requires free, personal access to foreign scientific and technical achievements. If Soviet scientists continue working in comparative isolation from the world scientific community, Soviet science will continue to lag. No-one made this point. Gorbachev apparently believes that Soviet science can be self-reliant and that co-ordination can be restricted to the CMEA countries. In fact, it is well known that self-reliance causes repetition, copying, redundant infrastructures and the waste of resources, including human resources and permanent backwardness.

One of the important practical results of the conference was the discussion of the difficulties of recruiting talented young people into science and the falling number of students who wanted to be engineers and technologists. One of the main reasons was the erosion of incomes. Salary scales had not changed since 1951, when they were well above average. Slow inflation had reduced them. While the income of industrial workers depended on performance, that of engineers did not and their salaries were usually lower than those of the workers they supervised. A few weeks later the salaries of research scientists, engineers, technologists, construction engineers and other groups of scientific and technical personnel were increased by up to 50 per cent by a system of flexible 'bonuses' linked to productivity and efficiency.[22]

At the end of June Gorbachev visited Kiev and other parts of the Ukraine. He paid particular attention to the industrial centre of Dnepropetrovsk, one of Brezhnev's power bases. The pattern repeated his Leningrad trip and seemed to mark a feature of his style of leadership. At a meeting of metallurgical workers he made a long speech without mentioning Brezhnev's name. It was less spontaneous than his Leningrad speech and he covered more general international problems which were not directly relevant to the economy (the arms race, the Geneva talks, etc.).[23] He paid a similar visit to Byelorussia on July 10, where he made a speech in Minsk.[24] In August a decision of the Central Committee and Council of Ministers linked the salaries of workers and other employees of factories and plants with the quality of their production.[25] The price of production was graded according to the quality of the product. Products which did not meet certain standards over a number of years were to be removed from the production list.

In September Gorbachev visited the Tyumen region, the most important centre of oil production. His speech on this occasion about the problems of the oil industry was published in full.[26] It was clear from the television coverage of the trip that the debates were rather heated. Oil was the main priority of the Soviet economy and the shortage was inhibiting Soviet industry and the industries of Eastern Europe. The Tyumen and Tomsk oil fields were the largest in the country, but they were producing less and less and were unable to fulfil their plans. On the way back Gorbachev toured the centre of the virgin land area, meeting farmers and Party officials in Tselinograd.[27] Next in this schedule of 'economic offensives' was a meeting in Moscow with veterans of the Stakhanovite movement (named after Stakhanov, a miner who overfulfilled his daily quota of coal production many times over in 1935). The two-day conference began with an appeal by Gorbachev to workers to continue the great traditions of Stakhanov.[28]

This marathon of trips and speeches on a wide range of topics was reminiscent of Khrushchev's cross-country tours, but in many ways it was counterproductive. The impact of the initial Leningrad speech could not be recaptured. Repeated long speeches left the public less fascinated, particularly because the main thrust of Gorbachev's argument had changed from current problems, corruption, mismanagement and poor leadership to long-term programmes and the future. Promises of a better future were familiar and too unconvincing to capture the popular imagination.

Nonetheless, long-term planning continued and accelerated. On October 1 newspapers reported that the Central Committee and Politburo had approved a programme of increasing the production of consumer goods and services for the period 1986–2000. This was said to be particularly important in developing the Party's 'implacable struggle against drunkenness and alcoholism'.[29] When the full text of the programme was published a few days later, it specified targets for increasing the production of hundreds of different consumer products (for example, cloth, television sets, cameras, radios, washing machines, vacuum cleaners, kitchen ware, furniture, etc.) in the periods 1986–90 and 1990–2000.[30] The services which would be developed in various parts of the country (public transport, clubs, cinemas, sports facilities, etc.), the research to improve the quality of these products and services and the development of industrial and trade facilities to guarantee their availability were listed. The total increase in this sector was to reach 30 per cent in 1990 and 80 to 90 per cent in 2000.

Although this kind of long-term planning is useful as a working draft for Gosplan and other planning agencies, turning it into a commitment and a law affects the credibility of the government. Failure will inevitably erode public support for the government. In any case, it is almost impossible to make long-term plans for consumer-oriented sectors of the economy. Public demand changes rapidly. The plan did not, for example, envisage the mass production of video cassettes, word processors, home computers or computer games. These goods are not yet produced in the Soviet Union and it is therefore impossible to predict future demand. But Western-made video systems have penetrated the Soviet Union and the long-term plan specifies the domestic production of 60,000 video cassette units by 1990 and 120,000 in 2000, clearly far too few. 12 million television sets are to be produced annually by 1990 and 13 million in 2000. 60,000 video cassette units will not even satisfy the demand in one large city. Clearly they must be meant for clubs and for official use, probably because the leadership disapproves of the 'video revolution' and is afraid that video equipment will become a channel through which foreign video films can have an adverse effect on Soviet viewers. There is no provision in the plan for producing desk copiers, the equipment to make video films and other popular items. The 'ideological' character of the plan is obvious and it was clear to intellectuals that neither their access to world information, nor their freedom of choice were expected to improve.

At the Central Committee Plenum on October 15 Gorbachev presented a comprehensive report on the draft Party programme and the general programme of social and economic development in 1986–1990 and until the year 2000.[31] The long-term plan was published in November.[32] It was comprehensive. In general terms, overall production was expected to double, living standards to rise by 60 to 80 per cent and labour productivity to increase 2.3 to 2.5 times by 2000. But the plan was more modest than previous programmes. No significant increase in the production of motor cars was envisaged (the current production of about 1.3 million passenger cars per annum is too low to satisfy public demand). The production of oil was not expected to rise from the 1982 level of 640 million tons by 1990 and no prediction was made for 2000. The production of coal, which had reached a peak of 723 million tons in 1978 and then declined in 1979–84, was not expected to rise beyond 700–800 million tons in 2000. For the first time in Soviet history the natural limits of the extensive development of natural resources were recognized in the development plans. The production of nuclear energy, however, was expected to rise by 400 to 500 per cent and to contribute at least 20 per cent of the available electric power. The target figures of the Food Programme for 1990 were confirmed despite the absence of any real progress in the first five years of the programme.

There was nothing particularly exciting to be expected by the year 2000 and the programme did not promise any reforms. *Pravda* and *Izvestiya* editorials maintained that the programme was a 'revolutionary strategy', but there was nothing particularly novel in its methods and approaches. In general, Gorbachev's economic strategy seemed to be constructed along traditional lines. But this should not have been surprising. There was no reason to believe that Gorbachev was ready to change course, or to invite the public to take a more active part in the discussion of economic priorities and the way to reach them. Most of these long-term programmes were introduced without any really open debate. What was impressive, however, was Gorbachev's involvement in economic planning. The active pressure from above had an immediate effect on the economy in 1985. The first three months of the year had registered a decline, but the economic results of the third quarter, July–September, were better.[33] The growth rate increased to 5 per cent (compared to the 1984 figures) and productivity increased by 3 per cent. But the growth occurred mainly in the 'flexible' industries (for example, the manufacture of television sets and washing machines). The oil and coal industries continued to perform badly, showing a 4 per cent decline in production and a 7 per cent decrease in productivity. The production of steel, iron, cement, timber and many food products was lower than in the same period in 1984. There was no increase in the production of mineral fertilizers.

The most dramatic changes were produced by the new drinking laws. The production of alcoholic drinks fell by 33 per cent and the the production of non-alcoholic drinks and mineral water rose by 25 per cent. The period of subsidizing economic development by revenues extracted from the general public by immoral means seemed to be over. An article in *Izvestiya* which openly linked the negative effects of drinking with the enthusiastic attempts of previous administrations to increase the production of low quality alcohol products summed it up frankly: 'Let's stop poisoning people . . . Enough is enough'.[34]

Agriculture: garden co-operatives and consolidation

Gorbachev's qualification as an 'agronomist–economist' was mentioned prominently in the brief biography released when he became General Secretary. He was the first Soviet leader to have an agricultural education. He was also the first to have done nothing other than agriculture before becoming leader. He will therefore be considered directly responsible for all the major decisions made about agriculture and he will be personally liable for any failures. Ryzhkov took over the industrial problems at the end of September, but he clearly has no experience in agriculture. Gorbachev's task was clear: he had to create a more efficient agricultural administration and eliminate the dualism of power and the fragmentation within the government system, while simplifying the decision-making system. It was only now that he really obtained full control over all the various lines of agricultural administration. He no longer needed to share agricultural power with Kunayev and Shcherbitsky in the Politburo, and Bodyl, Nuryev and others in the government. The system of agro-industrial councils which he himself had helped to create and which represented many different ministries and committees had become an obstacle.

The reorganization of the government and Party apparatus responsible for agriculture was dramatic. But it could not be brought into effect immediately. Gorbachev waited until the major work of the agricultural season was over. The new Central Committee secretary for agriculture, Nikonov, supervised the agricultural campaign while Gorbachev began to prepare for a more radical reorganization. His first act was to appoint A. Boldin, an agronomist and head of the agricultural department of *Pravda*, as his personal senior assistant (and probably speech writer on agriculture). The General Secretary's apparatus of advisers (the secretariat of the Office of the General Secretary) is the section of the Central Committee about which least is known. It is probably the most powerful section, comparable to the American President's White House advisers. In May Rasumovsky was moved from the North Caucasus to take over Ligachev's job as head of the Organizational Department of the Central Committee (Ligachev had moved up to take charge of the ideological departments). Rasumovsky became the key person in replacing local agricultural officials and supervising the election of delegates to the forthcoming Party Congress. Local officials were replaced throughout the summer, but more major reorganization had to wait until the end of the season. The sowing season had not been a success. The winter crops were damaged and resowing was necessary in many regions. The 1984 autumn sowing had been late and the winter was very cold. The North Caucasus was particularly badly hit and the reploughing of winter crop fields was not only expensive, but also took extra grain which had to be brought in from other regions and from the state reserves.

Gorbachev, unlike Malenkov in 1953 and Brezhnev in 1964, could not resort to making a popular gesture to encourage the private sector in rural areas. Rural depopulation and the absence of a technology suitable for small-scale agriculture meant that the existing private plots were underused. Private agriculture was in decline. Nonetheless, to stimulate some kind of private initiative Gorbachev announced measures to increase the number of garden allotments leased to industrial and office workers. The lease of small allotments to the urban population (usually not more than 0.05 hectares) had been legalized during the war and these allotments played an important role as a supplementary source of extra food (usually potatoes and vegetables) during food rationing, from 1941 to 1947. Later pressure from the urban population decreased, but interest in allotments rose again in the late 1950s when the government permitted them to be fenced off. A minute (no larger than 16–18 square meters) one-room summer house could be built on the allotments, but no heating, electricity or plumbing was permitted. Although the land was state property, the houses and trees were considered private property. The allotments turned into *de facto* small *dachas* for weekend use. The garden allotment movement became very popular and by 1980 there were more than 4 million allotments around Soviet towns.

Their economic role was rather small, since the total acreage was only about 0.25 million hectares, only 0.1 per cent of cultivated land. But their role in the production of fruit and berries was already significant. At least 0.5 million tons of apples, pears and other fruit grown on allotments was consumed. A significant proportion of the flowers and exotic products (for example, garlic) sold on the town markets came from garden allotments. Well-developed garden co-operatives consisting of 300 to 500 members had, in fact, grown into unregistered summer villages of small houses. It was, of course, impossible to prevent some owners from making a small fireplace to keep the *dacha* warm during the autumn or early spring.

These settlements finally became a source of political controversy. It is illegal in the Soviet Union for anyone to live anywhere unregistered by the police for longer than three days. The houses and allotments were not registered as anyone's abode and had no official residential status. Moreover, many of the houses had become much larger than the official limit and were perfectly suitable for living modestly for considerable periods of time. This spontaneous 'privatization' of unregistered houses and gardens was a source of alarm for some politicians. Local Party officials began to put the brakes on any further development of garden co-operatives by refusing to allocate more land. At the same time, the economic importance of the allotments had increased since 1979, when the food situation in the country deteriorated. Many families had built greenhouses to grow early vegetables and some had set up small rabbit farms – a good source of cheap meat and fur. The small black market in Russian fur hats was based entirely on such rabbit farms.

Attempts were made in 1982, 1983 and 1984 to control the development of allotments. But the decline of agriculture in the central non-*chernozem* areas and the programme of consolidating small villages into larger 'agrotowns' meant that many small fields far from roads were abandoned. They were ideal for private allotments. Gorbachev was strongly in favour of increasing the number of allotments, believing that outdoor work would serve as a pressure valve and be a healthy alternative to drinking. In his Leningrad speech in May he argued strongly in their favour in a way which must have been directed against high level opponents of the scheme:

> [The gardens and allotments] which we already have allow 20 million people to work and relax in summer in their leisure time. And many more are requesting the same kind of gardens and allotments. But we have been acting as if we are afraid of something, as if this was some kind of private entrepreneurial activity. What kind of private entrepreneurial activity can it be when the family is working its own small garden, spending its time out of doors? So we have now taken the decision to allocate annually from one million to one million two hundred thousand allotments to citizens.[35]

This was Gorbachev's second personal initiative which had a real practical and positive impact on the quality of people's lives. Of course, the garden co-operatives could not affect agriculture in general, but they did reduce the pressure slightly on state retail sales of vegetables and fruit, particularly in small towns.

The harvesting season in 1985 produced the usual problems. The Ipatovsky method was used in some Ukrainian regions and in the North Caucasus, although it was rarely called by that name, probably because the Ipatovsky district itself performed rather badly from 1979 to 1984. There were more open discussions about the method. Some experts, particularly the chairmen of contract brigades, opposed it because it made it difficult to distinguish the results of individual brigades or the quality of the grain from particular fields.[36] Local officials, on the other hand, liked the methods of harvesting by large consolidated groups of combines. It increased the productivity per combine and made it possible for regional and district authorities to use machinery where it was required without taking into consideration who owned it or from which farms the drivers and mechanics came.[37]

The discussion was significant in itself. The pros and cons were debated quite openly. This may have been a spontaneous effect of the changes in the administration, but it may also have been that more outspoken criticism of previous practices was being encouraged officially (and not necessarily by Gorbachev). Excellent essays were published about the poor state of agriculture, the erosion of the topsoil and the contradictions in the practical work of the over-organized agro-industrial councils in which members often had conflicting loyalties and responsibilities. Moreover, these essays were not merely published in the newspapers, but also in the popular, literary 'thick' journals.[38] It became clear that many of them had been written in 1983 and delayed by the censors. Yuri Chernichenko, for example, one of the best Soviet research journalists on agricultural problems, published an essay 'Our Bread' in August 1985 and deliberately signed it with the date August 1983 to indicate that he had been unable to publish it for two years.[39] The essays were not in favour of Gorbachev's previous initiatives and priorities. Their publication indicated either that Gorbachev had changed his mind, or that someone powerful was enabling them to be published. Ligachev was in charge of censorship and it was said in Moscow that he was displeased by the increasing development of private allotments and that he wanted to reduce the amount of food imported from the USA, even if it required austerity measures.

Until the end of 1984 the weekly reports of the Central Statistical Bureau and commentaries had been published on the right hand side or at the bottom of the front page of *Pravda*, *Izvestiya* and *Sel'skaya zhizn'*. In 1985 the reports were made more prominent, appearing on the left-hand side where the editorial used to be. Agricultural statistical reports were now being given top priority and considered more important than any other news of the day. By the end of August it was clear that the harvest losses were substantial. None of the southern regions (including Stavropol *krai*) could report that the harvest had been completed. In good years most of the work there is completed by the end of July. Winter sowing was taking place too slowly. Some articles and commentaries criticized the district agro-industrial councils (RAPO) for being too weak. In October the weekly statistical reports became even more pessimistic. But they also became more analytical – it was too late to put pressure on the country. Instead regret had to be expressed that some regions, and not only in the East, were still harvesting cereals, from which the grain had already dropped from the over-ripe ears. 'At least let's save the straw', an *Izvestiya* commentator remarked on October 17.[40] The winter sowing plan was not fulfilled and a large proportion of winter crops was sown later than was considered optimal. Autumn ploughing was delayed. In Siberia and Byelorussia the results at the end of October were even worse than they had been the previous very poor year. At the very end of October potatoes, vegetables and other crops were being collected from under the first snow in many regions. The general diagnosis of the failure was given as a shortage of the work force. It was increasingly difficult to keep up the pace of harvesting when the rural population was continuing to decline.

The problem of the rural exodus had reached a critical point. It is probable that fewer people left the villages in 1985 than in 1984, but the cost of each new departure was higher. The point had been reached where each single departure was now catastrophic. Moreover, it was a 'Catch 22' situation. Tractor drivers and milkmaids were leaving because their working day was intolerably long and they never had time off. But when one of them left, the burden on those who remained behind became even greater. The Politburo had discussed agriculture many times. But after approval by the Central Committee Plenum on July 2, the Central Committee and Council of Ministers passed a decree which was valid for 20 regions of the non-*chernozem* zones and parts of which would apply to other republics and zones. Investment funds would be increased above the already high levels of the Food Programme and subsequent decisions relating to the RSFSR. Target figures were given for the machinery to be sent to the rural areas in 1986–90. But the most significant feature of the decree was the provision to prevent the employment of the rural work force in industry or in towns in general. Peasants had once again lost their freedom of movement and choice of jobs.

Other alternative methods of keeping the rural youth in the countryside had been discussed in the press and in Party documents. They were all expensive, requiring the construction of better rural facilities. There had been some indication that Gorbachev was interested in the idea of allowing private 'family farms'. Positive remarks had appeared in the press about the very high productivity of European and American family farms.[41] It is known that the Central Committee had discussed it as a possible experiment, but that it was thought to be anti-Marxist Proudhonism (after Proudhon, the French socialist who was against centralized political organization and who thought that workers should own their own means of production). The Hungarian model had also been discussed, but the new secretary for agriculture, Nikonov, was known to be strongly opposed to it.

A few days later the Central Committee and Council of Ministers increased the procurement price for high quality wheat by 50 to 100 per cent and linked it to the protein content of the wheat grain rather than to weight, in an effort to deal with the protein defiency which was occurring in the diet of the population.[42] The best hard wheat could now fetch as much as 250–300 roubles per ton. On the official exchange rate this was more than the market price of American or Canadian grain. In the same month a further decision was made about increasing the production of various cereals in 1986 (introducing 'intensive' technologies).[43] In his speech in Tselinograd on September 7, Gorbachev appealed to *kolkhozniki* and *sovkhoz* workers to do everything possible to increase production. He made it clear that production costs were too high and that it would be difficult to continue subsidizing retail prices. It costs the state 20 billion roubles from the budget annually merely to subsidize the price of meat.[44] This is more than the annual budget allocation to the health service (which was 16 billion roubles in 1983). Gorbachev's speech was very critical of local officials, but it did not contain any fresh ideas about how to improve the situation in the new Five Year Plan, the draft of which had been published on November 9. The new Party Programme made an indirect provision for food prices to rise. This was long overdue. Retail prices of livestock products had not changed since 1962 and the prices of other food products were identical to 1953 prices. Continued food subsidies at this level would be impossible. In any case, they were inhibiting the introduction of food processing, improvements in sales practices, refrigeration and other developments in the food industry. The need to transform collective farms into state farms was mentioned in the draft programme. There was also a statement that prices should reflect production costs.[45]

The most dramatic and unexpected development in Soviet agriculture occurred on Friday, November 22. The Central Committee and Council of Ministers passed a resolution which completely reorganized the agricultural administration and practically transformed the remaining collective farms into state farms.[46] Most of the ministries which dealt with agriculture (the Ministries of Agriculture, Fruit and Vegetables, Meat and Milk Production, Food Production, Rural Construction, Procurement, the State Committees on Industrial and Technical Work in Agriculture with its *Sel'khoztekhnika* network) were simply abolished and merged into a consolidated State Agro-Industrial

Committee or *Gosagroprom SSSR*. Departments relating to agriculture in other ministries were also transferred to it (from the Ministries of Light Industry, Irrigation and Land Reclamation). Although the technical agricultural ministries (Tractor, Combine and Agricultural Machinery, Mineral Fertilizer, Livestock Farm Machinery, etc.) were not merged with *Gosagroprom SSSR*, they were put under its control. All the ministers with agricultural sectors and the chairman of the agricultural sector of Gosplan were included in the collegium of *Gosagroprom*, and so were the agricultural bureaucrats from the Ministry of Finance, the State Bank, *Tsentrosoyuz* (the rural trade organization), the Central Statistical Bureau and many others.

In effect a separate agricultural government of the USSR has been organized which can operate separately from the government responsible for the heavy, machine tool and defence industries. This is the most radical reorganization of the Soviet economic administration since Khrushchev's decentralization of the economy in 1957 and the creation of separate industrial and agricultural Party and local Soviet networks in 1962 (both of which were considered serious errors which contributed to Khrushchev's downfall and which were abolished in 1965). The Chairman of *Gosagroprom SSSR* was appointed that day by decree of the Presidium of the Supreme Soviet. He was to be Vsevolod Murakhovsky, first deputy prime minister and Gorbachev's close friend. It seems obvious that Gorbachev himself will be in charge of the system and that Murakhovsky will act as his deputy. He has neither the experience, education or knowledge to preside over the collegium of this new giant committee. A graduate of Stavropol Teacher Training Institute, he has worked all his life in Stavropol *krai*, and his years as *kraikom* first secretary (1979–84) were not the most successful in Stavropol agriculture. But it is not so much a question of qualification as of authority. The only way that Murakhovsky will be able to deal with former ministers and state committee chairmen is if Gorbachev is always behind him.

The new *Gosagroprom SSSR* was a product of another serious failure in agriculture. US estimates of the Soviet grain harvest (made on the basis of monitoring agricultural areas by satellite and other sophisticated methods) expected the harvest to be 195 million tons at first, well above the 1979–84 average. In July the figure was adjusted to 190 million tons. But the harvesting work was done so badly and the losses were so enormous that the final result was no higher than 170–180 million metric tons, if that. It was more difficult to mobilize the urban population to help with the harvest than usual. 1985 was the last year of the Five Year Plan and the Central Committee had made it clear that the usual 'adjustments' to take 'objective factors' into account (which usually means decreasing the targets) would not occur. The pressure on plants and factories to fulfil their plans was high and they could not afford to send millions of workers into the rural areas for the traditional annual 'assistance'. It was also obvious that the local agro-industrial councils were not functioning effectively. They included *kolkhoz* chairmen and *sovkhoz* directors who needed to work on their farms rather than discuss district problems in the local towns. The complex bureaucratic system which had been strongly defended in April 1984 as viable and praised by all present (except for the Georgian representative, who advocated a consolidated committee on agriculture instead) was simply disintegrating in October 1985 because everybody blamed everyone else for failure.

Gosagroprom SSSR was created in haste and without any discussion. A reorganization on this scale should be carried out by the Supreme Soviet, not by the government and Central Committee. The decision was published on November 23, only three days before the regular Supreme Soviet session. The Presidium of the Supreme Soviet confirmed the decision on the day it was published, but only in a brief statement. There was no proper law, signed by Gromyko, as would be expected even for the appointment of a new minister. It would appear either that the details of the decree were not ready, or that it involved too many changes for them to be specified. The inclusion of all *kolkhozy* in the consolidated system seems, for example, to violate the collective farm statutes, one of the basic laws of Soviet agriculture. According to the statutes, collective farms are self-administering co-operatives and their funds are the property of the members.

Despite the many organizational and legal problems which need to be resolved, it seems clear that the new administration will be better than the old. The fragmentation of agriculture along specialized lines has been halted. It may be possible to reduce drastically the enormous bureaucratic apparatus and to release agronomists for practical work. On the other hand, this is the tenth radical reorganization of the agricultural administration since the war and they have all followed similar patterns – fragmentation, followed by consolidation. The fragmentation, however, had never before been as irrational as it had become by 1970–84. Farm directors and chairmen had to deal with more than 13 local ministerial branches and networks. The attempt to rationalize this via APO and RAPO had been doomed from the start, but it had been Gorbachev's own initiative. He could not acknowledge that it was a failure. It was only now, as General Secretary, that he could afford to face the problem (and take the credit if the reorganization results in a better harvest in 1986).

The real problems of Soviet agriculture cannot, however, be resolved by bureaucratic reorganization. It will not cure the infertility of the topsoil, nor will it make rural residents want to stay in the villages. The experience of other countries indicates that progressive rural development is only possible when peasants become independent farmers. The transformation of peasants into specialized workers and state employees is not the best way to improve agriculture. Nor will tying the peasant to the land produce the desired results. When successful peasants are allowed to retain their organic links with the land and become successful farmers, agriculture benefits and so does the rest of the population. In November 1985 Gorbachev proved that he had the courage to make sweeping changes at the top of the agricultural bureaucracy. As a man who was born a peasant and who retains his ties with his village, perhaps he will have the vision and the courage to make the kind of change which will improve not only the bureaucracy, but also the harvest.

10
Domestic policy

Gorbachev's first year in power was marked by unprecedentedly large changes in the personnel of the Politburo and government and the rapid formulation of economic targets and methods of economic development for the next 15 years. In all other respects, however, the changes in domestic policy were merely cosmetic. Policies were better presented, the style was more modern, but there was little new in the contents. The reason was not just lack of time or preoccupation with the economy. There were particularly good opportunities to formulate new domestic policies in 1985. The new Party programme and statutes were being drafted, the long-term economic programmes provided opportunities and there were many international meetings at which statements were issued which concerned domestic policy.

After previous successions the new leader has often been under great pressure to take certain actions which have had immediate and serious ideological and international repercussions. In the case of Khrushchev, for example, Beria had to be removed and Stalin's crimes exposed to prevent the execution of the prominent doctors who had been tried and sentenced in February 1953. In foreign affairs it was urgent to end the Korean War. Brezhnev had fewer international crises to resolve immediately, but he and his colleagues acted rapidly and conservatively in the ideological and domestic spheres to reverse Khrushchev's liberal tendencies, preventing books from being published, films from being released, etc. When Gorbachev came to power he saw his most urgent tasks not in actions, but in formulating documents and particularly the Party Programme, which would contain recommendations about future domestic policy and about the position of the Soviet Union in the world. The final products made it clear that the new leadership was not yet ready to launch any active ideological and political initiatives.

Many social and professional groups nurtured the hope that the new leadership would resolve the problems which had been accumulating for years or even decades. There are always large numbers of letters from the public to the Central Committee, Presidium of the Supreme Soviet and editors of the major newspapers, but after a change of leaders they turn into an avalanche. It is these letters, rather than elections to the Supreme Soviet, which reflect public opinion. In the early 1960s *Izvestiya* sometimes reported receiving as many as 2,000 letters per day and *Pravda* probably receives more. Almost every citizen of the USSR sits down at least once in his lifetime to write a letter which starts 'Dear Comrade . . .' and is simply addressed to The Kremlin, Moscow. Now that this comrade was the charismatic and energetic Gorbachev, there must have been several million letters written to him, containing not just congratulations, but suggestions, projects, requests, complaints, demands for justice, appeals on behalf of those serving prison sentences (more than 2 million people), from prisoners themselves or from dissidents of all kinds (almost every known Soviet dissident began his dissident career by writing to the Central Committee or Politburo). This important aspect of Soviet political life is encouraged by the constitution which, in article 49, specifies:

> Every citizen . . . has the right to submit proposals to state bodies and public organizations for improving their activity, and to criticize shortcomings in their work. Officials are obliged, within established time limits, to examine citizens' proposals and requests, to reply to them and to take appropriate action. Prosecution for criticism is prohibited.[1]

This important article of the Soviet constitution means that even the most radical political criticism cannot be treated as 'anti-Soviet propaganda' if it is sent in a letter to the Politburo or Central Committee. Unless it is made public, distributed through *samizdat* or sent abroad, the author or authors cannot be taken to court. Of course, letters of this kind may be released for *samizdat* or published abroad not by the authors, but by KGB officials looking for a pretext to lay a criminal charge.

Gorbachev seems to have recognized the importance of these letters as a barometer of public opinion. He has quoted from them in his speeches on economic problems (in Tselinograd, for example, he quoted letters from ordinary people who believed that the price of bread should be increased to prevent people using it to feed farm animals). The problem of replying to these letters was the subject of his first domestic reorganization in the Central Committee. The volume had swelled beyond the capacities of the large section of 150 people whose job it was to deal with them, particularly since the law stipulates a one-month time limit for a reply. It was decided to abolish the section and distribute the mail instead to the relevant Central Committee departments. This was a sensible solution, since many of the letters were too specialized to be dealt with by the people who worked in the letter section.

The first ideological test faced by the new leadership, however, was identical to the one faced by Gorbachev's predecessors: the problem of Stalin. In March there were intense preparations for the celebration of the 40th anniversary of Victory Day. Before Chernenko died it had been announced that a film would be released, called *Pobeda* (Victory). Made in 1983–4, it depicted Stalin as the wise hero and Churchill and Truman as negative characters who did little to help the Soviet war effort. A decision had to be made about releasing the film. There was pressure from other groups, particularly war veterans, to rehabilitate Stalin. The Volgograd City Council and the Veteran Society had petitioned to change the name of the city back to Stalingrad and Chernenko was said already to have prepared a draft decree to do so. Gorbachev compromised. *Pobeda* was released, but Volgograd remained Volgograd. Most intellectuals were relieved by the decision.

Gorbachev's speech on the eve of Victory Day, May 8, was not very interesting. It seemed to have been written for him, since it was very official and descriptive, eschewing analysis. Gorbachev did, however, acknowledge the initial mistakes and miscalculations which had preceded victory and he only mentioned Stalin's name once. If there had ever been an intention to rehabilitate Stalin, it had clearly been abandoned. On the other hand, the traditional 'jubilee' amnesty was disappointing. The decree passed by the Presidium of the Supreme Soviet at the end of April was very selective, explicitly excluding all the articles of the Criminal Code which are used against political prisoners. It even excluded those people who had received sentences of less than three years under article 191 of the Criminal Code.[2] Political prisoners like Yuri Orlov and Sergei Kovalev, who had already served seven-year prison sentences and were serving their five-year terms of exile, were also excluded. This was an unmistakable signal that the new leader was not a liberal.

This was not the first sign that Gorbachev was no liberal, but intellectuals had gone on hoping that there would be some change after the succession. The Jewish *refusniks* had hoped that emigration, which had virtually ceased under Chernenko, would be liberalized. At first the situation seemed hopeful. In March, 98 people were allowed to leave.[3] In April another 166 arrived in Vienna, some of them from Moscow and Leningrad which had previously been the most difficult places from which to emigrate.[4] However, the various arrangements which must be made before emigrating are so complex that the applications of those who left in April must have been processed much earlier in the year. In the summer the number of people who received permission to emigrate began to decline and by August the level had fallen to 30 to 40 per month (this figure does not include Volga German emigrants, for whom annual figures only are available). This was well below the 1983 average, when about 100 Jews a month were given permission to leave (at the peak of Jewish emigration in 1979 the annual figure was 51,330. The 'new cold war' reduced it to 9,447 in 1981 and 2,692 in 1982).

Emigration figures are considered a valid index of Soviet respect for human rights. There are about 100,000 known applicants waiting for permission to leave and the *refusnik* community consists of about 30,000 people. However, the figures reflect both the general level of democracy within the country, and also the international situation. They began to rise slightly again in October, in connection with Gorbachev's visit to France and the preparations for the summit with President Reagan. In October 124 Jews left the Soviet Union, 44 of them from Moscow and one from Leningrad.[5] The November figure was 128.

In an interview on French television on September 30, Gorbachev maintained that emigration would only be considered to 'reunify families'. This meant that there would be no automatic right for Soviet Jews, Germans, Greeks or other minorities to emigrate for religious, ethnic or cultural reasons. In the same interview Gorbachev proved that he had very little knowledge of the essence of the Jewish problem in the USSR. He claimed that Jews were better treated in the Soviet Union than anywhere else in the world: 'The Jewish population, which accounts for 0.69 per cent of the entire population of the country, are represented in its political and cultural life on a scale of at least 10 to 20 per cent'.[6] He was correct about the proportion of Jews in the population, but it is very difficult to measure their representation in Soviet cultural life. After all, it is not only a question of government policy, but also of individual effort and inclination. And to say that they are represented in Soviet political life on a scale of 10 to 20 per cent is manifestly absurd. There is only one Jewish member of the government (Veniamin Dymshits), which makes the proportion less than one per cent. The proportion of Jews in the membership of the Communist Party was 1.4 per cent in 1983 and there is only one Jew (the ubiquitous Dymshits) amongst the 311 members of the Central Committee.

From the first visit to the Soviet Union of a group of American senators and congressmen in April onwards, Gorbachev has received many personal appeals on behalf of political prisoners and *refusniks*. His reply has been standard: 'Let us in the Soviet Union manage our affairs ourselves'.[7] He has also maintained that political dissidents are tried only when they violate the law, although he clearly must know that Soviet law turns dissent into a crime. Nonetheless, a goodwill gesture had to be made before the Geneva summit. Permission was given in November to Yelena Bonner, wife of the exiled Andrei Sakharov, to make a foreign trip. In fact, Sakharov had begun his third hunger strike over the issue in October, demanding that his wife be given permission to go abroad for medical treatment. His health was very poor, he was 64 years of age and weak after previous hunger strikes which had been ended in hospital by forced feeding. His life was considered to be at risk. If he were to die in November the outrage in the United States would be too great for Gorbachev to be able to gain any success at Geneva. The stakes were too high and at the end of October Yelena Bonner was told that she could go abroad immediately. Sakharov was Gorbachev's greatest 'human rights' problem. He had been exiled to Gorky in 1980 without trial or court action. It was a KGB operation under the false pretext that he was a security risk (false because he had been dismissed from his position at the Institute of Atomic Energy in 1968, 12 years previously, and had not been directly involved in military-oriented research since 1964).

The groups monitoring human rights violations in the Soviet Union (particularly those who had been members of the Helsinki Watch Group in Moscow and who had emigrated after serving prison terms) continued to report the arrest of dissidents and human rights activists. There was no discernible change in the second half of 1985 in the weekly reports of human right violations edited by Khronid Lubarsky.[8] The Moscow International Youth Festival in August was held under particularly heavy police guard – there were several times more policemen than there were visitors. The previous Youth Festival, in 1957, had been a joyful, free gathering of young people. This time the atmosphere was very different. The visitors were provided with badges bearing their photographs which had to be worn at all times. Most of the discussions which took place were political and anti-Western.

The situation in the Writers' Union and other unions of the 'creative intelligentsia' (journalists, composers, film-makers, etc.) is usually a good indication of the domestic political climate. There are always dozens of novels, films, plays, etc. which have been written and submitted for publication, or for permission to stage or screen. All plays and films require permission from a committee headed by the appropriate censorship official (at district level if the play is to appear in a provincial theatre). A significant proportion of these works are rejected, or delayed while changes are made. The authors, editors and directors (often well-known personalities) inevitably appeal to a new leader to resolve their problems with the censors. In April there were optimistic signs that change was in the air. Gorbachev refused to see the two most conservative leaders of the Writers' Union, the chairman, G. Markov, and A. Chakovsky, editor of *Literaturnaya gazeta.* It would have been normal for him to see them and familiarize himself with the people in charge (Andropov had seen them in December 1982 and expressed his confidence in them), but they were told that he was too busy. It was also noticed that Pyotr Demichev (Minister of Culture, candidate member of the Politburo and the former head of the Propaganda Department of the Central Committee) and his officials had become more polite to visitors. On the other hand, one of Chernenko's senior assistants, Pribytkov, was appointed Deputy Chairman of the Committee for the Protection of State Secrets in the Press (the official name of Soviet censorship). It was a demotion for Pribytkov, and boded ill for any relaxation in censorship. There were rumours that Gorbachev and Mikhail Zimyanin, the second secretary in the Ideological Department of the Central Committee who had acted as Suslov's second-in-command and was now fulfilling the same role for Ligachev, were not getting on. But there did not seem to have been any new instructions and the situation did not improve. Gorbachev's statements about ideology were ambiguous and did not suggest a new approach. He seemed to have left Ligachev in sole control of the ideological front while he concentrated on the economy.

In August Yevgenii Yevtushenko, the well-known controversial poet, wrote a letter to Gorbachev about the poor state of Soviet literature and the severe censorship restrictions. As a result, a short poem of his was published in *Pravda* on September 9.[9] The poem supported Gorbachev's economic policy, assailed timid bureaucrats who oppose innovation and hailed the six month Soviet moratorium on nuclear tests as an 'unprecedentedly brave deed of peace'. It also contained a veiled criticism of collectivization and an open criticism of Lysenko, relating current problems in agriculture with bureaucratic obstructionists. But the poem made it clear that it was not the Party, but bureaucrats that were responsible.

In the same month Gorbachev appointed Alexandr Yakovlev as Head of the Propaganda Department of the Central Committee to replace Stukalin, who was sent as Soviet ambassador to Hungary. This was considered to be a good sign. The department is the key sector of Ligachev's ideological secretariat. The appointment seems to have been made in haste (like the appointment of Razumovsky to head the Organizational Department), since the head of that department is usually a member or candidate member of the Central Committee and Yakovlev was neither. He had been a deputy chairman of the Propaganda Department but was dismissed by Suslov in 1970 (apparently because of articles he wrote criticizing the neo-Stalinist and Russophile tendencies in some political and literary journals) and sent to Canada as ambassador. In this capacity he had accompanied Gorbachev on his tour of Canada and the two men established a good rapport. Yakovlev was brought back to Moscow and appointed Director of the Institute of World Economy and International Relations. He came to Britain with Gorbachev in 1984. He is thought not to be conservative, but his influence will only be felt when he has been elected to the Central Committee.

The new appointments in the ideological sector seemed quite promising. Soviet 'ideological workers' divide roughly into a conservative, orthodox group which had been supported by Suslov and Demichev, and a more reform-minded, 'modestly progressive' group (Georgi Arbatov, Director of the Institute of the United States and Canada, Alexei Rumyantsev, former editor of *Pravda* and now Director of the Institute of Sociology, G. Shakhnazarov, senior member of the International Department of the Central Committee and a prolific writer on problems of socialism and communism, Alexander Bovin and Fyodr Burlatskii, both prominent journalists, fall into the latter group). The reform-minded group is progressive, rather than liberal. Its members enjoyed good relations with Andropov when he was a secretary of the Central Committee before 1967 and, after an eclipse, they had seemed to make a come-back after Brezhnev's death. It seemed that Gorbachev, who did not have his own circle of intellectuals, was recruiting advisers, assistants and officials from this group. But notorious conservatives like Zimyanin, Shauro, head of the sector of culture of the Central Committee and Khachaturov, editor of the journal *Voprosy ekonomiki* and Director of the Institute of Economy, also remained influential and probably enjoyed better relations with Ligachev than the progressives.

A third 'centrist' group includes people like Afanas'ev, editor of *Pravda*, and Richard Kosolapov, editor of *Kommunist*, the theoretical journal of the Party. Since the Soviet Union is an ideological political system, Party publications are usually the most authoritative indicators of current political and ideological trends. Marxism-Leninism is the essential link between various state institutions. It is also the way in which the supreme power of the Party and its General Secretary is legitimized. The ideological links between the different parts of the state machine must be kept strong if ideology is to continue to act in a cementing role. It was clear that the role of ideology had declined in the Brezhnev era, but this was not associated with any structural change. It was merely that a kind of 'ideological sclerosis' had set in. The top echelons of the Party simply could not produce the kind of ideological, political or social document which could be treated seriously by the educated public. In the 1970s and 1980s, for example, the best the Party could produce to inspire people was Brezhnev's 'works', a series of memoirs about the war years, the virgin lands, etc. primitively and poorly written by ghost writers and the source of innumerable jokes.

Gorbachev himself had not been above illustrating the primitiveness and sterility of the ideological material of the period. In a speech to an ideological conference in Stavropol *krai* in May 1978, for example, when he was still *kraikom* secretary, Gorbachev said:

> . . . the General Secretary of the CC CPSU, Chairman of the Presidium of the Supreme Soviet of the USSR, L.I. Brezhnev has revealed a talent for leadership of the Leninist type. His titanic daily work is directed towards strengthening the might of our country, raising the well-being of workers and strengthening the peace and security of nations.
>
> And not long ago we opened the pages of Comrade L.I. Brezhnev's remarkable book, *Malaya zemlya* in which the legendary heroes of the battles of the North Caucasus are portrayed in letters of gold. A short time has elasped since its publication, but the memoirs have provoked wide, truly national interest. To meet the innumerable requests of the workers of Stavropol, in February the memoirs were reprinted from the magazine *Novyi mir* in our *krai* newspapers, *Stavropol'skaya Pravda* and *Kavkazkaya zdravnitsa*.
>
> In number of pages the book *Malaya zemlya* is not very large, but in the depth of its ideological content, in the breadth of the author's generalizations and opinions it has become a great event in public life. It has evoked a warm echo in the hearts of Soviet people, the delighted response of front-line soldiers at readers' conferences and in the press.
>
> Communists and all the workers of Stavropol are boundlessly grateful to Leonid Il'ich Brezhnev for this truly party-spirited, literary work in which the sources of the great feat of our heroic nation, its spiritual and moral strength, its steadfastness and courage are depicted with deep philosophical penetration'.[10]

When one reads this extravagant praise of Brezhnev's superficial and mediocre work one cannot help but feel that its ideological value has been negative. Apart from everything else, Brezhnev's account distorts history. I myself was a soldier at the Taman front in 1943, of which *Malaya zemlya* ('small land') was a small coastal outpost, the result of an unsuccessful offensive to capture Novorossiisk in April and again in May 1943. Until Brezhnev transformed it into a major battle 30 years later, it was a minor episode of the war. Brezhnev was a political commissar who rose only one rank from colonel in 1941 to major general of the political service in 1945, but in 1978 he began to be treated in the official press as if he had been a more prominent military hero than Marshal Zhukov.

Many other more important Party figures than Gorbachev lavished extraordinary praise on Brezhnev's literary *oeuvre* in 1978. This demonstrated how empty, degraded and corrupt ideology had become. It is easy to understand why 'cult' statements were made in Stalin's time, when officials and leaders were afraid for their lives. But the only risk in 1978 was delayed promotion or loss of privilege.

Thus when Gorbachev became General Secretary in 1985, the need for new ideas and plans in the field of ideology was urgent. Gorbachev himself was clearly not going to be able to satisfy this need except as the leader of an ideological 'think tank' which was beginning to emerge. A separate 'think tank' seemed to be forming around Ligachev as well. This raised the possibility of controversy between 'left' and 'right' deviations in the future, but the trends were not immediately visible. A perfect arena for controversy was available in the form of the preparation of the draft Party programme for the XXVIIth Party Congress. The task of the programme is to explain current internal and international problems and offer long- and short-term solutions. In other words, it is a latter-day 'Communist Manifesto'. A new programme was badly needed, since the existing one had been adopted in 1961 to cover the next 20 years. It specified goals which had never been fulfilled and it had therefore been an embarrassment for some time, and had begun to affect the Party's claim to political legitimacy. The new programme was required for the Party's own domestic purposes (there is a ritual whereby new members state that they agree with the programme) and also for international consumption. The programme of the CPSU serves as a model for other ruling communist parties.

Despite the success of Lenin's Communist Party and the fact that it controlled a significant part of the world, the formal programme had been the weakest aspect of the world communist movement throughout the 20th century. Each previous programme had become obsolete within two or three years of its adoption and for practical purposes a substitute (usually a collection of the latest Party documents and decisions) was studied by new recruits. The first official programme had been approved in 1903 at the Second Congress of the Party in Brussels and London, when the split occurred between the Bolsheviks and Mensheviks. It demanded unlimited freedom of conscience, speech, the press, meetings, strikes and unions.[11] The second programme was drafted by Lenin and Trotsky and approved by the VIIIth Party Congress in 1919. It reflected the Civil War and the system of 'war communism': it was both radical, expressing the expectation of imminent world revolution, and utopian, promising the abolition of money and an entirely new economic order. Although it became irrelevant when the New Economic Policy was introduced in 1921, no new programme was written until after Stalin's death. Since Stalin ruled as a dictator and the role of the Party was much diminished, this did not matter very much.

The third programme took from 1954 to 1961 to prepare, and it was adopted by the XXIInd Party Congress. Although the Party had survived without a formal programme for many years with Stalin in power, Khrushchev found himself in urgent need of a formal programme. He was criticized by Chinese, Albanian and other Communist leaders as a 'revisionist' and he needed a document which would legitimize his own ideas about communism and the Soviet political and economic systems and turn them into a model for other socialist states. He hoped in this way to counteract the split that had appeared in the international communist movement (both China and Yugoslavia offered alternative models of communist development and many communist parties around the world were splitting into rival factions). The international purposes of the third Party programme, therefore, were even more important than its domestic aims. As a result, it was filled with boasts, promises and pretensions. It contained a moral code borrowed from Christian teaching (and ignored by the leaders themselves) and specific economic and social targets for the 1970s and 1980s which were soon proved unrealistic and which showed up how unreliably and imperfectly the planning system of Khrushchev's administration functioned. The programme promised that Soviet per capita production and consumption would reach the American level by 1970 and outstrip it by 1980, when communism would be achieved and people would be rewarded according to their needs. The Soviet Union would have the highest labour productivity in the world, each family would have its own separate apartment or house, collective and state farms would all be prosperous and profitable and the nutrition of the population would be based on scientific norms.

None of these ambitions were achieved. The programme specified that the 1980 national income would be five times the level of 1960. By then the Soviet Union would produce 2700 billion khw of electricity per annum (the actual level in 1980 was 1295 billion), 700 million tons of oil (603 million tons were produced in 1980), 300 million tons of grain (the 1980 grain harvest was 189 million tons) and 30 million tons of meat (meat production in 1980 was 15 million tons).[12] None of the other specified target figures was reached (the closest was cotton – 9.96 million tons were produced in 1980 and the target was 10 million tons).

This brief history of the previous Party programmes makes it clear why a more modest tone was required in the new one. The draft had been under preparation since the XXVIth Party Congress in 1981, when a commission was set up under Brezhnev's chairmanship. Andropov inherited the commission and then Chernenko took it over. The draft kept changing to reflect the views of the current General Secretary. But the fact that many people had contributed to the final document which was published for general discussion in October 1985[13] is irrelevant. Gorbachev approved the final version and it will be known in Party history as 'Gorbachev's Programme'. In fact, although a variety of institutional interests are represented and there are obvious contradictions between sections prepared by different departments of the Central Committee, it reflects his personality. The final approval of every section, and therefore the final responsibility for the programme as a whole, lay with Gorbachev.

The details of the new programme are irrelevant in a political biography, but there are useful hints in it of the likely direction of Gorbachev's policies and methods. It is much shorter than Khrushchev's programme and far less eloquent. It was prepared by people who had fewer illusions about the future and it does not promise communism in the immediate future, but 'mature socialism'. Nor does it forecast the demise of capitalism in the immediate future – capitalism has remained viable because it has been influenced by socialism to make concessions to the people. Many historical facts are distorted or ignored and it is uncritical of past errors and tragedies. Some past shortcomings are admitted and can be related to specific leaders (Stalin's 'personality cult', Khrushchev's 'subjectivist and voluntaristic' errors, Brezhnev's 'unfavourable tendencies and difficulties'), but these problems are in the past and the Party, 'displaying Bolshevist fidelity to principle and a self-critical approach', has worked to remove the consequences.[14]

The international section of the programme blames all negative events on capitalism and attributes all positive changes to the socialist countries. The international situation is depicted in black and white terms and the analysis lacks objectivity. The false general impression is given that the Soviet Union is leading world technical and scientific progress. The language used throughout is ambiguous, however, allowing for possible differences in interpretation should this prove necessary. Thus democracy is referred to as 'real democracy', freedom of information as 'access to all sources of knowledge' (allowing for the depiction of the many aspects of information to which Soviet citizens do not have access as 'useless knowledge' and therefore irrelevant to their needs), and human rights are 'filled with really vital content' and linked with duties. There is no section on agriculture in the new programme (the 1961 programme discussed agriculture) and no discussion of the global problems of demography and the environment which have begun to dominate the development of the world in the 1970s and 1980s. On the other hand, minor problems like the proper combination of general and vocational education in Soviet schools are dealt with in considerable detail. The general impression created by the new Party programme is that the conservative ideological wing still dominates in the Central Committee.

Amongst the contradictions in the programme, in one section the need to make prices reflect production costs is acknowledged: 'Price-formation must be improved to ensure that prices reflect more accurately the level of socially indispensable inputs and quality of products and services'.[15] But the programme also makes a promise to increase the purchasing power of the rouble, which implies the exact opposite. If prices were to reflect production costs the price of food products would have to rise steeply. In the programme the discussion on prices is linked to the consideration of the connection between the ideas of socialism and communism and the level of consumption. Soviet leaders have always promised that the production of food, consumer goods and services will increase and that living standards will improve. In socialist theory these promises are linked to the ability of the socialist system to make substantial improvements in productivity, technological levels, etc., thereby decreasing production costs and allowing price reductions. The idea is simple, but in reality productivity has been growing extremely slowly, technological progress has lagged behind that of the capitalist countries, production costs have risen constantly, and the purchasing power of the rouble has steadily eroded.

The Soviet state subsidizes essential products and services (bread, milk, rent, heating, health services, education, public transport, pensions and social benefits, etc.) heavily. This is necessary in most societies. But Soviet leaders have gone further. Reluctant to deviate from dogma and to attempt to establish a reasonable connection between production costs and prices, products and commodities which are not absolutely essential and which are not replenishable have also been subsidized (ranging from petrol, electricity, the postal and telephone services to non-essential foods, butter, sugar, vegetable oil, hotel prices, air travel, tourism, taxi services, cinemas, theatres, political and literary books, the press, etc.). The state heats houses and provides gas, water and television services absolutely free and as a result these services are used uneconomically and excessively.

In the 1930s, when the urban population was between 30 and 40 million, it was relatively simple to provide these services. But in the 1980s, when the urban population has reached 180–190 million, it has become enormously difficult. The only way it has been possible to continue the subsidies has been by freezing incomes. As a result, there are curious disproportions between the prices of various goods, some of which are artificially low, others reasonable and still others excessively expensive (clothing, shoes, hi-fi equipment, refrigerators, watches, cars, calculators, etc. all fall into the latter group). The consequence has been decreased consumption of expensive items and, therefore, a shortage of funds for subsidizing cheap items. It is bad luck for Gorbachev that the acknowledgement of inflation and the increase of many prices has to be done after his succession, rather than by Andropov or Chernenko. It has been necessary for a long time. Gorbachev has seemed to be reconsidering economic priorities, at least by increasing the salaries of those who need to use products and commodities from the unsubsidized sector (for example, academic books or calculators) and those who are so badly paid that daily life has become difficult (low paid pensioners, war invalids and widows). But price increases in many sectors are inevitable.

The Party Congress in February will approve not only the new programme, but also the new Party statutes. The draft statutes were published in November 1985.[16] The basic rules remain unchanged, but new elements have been added which strengthen the power of the General Secretary. The previous Party statutes did not specify how the General Secretary is elected. The position emerged historically as an organizational necessity. In Lenin's time it was he who was leader of the Party and not the General Secretary. Stalin was both leader and General Secretary, but he abolished the title of General Secretary after the war. Khrushchev was First Secretary and the title General Secretary was reintroduced by Brezhnev in 1966, but without changing the Party statutes. In the new statutes the title is 'legalized' and recognized as belonging to the official Party leader. The existence of the Party apparatus is also legalized for the first time. The previous statutes justified the creation of the Central Committee and regional committees, but did not specify the structure and function of the apparatus to serve the committees. Thus the vast departments and sections of the apparatus which have not only existed, but have wielded enormous power, have, until now, been informal.

The new statutes reduce the level of legal immunity enjoyed by Party members. This is an important change. The previous statutes made it impossible to try a member of the Party charged with a criminal offence before he had been expelled from the Party. It was a response to Stalin's campaign of terror, when Party members had often been arrested without any charge. But the result was that Party officials who were suspected of corruption and other criminal actions could often not be investigated or tried, since local Party committees would refuse to expel them. Under the new statutes this immunity has been removed. The Party decision to expel a member must depend on the result of the criminal investigation and trial (a Party member who is found innocent will not be expelled). But this rule also increases the power of the KGB and MVD. From a strictly theoretical, legal point of view, the new rules are correct and appropriate. But in practice there is no independent legal system in the Soviet Union and the result is that the General Secretary and the Politburo have acquired significantly more power.

The anti-corruption campaign has been continuing and it has involved regional Party officials and some members of the Central Committee, for example, Asanbai Askarov, an *obkom* secretary from Kazakhstan. He was accused of appropriating large sums from the construction budget to build a private hunting lodge, etc.[17] In fact, the privilege of Politburo members and *obkom* secretaries having hunting lodges was introduced by Brezhnev and the case against Askarov was intended to serve as a warning to other *obkom* secretaries.

In general Gorbachev has introduced very few social and political changes in his first year in office. This reflects the instincts of a professional Party official who understands that liberalization or democratization may turn against him. It also reflects the interests of Gorbachev's new team, in which neither Ligachev, nor Chebrikov, nor Ryzhkov have any desire to make the system more liberal. They have not understood that some dissent is necessary if ideological development is to take place, that it is only in interacting with some form of opposition that the ruling Party can escape dogmatism, ideological stagnation and the theoretical irrelevance of its own political principles. The postponement in introducing progressive social and political processes after the succession has allowed the more conservative Party elements to consolidate their position. But there is a contradiction between the economic goals which Gorbachev has set and the modernization which is required to achieve them, and his attempt to reach these goals via the same politically inflexible and undemocratic system.

It would seem that Gorbachev has either not yet understood the urgent necessity of encouraging the more progressive and liberal elements in the Party or that he cannot bring himself to do so.

There are two ways to balance the inevitably unpopular economic decisions which will need to be made. The first way is through liberalism and attempting to create real popular support. The second is by conservative methods, increasing personal power and using coercion and restrictions. Unfortunately, it looks at present as if the second way has been chosen. But the failure to make any real economic progress by these means may re-educate Gorbachev, who still seems open to alternatives. The exercise of power changes people, however, and this process has only just begun to work on Gorbachev. Whether it will work to change him for the better or for the worse remains to be seen. 70 years after the revolution the Soviet public still has only one freely available commodity to rely upon – hope.

11
New diplomacy, but the same old foreign policy

There are a number of Western politicians who would argue that the goals of Soviet foreign policy have remained the same since the war, or even since the revolution – expansion and world domination. They believe that expansion is an essential part of communist ideology and the idea of world revolution. Others argue even more convincingly that expansionism predates the present regime. It was the policy of the Russian empire from as far back as the 15th century. They see expansionism as a distinctive feature of *Russian* governments irrespective of ideology.[1] Not very surprisingly both these views are rejected by Soviet historians. They explain the pre-revolutionary expansion of Russia as unification, or both pre- and post-revolutionary expansion as defensive action against invasion from Asia and from the West, particularly from Germany which has invaded Russia twice this century. The memory of the second German invasion and the war which followed still dominates the Soviet political mentality.

In fact, territorial expansion has been a prominent feature of the development of most nations for millenia. In general, however, territorial expansion has been replaced by two other forms of expansion – economic and ideological. Economic expansion and the creation of economic or trade 'empires' is a spontaneous result of the ability of industrial capitalist economies to progress technologically and scientifically by competing. The most flexible and powerful economic systems (for example, the American and the Japanese) have acquired the leading role in the world economy. Ideological (or political) expansion is usually linked to countries which have undergone internal political crises and the collapse of their corrupt, inefficient, authoritarian or colonial regimes. The collapse, or 'revolution', has often been followed by a move towards socialism. Socialist ideas have become attractive in the 20th century, particularly to the poorer countries of the world to whom the Western ideas of a 'free world' are even more utopian than Marxist ideas of a centralized economy and just distribution.

If Soviet foreign policy is considered in this simplified framework, it will be seen to be partly a reaction to world developments and partly the result of internal factors and traditions. And if Gorbachev's foreign political intentions are to be judged by the new Party programme, there will be less ideological expansion of the USSR in future, compared to what was promised in previous programmes. A section of the programme is devoted to the theory of the 'struggle between the forces of progress and reaction' in the modern world. Everything that is progressive is associated with the Soviet Union and socialism, while the capitalist world, and particularly the USA, is the cause of everything 'reactionary'. But the programme does not contain a master plan of how to fight the reactionary forces of world imperialism. As far as foreign policy objectives are concerned, the only clear statements are about co-operation with the socialist countries on a reciprocal basis, to bring about socialist economic integration and 'consistent pooling of efforts . . . to accomplish jointly a task of historical importance, namely that of emerging into the forefront of science and technology'.[2] The outcome of the competition between socialism and communism is said to 'depend to a great extent on . . . the success of each country in its constructive endeavours'.[3] The programme promises solidarity and co-operation with the 'Newly-Free Countries', but no new substantive help. 'Every people is developing, mostly by its own efforts, the material and technical base needed to build a new society', while the Soviet Union 'has been doing and will continue to do what it can to render . . . assistance in economic and cultural development, in training national personnel, in building up their defences and in other fields'.[4]

By 1985 the Soviet leadership had understood that the special 'superpower' position of the USSR, and its previous ideological and political expansion carried a very heavy economic price and brought few benefits. The Brezhnev leadership was very proud of its international successes which were visible in the form of the American defeat in Vietnam, socialist transformation in Angola, Mozambique and Ethiopia and the intensification of revolutionary movements in Latin America. However, after every successful socialist revolution, the newly emerged fraternal country required economic aid and had little to offer in return. The inability of the Soviet Union to render any real assistance to starving Ethiopia (the famine was not reported in the Soviet press for more than a year and when details emerged they were distorted) or to find a political or a military solution in Afghanistan were indications of the limits of Soviet economic and military power. The energy crisis in Eastern Europe in 1984 and 1985 was a further alarming symptom. Soviet dependence on the Western capitalist countries for the development of high technology and for vital commodities like grain, meat, sugar and butter to prevent domestic malnutrition also contributed to a reorientation of foreign policy priorities.

The increasing complexity of Soviet foreign relations and the different levels at which foreign policy is conducted (diplomatic, economic, military, intelligence, political, direct or via proxies), often without co-ordination between the levels because of compartmentalization, secrecy and bureaucratization, had finally created a situation at the end of the Brezhnev era when the Soviet Union could no longer afford the cost of its 'empire'. There were too many client states and too few benefits. The collapse of detente and the new arms race entailed negative consequences, but the Soviet Union consistently denies that the intervention in Afghanistan in 1979 and the economic and political crisis in Poland in 1980–81 were even partially responsible for the deterioration.

Gorbachev has better personal qualities for foreign activities than his predecessors. This was recognized during his visit to Britain in 1984, when he became the favourite of the Western press. The fact that he is an impressive political figure has been acknowledged by all the foreign politicians who have had the opportunity to meet him and to get into discussion or dispute with him. He seems to enjoy press conferences and he has been a dominating figure with logical (but not always accurate) answers. His ability to discuss a range of issues is particularly remarkable given his limited foreign relations experience before 1984. But he is sometimes over-confident, tackling problems with which he is unfamiliar. Talking with French reporters just before his visit to

France, for example, he made the surprising statement that the Soviet record on political rights could be judged by the number of workers in the Supreme Soviet. There were more working class deputies 'than in all the parliaments of the developed capitalist countries put together'.[5] In fact, the Supreme Soviet has often been criticized for the dominance of professional Party and state officials within it. In 1950 only 7 per cent of the deputies were workers. The number rose to 11 per cent in 1962 and 18 per cent in 1974 (the proportion of the full-time Party and state bureaucrats was 45, 40 and 36 per cent respectively).[6] But it was also obvious that Gorbachev did not understand that Parliamentary membership is a full-time job in the West. Thus his excellent 'personal diplomacy' sometimes merely underlines the weakness of his opponents.

The fact that Reagan was extensively prepared for his meeting with Gorbachev produced the positive effect of raising the intellectual level of their meetings. They were shown on Soviet television and the Soviet public had not seen anything like this since Khrushchev's time. Even usually apolitical young people became interested. Gorbachev's charm, sense of humour, prompt responses, attempts to find convincing arguments and his less frequent recourse to demagoguery suddenly introduced the human factor into East–West confrontation. This in itself served to reduce tension. Gorbachev clearly did not resemble a person who was waiting for the opportunity to drop a nuclear bomb on the West.

In April US Congressmen visited the Soviet Union and had a four-hour meeting with Gorbachev. Tip O'Neill, the House Speaker, handed Gorbachev a letter from President Reagan suggesting a meeting. O'Neill was very impressed by Gorbachev's performance and he was quoted widely as saying that Gorbachev 'would be an excellent trial lawyer, an outstanding attorney from New York. He is a master of words, and a master of the arts of politics and of diplomacy'.[7] Although American journalists called him 'well informed, urbane, energetic, tough, witty and above all in possession of a disciplined intellect',[8] they did not detect any change in the Soviet political line. Gorbachev's statements contained 'the same elements of the traditional Soviet hard line, but not in a familiar pedantic Soviet style'.[9] They recognized that a combination of the ideological dogmatism of a convinced communist and intellect, political skill and force of personality had brought Gorbachev to the top.

In many ways Moscow was the diplomatic capital of the world in 1985. World leaders were queueing up to visit Gorbachev. But he had his own schedule and objectives. He knew that some of his tough domestic measures (particularly the economic measures and the campaign against drinking) would not be popular, and that continuing the anti-corruption campaign and rapidly replacing local officials as well as central ministers would cause apprehension amongst the Party elite. The international arena, on the other hand, gave him the perfect opportunity to project himself as an outstanding leader who was doing a great deal for his own country and for world peace. Although he was General Secretary and the most influential person in the Politburo, he still needed a consensus. All major decisions were presented as joint resolutions of the Central Committee and the Council of Ministers. Things could not be changed overnight in the economy or in agriculture. Results would take several years and, in agriculture particularly, there was a risk that there would be none. But while his personality could not increase crop yields rapidly, his power and political skill could reap a rich diplomatic harvest. It must have been clear to him that this was an area in which he could build up his popularity and his 'personality cult'. It was also an area in which he could be sure that the country was behind him. It was not only ideology and Party discipline which would make Soviet people watch his performance, but also national pride and patriotism.

What Gorbachev required from foreign policy was concrete success. And the only success which would matter was improving relations with Western Europe and, more importantly, with the USA. The key issue here was the problem of the arms race, although it was part of a more complex set of East–West relations. His second priority was Afghanistan, which was important in both domestic and foreign policy. The war had gone on for too long (it had already lasted longer than the Great Patriotic War) and there was no end in sight. It was a political and a military embarrassment. There were other pressing problems – China, India, Pakistan, the Middle East, Ethiopia, Cuba, Nicaragua, Angola, South Africa, Vietnam and Kampuchea, the Gulf War – but none of them was quite so urgent. If he wanted to accelerate economic development, the main task of his diplomacy should be to reduce the cost of foreign policy and that meant substantial arms reductions.

Gorbachev's strategy was not very difficult to predict. In early April former US President Richard Nixon made this prediction:

> Gorbachev has got major problems at home with the economy. Therefore where we in the West are strong, he needs our help. He's got to be concerned about Eastern Europe and the outer perimeters of the Soviet empire. Every one of the Soviet Union's 'colonies' is a drag and has to be subsidized.[10]

His first move was in the traditional form of an 'interview' with an unnamed editor of *Pravda* published on April 8. He offered the usual formula that international relations are dominated by the existence of two opposing social systems and that the main issue was 'peaceful coexistence' between socialism and capitalism. He then proceed to make what sounded like an off-the-cuff demonstration of Soviet goodwill:

> As of to-day – and I would like to emphasize this – the Soviet Union is introducing a moratorium on the deployment of its medium range missiles and suspending other countermeasures in Europe.[11]

There was a condition attached, however. The United States should follow suit and stop deploying medium range missiles in Europe. The Soviet moratorium would last until November (in fact, it has not been lifted). The decision was apparently more popular in Eastern Europe (where Soviet medium range missiles were to be deployed) than in the USA, which believed its own deployment to be a reaction to an earlier Soviet build up. Predictably, the USA rejected the freeze on the grounds that it would freeze a Soviet advantage and that it was designed to drive a wedge between the USA and its European allies. In particular, it was thought to be meant to influence the Dutch government which was to decide in November whether to permit the deployment of 48 cruise missiles (they responded with a compromise – cruise missiles could be deployed, but the number of other NATO weapons systems on Dutch soil would be reduced).

Gorbachev's diplomatic schedule in the spring held no surprises. He made a trip to Warsaw in April to sign the 20-year extension of the Warsaw Pact Treaty and while he was there, held intensive discussions on the other problems of the Pact countries. This was the first opportunity for many East European leaders to meet him again after Chernenko's funeral. In May the Indian Prime Minister, Rajiv Gandhi, paid an official visit to Moscow. Despite Gorbachev's wish to reduce the cost of Soviet commitments abroad, India was an important friend in South Asia and a large importer of Soviet industrial and military equipment. India has a negative trade balance with the Soviet Union and requires periodic credits. Several agreements were signed and reported in the Soviet press. However, a credit agreement for $1.2 billion remained unreported (this was not unusual – details of credits and financial assistance are not publicized and do not require Supreme Soviet approval).

The main diplomatic events of the year were scheduled for the autumn. The first was Gorbachev's official visit to France at the beginning of October, followed by a Warsaw Pact summit in Sofia at the end of that month, and the summit meeting in Geneva with President Reagan in November. The spotlight of the world was on the latter meeting. But first Gorbachev had to form a foreign policy team. A number of ambassadors were replaced, but the main event was the promotion of Gromyko, the longest serving foreign minister in the world, and his replacement by Shevarnadze, completely unknown outside the Soviet Union. In fact, Shevarnadze's inexperience in foreign policy could be an advantage if there were foreign policy changes. There were other new foreign policy appointments in the government. Nikolai Patolichev, the veteran Minister of Foreign Trade (he had held this post since 1958), was retired and replaced by Boris Aristov, the Soviet ambassador in Poland since 1978. This Ministry deals primarily with trade with capitalist countries. The Soviet ambassador in Cuba, Konstantin Katushev, was brought back to Moscow to become Chairman of the State Committee on External Economic Affairs, which deals with trade with socialist countries. He had previously been a prominent figure, a secretary of the Central Committee from 1972–7, a Deputy Chairman of the Council of Ministers and the Soviet representative in the Council for Mutual Economic Assistance (CMEA). He had seemed a possible successor to Kosygin as Prime Minister, but had lost his international position in 1980 and replaced Vorotnikov in Cuba in 1982.

The 10th anniversary celebrations of the Helsinki Accord in August gave both sides the opportunity for liberal gestures. At the beginning of August 35 delegations assembled in the Finnish capital. Human rights would clearly be discussed at the three-day conference. Reagan's public relations gift consisted in inviting the Soviet Union to send experts to monitor US nuclear tests in Nevada. Gorbachev rejected the idea and declared a unilateral five-month moratorium on all nuclear tests, beginning on August 6, the 40th anniversary of the dropping of the atom bomb on Hiroshima. He did not offer any goodwill gestures in the field of human rights. There was, in fact, something he could have offered. The Helsinki Accord provided many joint resolutions about the development of the exchange of information. Nothing contradicted these resolutions quite as much as the Soviet practice of jamming radio broadcasts by the BBC, Voice of America, Deutsche Welle and other stations broadcasting in Russian and other Soviet languages. Moreover, the jamming (done by several thousand specially designed transmitters) costs the Soviet government a great deal of money. It is also very unpopular both within the Soviet Union and without, since the noise interferes with normal shortwave broadcasts. Although it had been lifted at various periods in the past (from 1954, for example, until Soviet tanks entered Budapest in 1956, and again in 1960 and at various relaxed periods in the seventies), it had been particularly intensive and effective in the 1980s. The Helsinki anniversary presented an ideal opportunity to make a gesture by stopping what was essentially a policy of paranoia. Gorbachev let the opportunity pass, however, and none of the Westerners pointed out that jamming violated the Helsinki spirit.

After several months in office, Gorbachev seemed to be approaching his meetings with Western leaders without any indication that there was to be a change in Soviet foreign policy. New disarmament offers had been made, but they were so tightly linked to the demand for a cessation of 'Star Wars' (or, more properly, the Strategic Defence Initiative) that there was little likelihood that there would be an early agreement. There were rumours that diplomatic relations with Israel might possibly be restored although, in fact, Soviet anti-Zionist propaganda increased during the summer. The most serious foreign policy problem remained Afghanistan. The presence in Afghanistan of seven or eight divisions (120,000 men) was a major foreign policy liability. The fighting had intensified since March and the time had come for new suggestions or initiatives. A war of this kind could not be continued indefinitely. Seven, or even ten divisions would not be sufficient to keep the country under effective occupation. The refugee camps, in which two or three million refugees were living in Pakistan close to the border were an ideal breeding ground for young Islamic fighters. The situation was very similar to the one experienced by Israel from the Palestinian refugee camps in Jordan, Syria and the Lebanon, but it would be more difficult to create a sophisticated, sealed border area around the large, mountainous and sparsely populated country of Afghanistan than it was for Israel. There seemed to be no solution to the war. A Soviet invasion of Pakistan (like the Israeli invasion of the Lebanon in 1982) was an unattractive proposition which could lead to a major war in an area which is already difficult to control. The danger was that Gorbachev would be tempted to try a military solution before looking for a political way out, fulfilling Kissinger's prediction in 1978 of the possible consequences of a new generation of Soviet leaders who 'might be freer of self-doubt; with no inferiority complex . . . who may believe their own boasts [and] . . . may prove far more dangerous'.[12]

The sudden reappearance of Marshal Ogarkov (to launch his book *History Teaches Vigilance*) in June was seen as an indication of his rehabilitation. He was expected to be appointed commander-in-chief of the Warsaw Pact forces, but it is equally likely that he had become Gorbachev's military adviser. The General Secretary normally has personal military advisers, although their names are never revealed. Brezhnev's most trusted military adviser was Colonel-General Konstantin Grushevoi, a friend since their student days in Dneprodzerzhinsk and a colleague on the Dnepropetrovsk *obkom*. He had remained in the army after the war, becoming Commander of the political department of the Moscow military district. His close links with Brezhnev were only revealed after he died in 1982, when he was unexpectedly given a Red Square funeral. Brezhnev also had an adviser on missiles who accompanied him to the SALT II negotiations. Gorbachev would need a younger group of military advisers to take a fresh look at the problems of Soviet military involvement around the world. Ogarkov, an energetic and technically oriented marshal who had been dismissed by Chernenko, would be an excellent person to form the group.

It was presumably Gorbachev's military advisers who suggested stepping up military activity in Afghanistan. In 1979 Brezhnev's main objective in Afghanistan had been to secure Kabul, the other major towns and all roads and communications within one or two days. This tactic had proved very successful in Czechoslovakia in 1968. In Afghanistan, however, it sparked a protracted partisan war of attrition and produced millions of refugees from the rural areas. Andropov had favoured an enlargement of the powerful security wing of the KHAD, the Afghan State Security Service which was modelled on the KGB and which had specialized, elite frontier units. Many new agents were recruited by KHAD and infiltration of the resistance forces was increased. Some KHAD groups were disguised as guerrillas to create suspicion and confusion in the local population in the hope that the disunited resistance would become demoralized. The technique of infiltration had been used successfully against the dissident community within the Soviet Union and it had contributed to the 'normalization' process in Czechoslovakia. When Chernenko succeeded Andropov, he added his method to the repertoire – the creation of a people's militia alongside the regular Afghan army. Since the population resisted regular military service, it was hoped that the militia units would be a substitute which would enable the war to be 'Afghanized'.

Gorbachev launched fresh offensives on both the military and the political fronts. The newly established Ministry for Islam Affairs sought to reduce the conflict between Marxism and Islam, councils of elders were re-established in tribal areas and military action was escalated. Border roads were mined more intensively and commando-type Soviet units replaced some ordinary army units. Pressure was increased on Pakistan to stop the flow of arms to resistance groups and Pakistani territory was bombarded more frequently in April.[13] The Soviet press intensified its coverage of the fighting, imputing direct American involvement (one *Izvestiya* article, for example, claimed that in Peshawar alone at least 200 American volunteers had taken part in the fighting disguised as Afghan rebels[14]). Attempts were made to popularize the war and to use the upsurge of patriotism engendered by the 40th anniversary of the victory in Europe. War heroes were created of Soviet soldiers who were prepared to sacrifice themselves for their native land. Soviet television showed some combat scenes, which was an unprecedent event.[15] Although Gorbachev stated that he preferred a political solution, he seemed to be aiming for a quick military end to the war. Depicting the war as a heroic battleground may have been the first move in preparing the population for the escalation of Soviet involvement. The intention may also have been to create a military zone along the border with Pakistan like the one between the Soviet Union and China or Iran. Foreign speculation during the summer that Gorbachev might be contemplating a 'phased withdrawal of Soviet troops . . . thus freeing up roubles for his domestic reforms'[16] exaggerated the economic effects of the war. The operation is still a very limited one for the Soviet army, and the political price of a solution which could be interpreted as defeat would be far higher for Gorbachev than it would have been for Andropov or Chernenko. The only political settlement which Gorbachev could find acceptable would have to include the preservation of Babrak Karmal's government and a limited Soviet military presence in Afghanistan.

The war in Afghanistan has a high price for the United States as well. In 1985 alone, the US Congress allowed $470 million to the CIA to provide the Afghan resistance with arms and training.[17] Part of the arms supplied by the US never reaches the guerrillas, being taken by the Pakistan army, by feuding tribesmen in the border area or by opium traders in the region which is now the world's largest supplier of opium and heroin (most of which lands up in the West). The large frontier province in Pakistan has become a semi-autonomous, highly militarized zone which cannot be controlled effectively by the Pakistan army and which will remain a source of instability in Afghanistan for many years, playing a similar role to that North Vietnam played for the Vietcong in South Vietnam. Soviet military activity in Afghanistan is not, of course, as well, or as objectively, publicized as US military activity was in Vietnam. On the other hand, the USSR has far less international support (practical and moral) than the USA enjoyed in Vietnam in 1963–73.

The war in Afghanistan has had serious implications for the Soviet military establishment. It has proved difficult to fight a protracted war, even with small forces, on the basis of a conscripted army. In a larger war, seasoned soldiers continue fighting and the army gets more and more front-line experience. The soldiers and junior officers continue fighting until the war is over. A peace-time conscripted army which is rotated can only keep a limited contingent at the same level over a long period. Soldiers have to be demobilized when they have completed their two-year service. Moreover, the population is finding out more and more about the war from rumours and stories passed on by word of mouth. As it does so, the war becomes less and less popular. The government faces the difficult problem of needing to create another 10–20 divisions of professional soldiers with better training in real combat. This will change the whole political rationale of Soviet military service. While the resistance army is improving and the rebels are becoming more and more professional, Soviet army morale is low and the young conscripts are poorly prepared for this type of war. As a result, the Soviet military is introducing increasingly sophisticated weapons and limiting the fighting to defence of strategic points and raids carried out by professional commando units. But it has become more and more clear to the Soviet military command that a partisan war with Islamic fundamentalists is much more difficult than they ever expected.

Gorbachev is known to have created a special advisory commission on Islamic affairs which is to report to the Politburo. It is likely to have some influence on the policy towards Afghanistan. But it is also likely that the generals and officers with experience in Afghanistan will be promoted in 1986, when Gorbachev's power is more consolidated and he begins the task of rejuvenating the Soviet military establishment. Until now the top brass in the Soviet Union has been composed of officers with experience in the Great Patriotic War. They are now elderly and old-fashioned. When veterans of Afghanistan begin to replace them, they may advocate an increase in the Soviet military presence, with withdrawal taking place only after 'normalization'. This prospect does not augur well for Soviet–American relations. Gorbachev's statements about a possible political solution are misleading. He has nobody to negotiate with, except his colleagues in the Politburo. If the neighbouring Islamic countries negotiate on behalf of the resistance, an inevitable precondition will be the withdrawal of Soviet troops. But the 'Afghanization' of the war has little chance of success. Thus the 'Sovietization' of Afghanistan after a substantial increase of Soviet troops is not an unlikely option.

There have been no real surprises in Gorbachev's Western policy. He hoped to obtain support from Western Europe in his campaign against SDI and for nuclear disarmament. He also wanted Western Europe to contribute to the Soviet and Eastern European technological modernization programmes and separate talks with Britain and France about their nuclear forces. His wishes might have been reciprocated if he had shown any sign of domestic liberalization, as Khrushchev had done prior to and after the invasion of Hungary in 1956. Brezhnev's detente policy had been a continuation of Khrushchev's initiatives and had also been related to limited domestic liberalization (particularly allowing Soviet Jews, Germans, Greeks and Armenians to emigrate). But in 1985 with continuing semi-martial law regulations in Poland, the war in Afghanistan, a freeze on emigration and limited access for the Soviet Union to cultural and scientific exchange, the objective factors for better relations with Western Europe were absent. Soviet hopes for success were based on two factors: European economic problems and unemployment in Western Europe and the attractive personality of the new leader. Gorbachev was certainly a better salesman of the idea of Soviet–European co-operation than his predecessors. But Western Europe was too sophisticated to be simply charmed by him.

Gorbachev's trip to France in October was a test of the reality of Soviet expectations. It was a personal success for Gorbachev, but the political and economic results of what the Western media called 'Gorbachev's Charm Offensive' were non-existent. He confirmed his political skills, his ability to use modern, 'public relations' methods, his energy and style, but he did not deviate from the pursuit of traditional Soviet goals. He simply could not accept responsibility for any possible Soviet misconduct or error in the past. His position, based on the assumption that everything the Soviet Union was doing or had done was right, did not make a good impression on Western Europe. Khrushchev's style had been less polished, his suits had been more old fashioned and his manners less than diplomatic. Yet he was obviously initiating a new policy and he was able to accept that the Soviet Union had not always been right. If Gorbachev could add some political flexibility to his excellent diplomatic performance, he would be more successful in Europe. But he reacted angrily to questions on human rights and emigration and he misjudged France's nuclear policy by expecting to be able to woo Mitterand into agreeing to separate nuclear arms negotiations.

At the end of October Gorbachev took part in a two-day meeting of the Political Consultative Committee of the Warsaw Pact countries in Sofia. An official statement was released which repeated well-worn previous declarations. There were no new political initiatives during the meeting to attract interest inside or outside the Soviet bloc. The East European leaders are said to have discussed mutual economic problems, but the substance of the discussions was not revealed. East European leaders have no choice but to endorse Soviet policy and disagreements are kept well behind closed doors. It is almost certain that the approaching winter made countries like Rumania, Czechoslovakia and Poland try to get more Soviet oil and petrol to prevent similar energy crises to those which had occurred in 1984. Soviet oil supplies to East Europe had been reduced in 1985 because of production problems. Gorbachev could make no promises and in November the price of petrol was increased sharply in Poland and other countries to reduce consumption.

On his return from Sofia, Gorbachev began preparing for his main diplomatic challenge of the year, the meeting with Reagan in Geneva. The Soviet position for Geneva was already well known and had been endorsed by the Soviet allies in Sofia. Substantial reductions in the total number of nuclear warheads on strategic systems (weapons which could reach American territory) were possible: the total number of warheads allowed to each side was proposed to be 6000. This still represented an 'overkill', but it was a 50 per cent reduction from the SALT II ceilings. The United States agreed in principle, but the two superpowers disagreed about the distribution of the proposed reduction. The USA wanted a substantial reduction of Soviet land-based missiles (the main part of the Soviet nuclear arsenal). The Soviet Union, on the other hand, wanted to include the American intermediate range weapons stationed in Europe which can reach Soviet territory, while discussing the SS-20s (which can reach Western Europe) in a different forum. Clearly, these details could only be resolved by experts in professional negotiations and not by the leaders during a two-day meeting. In principle, however, the Soviet offer was realistic and negotiable, except for the fact that it was linked to a demand that all SDI research projects be halted. The Soviet fear of SDI was understandable. If the USA was successful in developing a shield which would protect its territory from ballistic missiles, it would, in effect, have a first strike capability. Even if the shield did not guarantee foolproof protection, it would substantially alter the strategic balance. The Anti-Ballistic Missile Treaty signed in 1972 allowed each superpower one land-based system to protect a population centre. But space-based defence systems represented an entirely new technological principle and the United States, with its technological superiority, had the lead.

Research for the system would be enormously expensive ($20–30 billion), but the cost of research was not the greatest problem (though it would be even greater for the Soviet Union since it lagged behind in the field of high technology). The cost of deployment would be even greater. Scientists objected to the idea because they understood how difficult it would be to make an impenetrable shield. But these objections rested on the American assumption that the Soviet Union would launch a first strike. The real problem lay in the fact that if the US went ahead with SDI research, the Soviet Union would have to replace practically all its strategic weapons. SALT II, which restricted the development of new types of missiles, would be scrapped entirely and a new and highly technological stage of the arms race would begin. In order to reduce the objections of its European allies to SDI, the USA offered to share research efforts and to subsidize research carried out in other countries. Very large funds were involved and both West Germany and Britain decided to join in. At the same time, it was difficult for the Soviet Union to object to the research stage. There were no international treaties to invoke which prohibited research work in this field.

The Soviet objection that these 'defensive' missiles were actually offensive, was not entirely unreasonable. If the shields could destroy ballistic missiles in flight, they would, with minor modifications, also be able to be used against other targets. It would be enormously difficult for the Soviet Union to develop a similar system, partly because of the technology gap (the American offer to share the technology was not taken seriously by anyone).

But the Soviet Union also has a far larger territory to protect. Moreover, the shields would not offer protection against the Pershing 2 missiles deployed in Europe, since their flight time to their targets would be too short. In any case, it was unlikely that Reagan was right in seeing SDI as the means to end nuclear arms. All it would mean would be a new and very expensive stage of the arms race.

It was clear that Gorbachev would concentrate his attention on the arguments against SDI at Geneva, while Reagan would continue to argue the right of any country to defend itself and to make empty promises to share the technology later. Regional conflicts were also expected to be on the agenda. There was no sign during the preliminary talks that the summit would produce any arms agreements. Pessimists expected that the meeting would only cause relations between the superpowers to deteriorate still further, with both leaders shouting at one another. Even optimists expected that nothing substantial would be changed, except that the two leaders would become personally acquainted. They did not believe that a personal rapport would emerge, since each leader was expected to show contempt for the other's point of view. In the innumerable discussions, interviews and media analyses before the event, the consensus was that the meeting would fail. If Gorbachev had followed the advice of his advisers (for example, Zamyatin, an influential Central Committee figure and chief spokesman on foreign affairs, or Kornienko, First Deputy of the Minister of Foreign Affairs and Gromyko's favourite as his successor) the meeting would have been a failure and the 'human factor' would not have been able to play a role in the outcome. It was entirely to Gorbachev's and Reagan's credit that the summit can be considered a relative success, even without substantial results on the main issues.

An important contributory factor to the success was the arrangement of the meeting, with private sessions as an important part of the agenda. This allowed personal relations between the leaders to improve and thus mutually hostile propaganda became difficult. Both leaders probably realized (and possibly they discussed the problem in their private talks) that the other was more moderate than the hawkish politicians each had to deal with back home. Both had a considerable stake in making the meeting seem a success. Gorbachev once again proved himself an excellent diplomat and performer. This did not surprise the Western media who knew that he was formidable in this respect. What was surprising was how well Reagan performed. The members of Gorbachev's team, used to a system of collective responsibility, were probably disturbed that their boss managed to hold his own without their constant support and advice. The American team, on the other hand, must have been very relieved that Reagan was able to keep the negotiations going at the personal level, while being impressive and tough. The final statements, a few small agreements on cultural exchanges etc., were of secondary importance. The most important outcome was the reduction of mutually hostile rhetoric and attempts to damage the reputation of the other side. Mutual respect was generated, but it is a fragile result. A minor international crisis, always possible in areas of confrontation, could unleash the hostile propaganda. Gorbachev's visit to the USA in 1986 and Reagan's visit to the USSR in 1987, if they take place as agreed, will continue the process of improving superpower relations.

On his return to Moscow, Gorbachev gave a detailed report about the Geneva meeting at a Supreme Soviet session.[18] He was already more restrained and moderate in describing the American position (the Americans were not called aggressive, for example, although Gorbachev did maintain that they were trying to achieve superiority). International relations looked frail, but more hopeful than they had been for some time.

There are far simpler problems than SDI to which Gorbachev could apply common sense and improve the international situation. At a press conference in Paris on October 4 he had been asked: 'Do you contemplate in the near future opening the doors of the Soviet Union more widely and allowing Soviet people to travel freely to the West, and people from the West to travel to the Soviet Union?'[19] Gorbachev ignored the first part of the question. He apparently had no plans for opening the doors to his own people. As far as Westerners were concerned, they were welcome in the Soviet Union on condition that: ' . . . it was not linked with attempts to use [their trips] for political, provocative aims, to poison the situation, to interfere in internal affairs'.[20] He gave the example of a group of American tourists who enjoyed a Volga cruise. What he did not yet seem to understand was that when Soviet citizens were able to make individual decisions to buy package tours for a Mississipi cruise, this would be the greatest leap in the development of socialist democracy and the greatest achievement of world peace. Gorbachev and his colleagues in the Politburo have the power to make this possible. It is a better way to match the US than trying to construct a Star Wars programme. It is cheaper and easier. Competing in levels of individual freedom would be more popular in both countries than competing in levels of possible mutual annihilation. When the Soviet leadership begins to trust its own public with a wide range of individual choices and freedoms, the public in other countries will begin to trust the peaceful intentions of the Soviet leadership.

Conclusion

Within a year Gorbachev has become the most celebrated and best known political leader in the world. It is, of course, natural for the leaders of the superpowers to attract more attention than the leaders of smaller nations. Is it also inevitable that communist leaders, who tend to stay in power for life, are taken more seriously than the leaders of democratic societies who are subject to criticism and opposition and rarely survive more than two terms in office. When Brezhnev died in 1982 the question everyone within and without the Soviet Union asked was 'is this the end of an era?' When Andropov succeeded him there were hopes, but no clear answer. When Chernenko succeeded Andropov the answer was a definite negative. It is now obvious, however, that a distinctively new era in Soviet history has begun: there is a new leader and a change in political generation. From the programmes they have adopted it is clear that Gorbachev and his colleagues intend to stay in power for a long time. They expect to see the Soviet Union into the next millennium.

Communist leaders enjoy a far greater concentration of political and executive power than the governments of pluralist societies. At the same time the limitations of the ideology from which they claim legitimacy leave them with fewer choices of goals. They receive their mandate from the Party, not from the public at large and the Party considers that the 1917 revolution has given it eternal power. But even given these limited choices, there are alternative options which would make a real difference. This has been proved by such Communist reformists as Khrushchev, Gomulka, Tito, Kadar, Dubček and Deng Xiaoping. But these reformists have usually wanted to break with a past from which they had suffered either directly or morally. Their ideas have developed under the influence of revolution, war and repression. The generation of communist leaders to which Gorbachev belongs has not experienced of suffering and fear. From the beginning of their political careers they have been amongst the privileged. But they are better educated and they have better adminstrative skills than their predecessors. They are the products of the system, not its creators. They tend to prefer improvement and continuity rather than broad, bold reform.

We have traced Gorbachev's life and the formation of his personal ambitions. We have also tried to analyse his capabilities, methods, ideas and limitations. It is natural to ask whether his vision of the year 2000 is realistic. Will he be able to make life in the Soviet Union safer and more attractive?

The social psychology and value system of the United States have changed far less in the 20th century than have those of the Soviet Union. Americans live under the same constitution, the same system of government, the same general economic system, with the same two parties providing alternative sources of leadership. Many of the laws and economic principles which were valid in the United States at the beginning of the century are still valid. Russia, on the other hand, has passed through a series of dramatic historical experiences from 1904 to 1964 and it is only in the last twenty years that there has been a degree of stability. Every group in society, the elite as well as the masses, has suffered the traumatic effects of war, revolution and repression. The post-Khrushchev leadership assumed power on the basis of a promise that the stability of their positions would bring consensus based on significant economic and social improvements. They linked their legitimacy with the expectation of a better life, a better diet, better health and a better international climate. They failed on every count. The official statistics use figures selectively, but even they do not indicate real success. The general per capita consumption has begun to increase more slowly, the food situation has deteriorated, the average diet has developed protein deficiencies, life expectancy began to decline after 1964 for all groups (but particularly seriously for men), mortality began to rise, environmental pollution reached dangerous levels. Crime, accidents, alcoholoism, smoking, drug addiction, industrial accidents, and the population of the prison camps have all risen. The divorce rate has more than doubled, reaching 50 per cent in the European part of the Soviet Union. The Soviet army is still the largest in the world and Soviet soldiers are dying in Afghanistan in a war which has been going for longer than any war in the last two centuries of Russian history. The political and social atmosphere in the country is worse now than at the beginning of the 1960s. Nothing can be done about the past (except, of course, the familiar technique of re-writing history), but the future is in Gorbachev's hands.

It has already been abundantly clear that Gorbachev is neither a liberal nor a bold reformist. He prefers small modifications, administrative methods and economic adjustments to structural reform. But there are indications that he has not yet made his final choice. He has been careful not to link his credibility to a single option. If, however, he merely continues the course he has adopted in his first year in office, trying to modernize and repair the existing system without lifting the many artificial and unjust political and economic restrictions, there will be little improvement in Soviet material and intellectual life and the acceleration which has been predicted in the new programmes will not take place. Computers alone cannot bring about miracles. If administration remains strictly centralized, coercive and disciplinarian, if conservative dogmatism continues to dominate intellectual life and if the unearned privileges of the elite continue to widen the gap between leaders and led, economic and social progress will not last beyond the initial short-lived improvement which naturally follows a period of succession when the previous most obvious mistakes and miscalculations are removed.

Liberalization is not only desirable from a political point of view. It has great economic and international value. Freedom of the press and a better exchange of information between countries, a radical relaxation of arrangements for foreign travel, the abolition of the notorious articles of the Criminal Code which make the expression of political dissent a criminal offence would mean that Soviet science and technology would develop more rapidly, there would be a healthy diversity in cultural life and a complementarity between individual and collective efforts in the economy. The policy of 'open borders' and the cancellation of the wasteful jamming of foreign radio broadcasts would make it more likely that agreements could be negotiated to reduce nuclear and conventional arsenals. It would also increase Western doubts about the wisdom of the Star Wars programme far more than a dozen summit meetings and years of negotiations. This in turn would release a vast amount of funds for better health and social services, for rationalizing the income and prices system and for increasing economic assistance to poorer nations. Without liberalization, Soviet science and technology will continue to develop by copying and assimilating technologies and services which have already been tested in other developed countries. Capitalism, which is 'doomed' in Soviet theory, will remain the main source of Soviet technical innovation and Soviet agriculture will continue requiring huge imports to make up for its inability to provide the population with the long promised better diet.

Whether there is authoritarian or liberal rule, the eventual emergence of Gorbachev's own 'cult of personality' is inevitable. It is an important feature of Soviet-style political systems. Gorbachev will almost certainly use his power and influence more wisely than Stalin, Khrushchev and Brezhnev did. But genuine popularity, which can be an important factor in economic and political development, is the product of a liberal or democratic society. The 'cult of personality' should not be confused with real popularity. Popular leaders are those who try to fulfil the aspirations of their people and they are remembered with gratitude.

It is possibly a mistake to expect too much from Gorbachev. The very fact that he has a better intellect, better education, and is a more decent person than his predecessors may contribute to a gradual improvement in the quality of the Soviet political and administrative elite and help to cultivate a more flexible and less dogmatic future generation of leaders. We have seen that Gorbachev has inherited his power from sponsors like Suslov, Andropov, Ustinov and Gromyko. This means that he possessed the proper combination of orthodoxy, efficiency, toughness and political and diplomatic skill to move all the way up through the Soviet political system. But if he wants the best possible role for the Soviet Union in future world history, he needs to share his decision-making power not only with his Kremlin colleagues, but with his people as well. If he does that, he will change from being the ruler to being the leader.

Notes and references

1 The General Secretary is dead, long live the General Secretary

1 Dusko Doder, Moscow correspondent of the *Washington Post*. Washington Post Service, *International Herald Tribune*, March 19, 1985.

2 Instructions were sent from the Central Committee to local organizations to start preparations for the Party Congress due to be held in November 1985. They were not intended for publication, but some local newspapers published information about the early date of the Congress. See *Pravda Vostoka*, March 3, 1985.

3 Foreign Agricultural Circular. 'Grains. USSR Grain Situation and Outlook', United States Department of Agriculture, May 1985, p. 5.

4 *Izvestiya*, December 22, 1984.

5 Mark Frankland, 'Russia's Changing Face', *The Observer*, March 17, 1985.

6 Seweryn Bialer, 'Gorbachev: the tailwinds in his spring to power', *International Herald Tribune*, March 19, 1985.

7 For the figures of the election results in the RSFSR elections in 1985, see *Sovetskaya Rossiya*, March 2, 1985. For the 1980 results, see *Sovetskaya Rossiya*, February 27 and 28, 1980.

8 Roy Medvedev, *Khrushchev*. Oxford, Blackwell and New York, Doubleday, 1982, pp. 116–119.

9 Mark Frankland, *The Observer*, June 2, 1985

10 Dev Murarka, 'The Making of Gorbachev', *Mainstream*, March 30, 1985, p. 8. Murarka is a freelance correspondent based in Moscow.

11 Zhores Medvedev, *Andropov: His Life and Death*. Oxford, Blackwell, 1984 (revised edition), p. 219.

12 Rumours about Romanov's attempt to block Gorbachev's nomination were circulating in Moscow after Romanov's dismissal in July. They were reported in many Western newspapers on July 2, 1985. See, for example, the report by Dusko Doder in *International Herald Tribune*, July 2, 1985.

13 Dusko Doder, Washington Post Service, *International Herald Tribune*, March 19, 1985.
14 A. Gromyko's speech at the Plenum of the CC CPSU, March 11, 1985, *Kommunist*, No. 5, March 1985, pp. 6–7.
15 Dev Murarka, 'The Making of Gorbachev'.
16 Zhores A. Medvedev, *The Observer*, colour supplement, November 20, 1982, pp. 18–21.
17 *Pravda*, November 23, 1982.
18 *Pravda*, March 15, 1984.
19 *Pravda*, April 26, 1985.
20 *Narodnoye khozyaistvo SSSR v 1983 godu* (henceforth *Nar. khoz.*). Moscow, Statistika, 1984, pp. 18–23.
21 *Izvestiya*, May 27, 1985.

2 Childhood and Youth

1 The previous leaders were Lenin, Stalin, Malenkov, Khrushchev, Brezhnev, Andropov and Chernenko. In Western literature Malenkov is often left out of the list because his tenure was so short (less than a year). However, for Soviet citizens the few months after Stalin's death are associated with enormous changes. The abolition of taxation on private plots in rural areas and the programme which was adopted in August 1953 to increase the production of consumer goods, in particular, are associated with Malenkov's name, not with Khrushchev's.
2 These details abour Gorbachev's parents were included in a brief official biography of Gorbachev released in English only by Novosty Press for an English edition of Gorbachev's collected speeches: Mikhail S. Gorbachev, *A Time for Peace*. Richardson and Steirman, New York, 1985, pp. 9–15.
3 S. P. Trapeznikov, *Leninism and the Agrarian and Peasant Question*, Vol. 2: *The Historical Experience of the CPSU in Carrying Out Lenin's Cooperative Plan*. Moscow, Progress Publishers, 1981, p. 278.
4 *Ibid.*, p. 283
5 Trapeznikov, *Leninism* Vol. 2, p. 285.
6 E. Oskolkov, *Pobeda kolkhoznogo stroya v zernovykh raionakh severnogo Kavkaza*. Rostov on Don, 1973, p. 286.
7 A. Radin and L. Shaumyan, *Za chto zhiteli stanitsy Poltavskoi vyselyayutsya s Kubani v severnye kraya*. Rostov on Don, 1933, quoted in Roy Medvedev, *Let History Judge*, New York, Knopf and London, Macmillan, 1971, p. 399.

8 Roy Medvedev, *Let History Judge*, p. 95. The Kosterin manuscript circulated in the USSR in unpublished *samizdat* form. It was given to Roy Medvedev by Kosterin himself.
9 Roy Medvedev, *Let History Judge*, p. 399.
10 Roy Medvedev, 'Suslov: Ideologist-in-Chief', Chapter 3 of *All Stalin's Men*. Oxford, Blackwell and New York, Doubleday, 1983, pp. 61–81.
11 A. M. Nekrich, *The Punished People*. New York, Norton, 1978.
12 *Pravda*, October 22, 1980 and March 12, 1985.
13 *Nar. khoz. 1972 gody: Statisticheskii ezhegodnik* Moscow, TsU SSSR, 1972, p. 284.
14 Zdenek Mlynar, 'Il mio compagno di studi Mikhail Gorbaciov', *I'Unita*, April 9, 1985. A shorter version of this article was published in Vienna in *Kurier*, April 19 and 20, 1985.
15 Ibid.
16 Ibid.
17 Interview with L. Yudovich, *The Wall Street Journal*, March 12, 1985.
18 F. Neznansky, part of a discussion published in *Possev*, No. 4, 1985, p. 22.
19 *Nar. khoz.*, 1965, p. 689; 1983, p. 495.
20 A. A. Piontovsky and V. D. Men'shagin, *Kurs sovetskogo ugolovnogo prava. Osobaya chast'*, Vol. 1. Moscow, Gosyurizdat, 1955.
21 Dina Kaminskaya, *Final Judgment: My Life as a Soviet Defence Lawyer*, London, Harvil Press, 1983, p. 1983. Dina Kaminskaya emigrated from the Soviet Union in 1977. Her description of Soviet defence lawyers applies not only to the 1950s, but to the 1960s, 1970s and 1980s as well. Some attorneys were officially disqualified in the 1960s and 1970s for defending political dissidents too vigorously. This made it impossible for dissidents who were tried later in the 1970s and in the 1980s to be defended properly.

3 The young Gorbachev in Stavropol

1 *Ezhegodnik Bol'shoi Sovetskoi Entsyklopedii*. Moscow, Sovetskaya Entsiklopediya, 1981, p. 591.
2 Mlynar, 'Il mio compagno di studi Mikhail Gorbaciov', *L'Unita*, p. 9.
3 *Nar. khoz.*, 1956, p. 31.
4 *Ustav VLKSM*, Moscow, Molodaya Gvardiya.
5 *Pravda*, January 29, 1960.

6 *Pravda*, June 26, 1960.
7 Roy Medvedev, *Khrushchev*, p. 235.
8 Zhores A. Medvedev, *The Rise and Fall of T. D. Lysenko*. New York, Columbia University Press, 1969, pp. 206, 208, 229.
9 *Nar. khoz.*, 1965, p. 37.
10 R.M. Gorbacheva, *Formirovaniye novykh chert byta kolkhoznogo krest'yanstva. Po materialam sotsiologicheskogo obsledovaniya v Stavropol'skom krae. Avtoreferat dissertatsii*. Moscow, MGPI, 1967.
11 Mlynar, 'Il mio compagno di studi Mikhail Gorbaciov.'
12 Ibid.
13 Wolfgang Leonhard, *Eurocommunism: Challenge for East and West*. New York, Holt, Rinehart and Winston, 1979, pp. 106–107.

4 Kraikom secretary

1 *Constitution of the Union of Soviet Socialist Republics*. Moscow, Novosti Press, 1980, pp. 107–108.
2 *Itogi Vsesoyuznoi perepisi naseleniya 1970 goda*. Moscow, Statistika, 1972, Vol. 1, pp. 12–13.
3 *Izvestiya*, June 16, 1985.
4 *Pravda*, June 8, 1974.
5 *Izvestiya*, July 26 and 27, 1974.
6 *Constitution of the Union of Soviet Socialist Republics*, pp. 91–92.
7 T. Rakowska-Harmstone, 'Toward a theory of Soviet leadership maintenance', in P. Cocks, R. V. Daniels and N. W. Heer (eds), *The Dynamic of Soviet Politics*. Cambridge, Mass., Harvard University Press, 1976.
8 The campaign has been described in detail in a number of articles, as well as in a book written by the Ipatovsky *raikom* secretary. See, for example, V. V. Kalyagin, *Novatorskii poisk ipatovtsev*. Moscow, Kolos, 1979.
9 'Upravlyaya zhatvoi', *Pravda*, July 16, 1977.
10 *Pravda*, July 18, 1977.
11 *Agitator*, No. 5, 1978, p. 7.
12 *Pravda*, February 4, 1978.
13 *Pravda*, February 10, 1978.
14 *Pravda*, July 21, 1978.
15 *Soviet Analyst*, No. 15, 1978.
16 V. Solovyov and E. Klepikova, *Yuri Andropov*. New York, Macmillan and London, Collier Macmillan, 1983, p. 168.

17 P. J. Murphy, *Brezhnev: Soviet Politician*. Jefferson, NC, McFarland & Co., 1981, p. 294.
18 S. Bialer, *Stalin's Successors*. Cambridge, Cambridge University Press, 1980, pp. 76–77.
19 A. N. Shevchenko, *Breaking with Moscow*. New York, Knopf, 1985, p. 185.
20 *Pravda*, September 21, 1978.
21 *Pravda*, November 28, 1978.
22 Roy Medvedev, *All Stalin's Men*.

5 In charge of agriculture in the Politburo

1 *Nar. khoz.*, 1979, p. 242.
2 For a more detailed description of the structure and responsibilities of the Secretariat, see R. J. Hill and P. Frank, *The Soviet Communist Party*. London, Allen & Unwin, 1983.
3 *Pravda* and *Izvestiya*, February 3, 1979.
4 Ibid.
5 *Izvestiya*, March 7, 1979.
6 Roy Medvedev, 'How I ran for election and how I lost', *Spokesman pamphlet*, No. 68, 1979.
7 *Nar. khoz.*, 1979, p. 220.
8 R. L. Paarlberg, *Food Trade and Foreign Policy*. Ithaca and London, Cornell University Press, 1985, p. 88.
9 *Nar., khoz.*, 1979, p. 247.
10 T. G. Butson, *Gorbachev*. New York, Stein and Day, 1985, p. 52. His speculation seems to be based on the book by Solovyov and Klepikova, *Yuri Andropov*, p. 183, which contains a number of rumours and speculations without citing reliable sources to confirm them.
11 *Izvestiya*, February 2, 1980.
12 Interview with A. G. Aganbegyan in *Khimiya i zhizn'*, No. 10, 1979, p. 4.
13 *Pravda*, April 16, 1980.
14 M. Gorbachev, 'Aktual'nye voprosy sel'skogo khozyaistva i ego effektivnosti', *Kommunist*, No. 11, 1980, pp. 39–49.
15 E. Manevich, *Voprosy ekonomiki*, No. 9, 1981.
16 *Nar. khoz.*, 1980, p. 202.
17 *Pravda*, October 22, 1980.
18 *Stavropol'skaya Pravda*, August 14, 1981.
19 Foreign Agricultural Circular: 'Grains. USSR Grain Situation and Outlook', US Department of Agriculture, May 1985, p. 5.

20 Paarlberg, *Food Trade* p. 88.
21 *Kommunist*, No. 9, 1982, pp. 3–63.
22 *Pravda*, May 25, 1982.
23 M. Gorbachev, 'Prodovol'stvennaya programma i zadachi eyo realizatsii', *Kommunist*, No. 10, 1982, pp. 6–21.
24 Ibid.
25 *Stavropol'skaya pravda*, August 17, 1982.

6 Andropov's ally

1 S. F. Cohen, *Sovieticus: American Perceptions and Soviet Realities*. New York, W. W. Norton, 1985, p. 81.
2 Milovan Djilas, *The New Class*. New York, Praeger, 1957.
3 *Sel'skaya zhizn'*, December 10, 1982.
4 See, for example, Martin Ebon, *The Andropov File*, New York, McGraw-Hill, 1983; Zhores A. Medvedev, *Andropov*; A. Beichman and M. S. Bernstam, *Andropov: New Challenge to the West*, New York, Stein and Day, 1983; Jonathan Steele and Eric Abraham, *Andropov in Power*, Oxford, Martin Robertson, 1983; Solovyov and Klepikova, *Yuri Andropov*.
5 *Pravda*, April 23, 1983.
6 *Minutes of the Proceedings and Evidence of the Standing Committee on External Affairs and National Defence*. Issue No. 95, May 17, 1983, Ottawa, Queen's Printers.
7 Ibid.
8 *Pravda*, June 15, 1983.
9 See Zhores A. Medvedev, *Andropov*, p. 65.
10 *Pravda*, June 22, 1983.
11 *Newsweek*, July 25, 1983, p. 39.
12 Foreign Agricultural Circular: 'Grains. USSR Grain Situation and Outlook', US Department of Agriculture, May 1985, p. 7.
13 *Pravda*, March 2, 1984.
14 *Ekonomicheskaya gazeta*, No. 9, February 1983; *Izvestiya*, July 22, 1983.
15 *Izvestiya*, September 29, 1983.
16 *Izvestiya*, October 28, 1983.
17 *Pravda*, November 7, 1983.
18 Mark Frankland, 'Shake-up fails as Andropov loses his grip', *The Observer*, February 4, 1984.
19 *Izvestiya*, November 18, 1981.
20 *Izvestiya*, November 24, 1982.

21 *Izvestiya*, June 18, 1983.
22 *Radio Liberty Research Bulletin*, March 29, 1984.

7 Second-in-Command

1 Martin McCauley, 'Leadership and the Succession Struggle', in Martin McCauley (ed.), *The Soviet Union after Brezhnev*. London, Heineman and New York, Holmes and Meier, 1983, p. 29.
2 *Pravda*, November 20, 1982.
3 *Izvestiya*, March 1, 1984.
4 *Izvestiya*, April 12, 1985.
5 *Constitution of the Union of Soviet Socialist Republics*, p. 94.
6 Richard Owen, 'Door closes on the last dissident', *The Times*, May 4, 1984, p. 8.
7 *Pravda*, March 27, 1984.
8 Ibid.
9 *Izvestiya*, May 25, 1984.
10 *Izvestiya*, October 4, 1984.
11 Foreign Agricultural Circular, 'Grains'. USSR Grain Situation and Outlook, US Department of Agriculture, May 1985, p. 5.
12 *Izvestiya*, July 16, 1984.
13 *Izvestiya*, August 2, 1984.
14 *The Times*, September 8, 1984.
15 *The Times*, October 20, 1984.
16 *Pravda*, October 24, 1984.
17 *Pravda*, November 16, 1984.
18 *Newsweek*, November 5, 1984, p. 12.
19 Ibid.
20 *Izvestiya*, December 11, 1984.
21 Denis Healey, 'Gorbachev face to face', *Newsweek*, March 25, 1985, p. 15.
22 *Ibid.*

8 Changing the Kremlin Guard

1 S.F. Cohen, *Soveticus: American Perceptions and Soviet Realities*. New York, W. W. Norton, 1985, p. 81.
2 R. J. Hill and P. Frank, *The Soviet Communist Party*. London, Allen & Unwin, 1983, p. 65.

3 *Pravda*, March 17, 1985.
4 *Time*, March 25, 1985, p. 15.
5 *International Herald Tribune*, March 19, 1985.
6 *Pravda*, March 27, 1985.
7 *Pravda*, April 23, 1985.
8 *The Sunday Times*, April 28, 1985, p. 2.
9 Ibid.
10 *Izvestiya*, March 2, 1985.
11 *Izvestiya*, May 10, 1985.
12 *Kommunist*, No. 8, May 1985, pp. 23–34.
13 *Pravda*, June 13–14, 1985.
14 *Pravda*, July 2, 1985.
15 *Izvestiya*, July 3, 1985.
16 *Vedemosti Verkhovnogo Soveta Soyuza Sovetskikh Sotsialisticheskikh Respublik*, No. 40, October 2, 1985, pp. 631–632.
17 *Izvestiya*, November 3, 1985.
18 *Izvestiya*, November 23, 1985.

9 Getting the country moving

1 Roy Medvedev, 'New Man in Moscow', *The Los Angeles Times*, March 17, 1985; 'A View from Moscow', *Newsweek*, March 25, 1985, p. 27.
2 *Izvestiya*, April 19, 1985.
3 *Izvestiya*, May 15, 1985.
4 *Nar. khoz.*, 1983, p. 411.
5 *Izvestiya*, July 14, 1985.
6 I. V. Stalin, *Works*, Vol. 10. Moscow, Foreign Languages Publishing House, 1954, pp. 237–238.
7 A. Krasikov, 'Commodity Number One', in R. A. Medvedev (ed.), *Samizdat Register*. No. 2, London, Merlin Press, 1981, p. 171.
8 *Nar. khoz.*, 1983, p. 190.
9 *Vestnik Statistiki*, No. 8, 1985, p. 73.
10 *Pravda*, May 17, 1985.
11 *Vedemosti Verkhovnogo Soveta*, No. 39, 1985, pp. 714–715.
12 Y. V. Andropov, *Speeches and Writings*. Oxford, Pergamon Press, 1983, p. 11.
13 Ibid., p. 9.
14 Zhores A. Medvedev, *Andropov: His Life and Death*. Oxford, Blackwell, 1984, p. 206.

15 *Izvestiya*, April 20, 1985.
16 A. Aganbegyan, 'Obuchat' nauke upravleniya', *Izvestiya*, March 25, 1985.
17 *Izvestiya*, April 12, 1985.
18 *Izvestiya*, April 14, 1985.
19 *Izvestiya*, April 30, 1985.
20 *Kommunist*, No. 8, 1985, pp. 23–24.
21 *Pravda*, June 12, 13, 1985.
22 *Izvestiya*, July 16, 1985.
23 *Izvestiya*, June 27, 1985.
24 *Izvestiya*, July 12, 1985.
25 *Izvestiya*, August 4, 1985.
26 *Izvestiya*, September 7, 1985.
27 *Izvestiya*, September 8, 1985.
28 *Izvestiya*, September, 21, 1985.
29 *Izvestiya*, October 1, 1985.
30 *Izvestiya*, October 9, 1985.
31 *Pravda*, October 16, 1985.
32 *Pravda*, November 9, 1985.
33 *Izvestiya*, October 20, 1985.
34 *Izvestiya*, August 17, 1985.
35 *Kommunist*, No. 8, 1985, p. 31.
36 *Izvestiya*, June 11, 1985.
37 *Izvestiya*, July 22, 1985.
38 See, for example, V. A. Kovda, 'Kak pomoch' nashim chernozemam', *Nash Sovremennik*, No. 7, 1985, pp. 117–128; G. Lisichkin, 'Za vedomstvennym bar'erom', *Novyi Mir*, No. 10, 1985, pp. 167–190.
39 Yu. Chernichenko, 'Svoi khleb', *Novyi Mir*, No. 8, 1985, pp. 6–48.
40 *Izvestiya*, October 17, 1985.
41 A. Nikitin, 'Ot okolizy do okrainy', *Novyi Mir*, No. 7, 1985, pp. 179–199.
42 *Izvestiya*, July 7, 1985.
43 *Izvestiya*, July 20, 1985.
44 *Izvestiya*, September 11, 1985.
45 *Izvestiya*, October 26, 1985.
46 *Izvestiya*, November 23, 1985.

10 Domestic policy

1 *Constitution of the Union of Soviet Socialist Republics*. Moscow, Novosti Press Agency, 1980, p. 46.

2 *Izvestiya*, April 28, 1985.
3 *Jews in the USSR* (A Weekly Information Bulletin), Vol. 14, No. 14, April 11, 1985, p.4.
4 Ibid., Vol. 14, No. 17, May 2, 1985, p. 4.
5 Ibid., Vol. 14, No. 42, November 7, 1985, p. 4.
6 M. Gorbachev, *A Time for Peace*. New York, Richardson and Steirman, 1985, p. 253.
7 Ibid., p. 252.
8 E. Lubarsky (ed.), *Vesti iz SSSR*. Munich.
9 Y. Yevtushenko, 'Kabychegonevyshlisty', *Pravda*, September 9, 1985.
10 *Stavropol'skaya Pravda*, May 6, 1978.
11 L. Schapiro, *The Communist Party of the Soviet Union* (2nd edition). London, Allen & Unwin, 1970.
12 *The Programme of the CPSU*. Soviet Booklet, No. 83, 1961.
13 *Pravda*, October 26, 1985. The English text was published in *Soviet News*, October 30, 1985.
14 Ibid.
15 Ibid.
16 The English text of the statutes was published in *Moscow News*, No. 45, November 10, 1985.
17 *Pravda*, July 14, 1985.

11 New diplomacy, but the same old foreign policy

1 Richard Pipes, *Russia under the Old Regime*. Harmondsworth, Middx, Penguin, 1979, p. 79.
2 'Programme of the CPSU', *Soviet Weekly*, November 9, 1985, p. 23.
3 Ibid., p. 24.
4 Ibid., p. 25.
5 Mikhail Gorbachev, *A Time for Peace*. New York, Richardson and Steirman, 1985, p. 252.
6 J.F. Hough and M. Fainsod, *How the Soviet Union is Governed*. Cambridge, Mass., Harvard University Press, 1979, p. 364.
7 *Time*, April 22, 1985, p. 7.
8 *Time*, September 9, 1985, p. 4.
9 Ibid., p. 5.
10 *Time*, April 22, 1985, p. 8.
11 *Pravda*, April 18, 1985.
12 Henry Kissinger, *The White House Years*. London, Weidenfeld & Nicolson and Michael Joseph, 1978, p. 1141.

13 *The Sunday Times*, April 21, 1986, p. 22; *Time*, April 22, 1985, p. 16.
14 V. Krotkov, 'Dushmany s amerikanskami passportami', *Izvestiya*, November 6, 1985.
15 Serge Schmemann, 'Afghanistan war creates Soviet heroes', *International Herald Tribune*, November 13, 1985.
16 *Newsweek*, August 19, 1985, p. 26.
17 *Time*, December 9, 1985, p. 10.
18 *Izvestiya*, November 28, 1985.
19 *Izvestiya*, October 6, 1985.
20 Ibid.

Note on spelling

There are several ways of spelling in English the Russian surname 'Gorbachev': Gorbachev, Gorbachov, Gorbachyov and Gorbachëv. The letters 'e' and 'o' in the Russian alphabet are used to indicate the same sounds as 'e' and 'o' in English, and in Russian Gorbachev is spelt with an 'e'. However, the sound required in this name is slightly different from the normal 'e' and was best represented by the letter 'ë', which was dropped from the Russian alphabet for simplification in 1970 and which signified a vowel sound similar to that in Ch*u*rchill. This sound is now covered in Soviet literature by 'e', and rules for transliteration of Russian words recommend the usage of 'e', in place of 'ë'. Therefore, while the various spellings noted above have come into use in English-language literature, 'Gorbachev' remains the most direct translation from Russian usage and is consistent with other names with the same Russian form, e.g. Ligachev, Khrushchev.

Glossary

apparat, apparatus	The machine, the organization of offices and officeholders; for example, the Party *apparat*, the state *apparat*, and so on. The English expression, 'political machine', would be an accurate translation, except that it is pejorative, while *apparat* is not.
apparatchik	Familiar term for an official in the Party *apparatus*.
cadre	The most important members of an organization or institution, those who constitute its nuclei of leaders at various levels. By extension from the term for the skeleton organization of a military unit.
Central Committee or CC	A high policy-making and administrative organization of the Communist Party, nominally elected by and responsible to the Party Congress. Directs the activities of the Party between Party Congresses; each republic has its own Central Committee.
CPSU	Communist Party of the Soviet Union.
dacha	Holiday house, usually in the country or at a resort. For officials it usually means a special, state-owned villa, given either for a certain period or indefinitely as a property of a family.

gorkom — The Party committee in town or city.

Gosplan — The state planning committee.

hectare — A unit of land measure equivalent to 2.47 acre.

ispolkom — Executive committee. *Ispolkoms* in districts, towns or regions are parts of the local governmental network.

Izvestiya — Central governmental newspaper. Second in importance after *Pravda*.

KGB — Abbreviation of *Komitet gosudarstvennoi bezopasnosti* (Committee of State Security).

kolkhoz — Collective farm, formed on the basis of common means of production and collective labour; an agrarian producers' cooperative which is obliged to make deliveries to the state at prices fixed by the state. Each member receives advance payments, checked later, as a share of the net income commensurate with the share of 'labour days' he contributes to the collective operations. Members also have private plots (up to 0.5 hectare) around their family homes.

kolkhoznik — Member of a collective farm.

Kommunist — Main theoretical journal of the Central Committee of the CPSU.

Komsomol — Abbreviation of *Kommunisticheskii soyuz molodezhi* (Young Communist League), the mass movement to which the majority of young people belong.

krai — A large territorial subdivision of RSFSR. Different from *oblast'* by presence of non-

Russian ethnic minorities separated into Autonomous regions.

kraikom — The Party Committee, i.e. the Party's chief organization, in a *krai*.

kulak — Russian term specifying class differentiation in the countryside. The *kulak* (literally, a 'fist') was a wealthy peasant who rented land from others and produced on a relatively large scale for the market. The middle peasant (*seredniak*) had average-size holdings, mostly worked by family labour, and sold some surplus on the market. The poor peasant (*bedniak*) did not have enough land to feed his family and usually had to borrow or hire himself out.

MTS — Machine Tractor Station. Machinery depot servicing several collective farms with machines, drivers and mechanics for many works (ploughing, sowing, harvesting, etc.).

MVD — Abbreviation of *Ministerstvo vnutrennikh del* (Ministry of Internal Affairs).

New Economic Policy (NEP) — Introduced by Lenin in 1921 in order to alleviate the heavy burden on the population that was imposed by the Civil War (1918–21). It permitted private enterprise and was expected to last many years, but was terminated by Stalin at the end of the 1920s and replaced by collectivization and the Five Year Plans.

nomenklatura — The list of important tenured positions in the Party and state apparatus, appointment to which requires approval from higher Party bodies. Originally from *nomenklaturnyi rabotnik*, which meant a professional official of the Party and state apparatus.

oblast'	A major administrative subdivision of a Soviet republic, comparable to a province or state.
obkom	Abbreviation of *oblastnoi komitet* (regional Party committee).
Politburo	The political bureau of the Central Committee of the CPSU. The top decision-making body in the Soviet political system. It was called the Presidium between 1952 and 1966. Members are either full members, with voting rights, or candidate members, who attend proceedings but cannot vote.
Pravda	The newspaper organ of the Central Committee of the CPSU.
raiispolkom	Executive committee in a *raion*.
raion	Administrative subdivision of an *oblast'* or of a city.
raikom	The Party committee, i.e. the Party's chief organization, in a *raion*.
RSFSR	Russian Soviet Federative Socialist Republic; the official name of Soviet Russia from 1917 to 1922, when the USSR was formed; now the name of the largest republic of the Soviet Union, the Russian Republic.
samizdat	Works of literature, politics, etc. reproduced by copying, photocopying, or typing, and distributed by individuals outside the official censorship system.
Soviet	Literally 'council' – the basic governmental unit of the Soviet system.

State farm or *sovkhoz*	A state agricultural enterprise. *Sovkhoz* workers receive their wages in cash, whereas on a *kolkhoz* labour is rewarded partly with money and partly with agricultural produce.
Supreme Soviet	Soviet parliament consisting of elected deputies in two chambers, one based on nationalities, the other on demographic electoral constituencies. Only one candidate – usually proposed by the local Party organization – stands for each seat.
Union republics	The Soviet Union is made up of fifteen republics which are called Union republics (or constituent or national republics). Where there are large and distinct national minorities, Union republics may be further subdivided into autonomous republics and autonomous regions.

Index